Revolution

to the memory of
Lewis and Beryl Michtom
and
Benjamin and Tina Kimmel

Revolution
A Sociological Interpretation

Michael S. Kimmel

Polity Press

Copyright © Michael S. Kimmel
First published 1990 by Polity Press
in association with Basil Blackwell

Editorial office:
Polity Press, 65 Bridge Street,
Cambridge CB2 1UR, UK

Marketing and production:
Basil Blackwell Ltd
108 Cowley Road, Oxford OX4 1JF, UK

ISBN 0 7456 0312 2
ISBN 0 7456 0313 0 (pbk)

British Library Cataloguing in Publication Data
A CIP catalogue record for this book is available from the British Library

Typeset in 10 on 12 pt Garamond
by Colset Private Limited, Singapore
Printed in Great Britain by
T.J. Press (Padstow) Ltd, Padstow, Cornwall.

Contents

Preface

Ten years ago, I sat in a small apartment in Paris, watching the snow swirl on the streets below and listening to the radio as the reports of the Iranian Revolution unfolded. At first, there were lengthy interviews with Ayatollah Khomeini, who was living in exile a few miles from my apartment. Suddenly, he had returned to Iran to lead one of the century's most dramatic revolutions. And again, that summer, I was captivated by reports from Nicaragua of the fall of the Samoza regime, and the success of the popular revolution led by the Sandinista Front.

Ironically, I was in Paris that year doing the research for my PhD thesis, trying to understand the causes, dynamics, and outcomes of two revolutionary upheavals in Europe over 300 years earlier, in the middle of the seventeenth century: the English Revolution and the Frondes in France. In that historical research, I was trying to understand both the similar causes of those two revolutionary struggles and their very different outcomes. Why did the English Revolution succeed and the Frondes fail?

To sort out these questions, I turned to the theories that social scientists had developed to explain the phenomenon of revolution. And I found most of those theories offered partial explanations at best, and wholly inadequate explanations at worst. And when I tried to explain the revolutions that were unfolding in 1979, I found most social scientific theories could not adequately explain them either. Few analysts were asking, for example, what the connections between the two revolutions were, because their analysis rested entirely on internal variables. Yet it seemed clear to me that the success of both revolutions depended, in part, on the withdrawal of American support to the Shah in Iran and to the Samoza regime as part of President Jimmy Carter's human rights policy. The international arena in which domestic politics is played out seemed of critical importance in 1979, both as I observed the revolutions in Iran and Nicaragua and as I researched mid-seventeenth-century Europe.

It also became clear to me that while macro-level institutional forces – the international economic and political arena, class relations at the level of agricultural production, the state – were the determinant structural levels upon which any explanation of revolution must depend, they were also insufficient. How to explain the remarkable divergence of the Nicaraguan and the Iranian revolution, except by recourse to ideological and cultural features unique to each case? Both revolutions expressed nationalist, anti-imperialist sentiments, but one did so through a seventh-century millennial theology embodied in a sternly anti-modernist charismatic leader and the other through a vaguely socialist, thoroughly populist nationalism. And how to explain the success of the English Revolution and the failure of the Frondes except by taking account of the way in which religious ideology, Puritanism, held the English revolutionary coalition together even after their political and economic interests had begun to unravel it.

It became clear to me that an adequate explanation of revolution required setting the structural stage, making state, class, and international arena decisive, and yet allowing room for the complex play of human agency, of people's hopes and angers, mediated by culture and ideology that are historically specific to the country in question. It was then that I determined eventually to write a book in which I explored the ways in which social scientists have treated the phenomenon of revolution, and to try to use my critiques of those theories to build a theory that would account for both the structural dynamics of revolutionary events and still preserve an emphasis on culture, ideology, and human agency.

In the ensuing decade, I completed the project on revolutions in Early Modern Europe, and went on to other projects. I knew I would eventually return to this, and when the circumstances presented themselves a few years ago, I was eager to write this book. For we live now in a revolutionary age, an age in which revolutionary struggles are occurring on almost every continent, from South Africa to Guatemala, from the Philippines to Northern Ireland. Nations and ethnic groups struggle for autonomy in the western industrial countries as well as in the Soviet Union and eastern bloc countries. Third World peasants, priests, and intellectuals attempt to rid themselves of foreign domination. And to live in such an age presents us with a special ethical imperative to attempt to understand it. I have written this book then with the hope that by exploring the theories of revolution offered to us by social science in the twentieth century, contemporary readers could have a better idea of how to explain the extraordinary events in the world in which we live.

Lenin once wrote that it was "more pleasant and useful to go through the experience of revolution than to write about it." He offered this as an explanation of why he interrupted the writing of the last chapter of *State and*

Revolution in November 1917. Perhaps he was right; I wouldn't know, although I do retain a vivid fondness for that moment in the late 1960s when I believed I was participating in a revolution. But writing about it hasn't been all that bad. Perhaps this is because writing is both a solitary activity and a profoundly social activity. Although it is only one person who sits in front of a blinking computer screen day after tedious day, I am constantly in imaginary (or real) dialog with teachers, friends, and colleagues. I've been fortunate that I've had such dedicated teachers, supportive friends and family, and generous colleagues. And I've been even more fortunate that many of those closest to me overlap those arbitrary categories.

As an undergraduate and graduate student, I was fortunate to study with Robert Bellah, Victoria Bonnell, Peter Evans, Jim Farganis, Elbaki Hermassi, William Kornhauser, Colin Loftin, and Neil Smelser. Although my ideas have diverged significantly from Smelser's, I have always found him intellectually supportive, and I am very grateful for his careful and critical reading of my work. Since graduate school, I found myself profoundly influenced by the work of a number of scholars, including Craig Calhoun, Randall Collins, Wally Goldfrank, Jack Goldstone, Irving Louis Horowitz, Scott McNall, Jeffrey Paige, Theda Skocpol, Charles Tilly, and Immanuel Wallerstein. My intellectual debts to them will be evident in this work; that a few of them have also become close friends has been an unanticipated pleasure.

I am grateful to David Held at Polity Press for shepherding this project through from its original proposal, and to Hazel Coleman for her exceptional copy-editing. Frances Goldin is more than a wonderful agent; she is an ally and a friend.

My friends and family have, as always, known how best to be supportive, whether it meant leaving me alone to work out a particular problem, talking it through with me, or insisting on distracting me with worldly temptation. I am grateful to Angela Aidala, Paul Attewell, Judith Brisman, Barbara and Herb Diamond, Martin Duberman, Kate Ellis, John Gagnon, Cathy Greenblat, Pam Hatchfield, Ed Kimmel, Sandi Kimmel, David and Deborah Levin, Martin Levine, Iona Mara-Drita, Mary Morris, Katherine Newman, and Mitchell Tunick.

Finally, I dedicate this book to the memory of my grandparents, who first taught me the love of learning, and also instilled in me the moral imperative to use the fruits of that learning to make the world a better place for having lived in it.

M.K.
New York City

1

Revolutions in the Sociological Imagination

> *Revolution is the sex of politics.*
> H.L. Mencken

There's a well-known story about King Louis XVI in France. As the king observed the protests in the streets of Paris in 1789, he turned to his friend, the duc de La Rochefoucauld-Liancourt, and exclaimed, "My God! It's a revolt!" "No, Sire," La Rochefoucauld is said to have replied. "That is a revolution."

La Rochefoucauld's reply is justly celebrated because it revealed how the king was unable to perceive what was occurring beneath his window, but it also suggests several questions – questions that lie at the heart of social science thinking about revolution. How could La Rochefoucauld know the difference between a revolt and a revolution? What are the distinguishing features of each? If we were standing at the window with the king and his duc, would we have known enough to agree with the duc?

The central questions in the study of revolution have plagued social scientists, philosophers, and even kings, for centuries. What are revolutions? Why do they occur? Why do some succeed and others fail? Are revolutions necessarily violent upheavals, or can there be non-violent revolutions? Why do people rebel? What motivates them to risk their lives for such a cause?

Revolutions are of central importance for social scientists not only because they are extreme cases of collective action, but also because revolutions provide a lens through which to view the everyday organization of any society. "[T]he understanding of revolution is an indispensable condition for the fuller knowledge and understanding of society" (Zagorin, 1976: 151). Revolutions are also important for us to understand not as social scientists but as citizens: we live in a world in which over half of the inhabitants of the planet live in a country that has undergone a revolution in this century. Our age is a revolutionary age, and in order to be responsible citizens, it is imperative that we begin to understand this phenomenon. Revolutions are events which deeply affect our lives. In fact, "excepting war, religion, and romantic love, nothing in ordinary human experience has so inflamed the imagination of men, encouraged so many romantic illusions, or broken so completely with the ordinary routine of existence, as has been true of revolution" (Park, 1955: 36).

What is more, revolutions make a moral claim on our sensibilities. Revolutions demand that we take sides, that we commit ourselves to a political position. It is difficult to remain neutral during a revolution. At the more international level, revolutionaries often make large claims about what they will accomplish if they are successful in an effort to enlist support from those of us in advanced industrial countries. The support of the major industrial powers, or a least the withdrawal of support for the established regime, has historically been central to the success of revolutions in the twentieth century. So revolutionaries will make moral and political demands of us, even if we do not live in a revolutionary society ourselves. The questions we will address in this book are therefore central to our lives as both social scientists and as citizens, who seek to act thoughtfully, compassionately, and ethically.

Revolutions are a centerpiece of all theories about society. If, for example, one assumes that societies are composed of organized interlocking parts that function smoothly together – a view that would suggest that social order, value consensus, and a division of labor that functions to create a harmonious blend of interests and ideals – then revolutions are of great significance because they are the polar opposite of the normal tendency towards order. The poet William Butler Yeats expressed this idea eloquently in his poem "The Second Coming" (1920):

> Things fall apart; the centre cannot hold;
> Mere anarchy is loosed upon the world;
> The blood-dimmed tide is loosed, and everywhere
> The ceremony of innocence is drowned;
> The best lack all conviction, while the worst
> Are full of passionate intensity.[1]

Revolutions are a negative case to theories of social order, when things fall apart and the world seems to go mad. And to the theorist of social order it is imperative to study revolutions because the better we understand how things change, the better we can understand how they stay the same.

If, on the other hand, one assumes conflict among various groups in society provides the underlying tension that both maintains social structures and propels the society towards social change, the revolutions are also vital to one's understanding. If the social change is ubiquitous, then revolutions are the most extreme case of social change – moments of discontinuity, of transformation, when the edifice of society is toppled and its structural foundations exposed.

Regardless of one's theoretical posture, revolutions are a central phenomenon to all theories of society, and have proven a popular subject to study. As the editorial forward to an issue of *Comparative Studies in Society and History* put it in 1980 "[o]utbursts of violence attract social scientists the way volcanic erruptions draw geoglogists, as specific events inviting measurement that promise to reveal subterranean forces which may in turn reflect still more basic structures" (1980: 144). As a result of this popularity, and the different theoretical postures which social scientists assume, there seem to be as many theories of revolution as there are theorists. How are these various theories to be assessed? What criteria should be applied to theories of revolution? Along what axes are the revolutions, and the theories about revolutions to be compared? Which theories are the most analytically useful in explaining the historical cases of revolution that have occured?

This book is an effort to make sense of the enormous amount of scholarly and popular writing about revolution that has appeared in the twentieth century. In an effort to build an adequate theoretical explanation of revolution, I will discuss the various theories of revolution that have been offered by other social scientists, compare them analytically, and then draw parts from each to build synthetic theory of revolution. A theory of revolution must be internally consistent; it must follow a causal argument, and make sense of a number of empirical cases that fall within its definition of the term. Theories of revolution must address five basic questions. (1) What is a revolution? (2) What is it that changes during a revolution? (3) What causes revolution? (4) Why do people participate in revolutions? (5) What are the consequences of revolution? How they answer these questions will determine their utility in explaining historical cases of revolution and their comparability as sociological theories.

The remaining chapters of this book will discuss the ways in which social scientific treatment of revolution has developed in the twentieth century. In chapter 2, I examine some of the theories of revolution offered by the "masters" of sociological theory, writers such as Karl Marx, Alexis de Tocqueville, Max Weber, and Emile Durkheim, whose work has continued to inform contemporary analysis of revolution. In chapter 3, I turn to "non-structural" theories of revolution which stress the historical process of revolution, the physchological motivations of groups to rebel, or the collapse of an otherwise harmonious functioning social system. My critique of these schools expands through chapters 4–6, in which I discuss the various levels of a structural theory that have been offered by social scientists: the international context for revolutionary activity (chapter 4); the struggle between social classes at the level of production (chapter 5); and the role of the state in revolution (chapter 6). Finally, in chapter 7, I return to the question of mobilization and motivation within a structural argument to build a theoretical synthesis of these earlier models.

In the remainder of this chapter, I will briefly explore the five questions that will dominate our discussion of revolution.

What is a Revolution?

The first question about revolution concerns what we mean by the term. Definitions abound, and there is little consensus about what a revolution is, let alone why it may occur. Let's start with a definition drawn from a non-social-scientific source: the *Oxford English Dictionary* defines revolution as ''A complete overthrow of the established government in any country or state by those who were previously subject to it; a forcible substitution of a new ruler or form of government.'' This definition implies that revolutions take place on the political level, involving governments and rulers, and that they must be ''complete'' and successful in order to count as revolutions. It also equates the imposition of a new ruler with a revolutionary transformation of society.

Aristotle understood revolutions to be qualitatively different from these simple changes in political leadership, although he agreed that success was a criterion of the term. In *Politics*, Aristotle wrote that there were ''two sorts of changes in government; the one affecting the constitution, where men seek to change from an existing form into something other, the other not affecting the constitution when, without disturbing the form of government, whether oligarchy or monarchy, or any they try to get the administration into their own hands.''

These two definitions resonate with many of those offered by social scientists. Most definitions, for example, imply that in order to be labelled a revolution, the uprising must be successful. Baecheler (1975: 91) defines revolution as a ''protest movement that manages to seize power,'' and Neumann (1949a: 333n) expands the definition to include a ''sweeping, fundamental change in political organization, social structure, economic property control and the predominant myth of a social order [thereby] indicating a major break in the continuity of development.'' Trimberger (1978: 12) calls revolution ''an extralegal takeover of the central state apparatus which destroys the economic and political power of the dominant social group of the old regime,'' which again implies success in the definition.

The last definition also implies the use of violence in a revolution, and many social scientists have placed violence in the center of their analysis. Thus

Friedrich (1966: 5) defines revolution as "the sudden and violent overthrow of an established political order," and Huntington (1968: 264) calls it "a rapid fundamental and violent domestic change in the dominant values and myths of a society, in its political institutions, social structure, leadership, government activity, and policies." Skocpol offers perhaps the most comprehensive and succinct structural definition: "Social revolutions are rapid, basic transformations of a society's state and class structure; they are accompanied and in part carried through by class based revolts from below" (Skocpol, 1979a: 4). One writer attempts to modify this requirement of violence by arguing that revolution refers to events "in which physical force (or the convincing threat of it) has actually been used successfully to overthrow a government or regime" (Calvert, 1970: 15).

But is success a *requirement* for a revolution to be called by that name? Such a definition would mean that revolutions that fail be called something else, thus restricting the number of empirical cases to about twenty. This would be unfortunate, because revolutions that fail can provide as many clues to the causes and the process of revolutions as those that succeed.

To posit success of the revolution as a definitional criterion also leads to a serious teleological problem, in which the theorist interprets the origins by their outcomes. During a potential revolution, an "urban mob" or a mass of "traditional peasants" may attempt to seize power, and they may think they are less making a revolution. Why would social scientists only permit a successful attempt to be labelled a revolution? Are not all such efforts revolutions – some that succeed and some that fail? Does the content of the revolutionary effort change after the fact if the rebels are unsuccessful?

By the same token, a theory of revolution must also be able to explain its opposite; our eventual understanding of revolution must also be able to explain counter-revolution as well. As Tilly (1964: 30) explains:

> Just as a theory of heredity which could not account for the occasional appearance of dramatically new genetic traits would be considered incomplete, a theory of revolution, or an analysis of a spcific revolution, which provides no understanding of the presence of counter-revolutionary forces in the midst of society in revolt must leave us unsatisfied. If a theory purports to tell us when and why a society is ready for rebellion, it also ought to tell us which sectors of the society will resist the rebellion, and why. Exceptions prove the rule. Counter-revolutions test our explanations of revolution.

Perhaps our definition will require expansion to include efforts at transformation, whether successful or not. Meusel suggests that a revolution occurs "when the upper class cannot and the lower class will not continue the old system" without making the success of that clash and the success of the lower class as explicit, formal criterion of the definition (Meusel, 1934: 368). Dunn

(1972: 12) defines revolutions as ''a form of massive, violent and rapid social change. They are also attempts to embody a set of values in a new or at least renovated social order.'' And Zagorin (1982, Vol 1: 17) provides perhaps the most useful definition of all, combining questions of success, violence, and the object of the revolutionary change:

> A revolution is any attempt by subordinate groups through the use of violence to bring about (1) a change of government or its policy, (2) a change of regime, or (3) a change of society, whether this attempt is justified by reference to past conditions or to an as yet unattained future ideal.

A revolution may succeed or fail – the emphasis is on the effort – and may choose as its object a political transformation, a social transformation, or a simple change of ruler. It is always purposive, develops ideological justifications, and invariably entails violence. But even this definition equates a change in the regime, perhaps even the replacement of one ruler by another (a *coup d'état*), with a revolution.

One useful suggestion might be to hold to a distinction between revolutionary situations and revolutionary outcomes. We can of course imagine situations in which a revolution takes place, but the outcome does not yield the type of society envisioned by the revolution, or in which the forces of the old regime are victorious, either by their own strength or by soliciting aid from abroad. But these are revolutions also, and they are far more numerous than the successful transformations. To include them in the definition, and to draw contrasts between them and the successful revolutions, will, I believe, prove instructive to students of the phenomenon.

To frame our discussion, I will offer a fairly fluid and simple definition, which we will modify as we proceed. *Revolutions are attempts by subordinate groups to transform the social foundations of political power*. Such efforts require confrontation with power-holders, and must stand a reasonable chance of success to differentiate a revolution from other acts of rebellion, such as a social movement or terrorist act. Such a definition is sufficiently broad to include successful and unsuccessful revolutions, to embrace a large number of sequences over various amounts of time, and yet it is specific enough to allow us to distinguish between revolutions and other forms of social change, such as *coups d'état* and rebellions. Although a revolutionary event must stand a reasonable chance of successfully carrying out a program of social transformation, success is not inevitable. Social movements and seemingly isolated acts of rebellion may trigger wider movements and become revolutions themselves. The definition does not yet specify the composition of the subordinate groups that make the revolution; that will be the task of succeeding chapters. Nor does it insist that violence be a part of the insurgents' scheme, since we may want to investigate non-violent revolu-

tionary efforts and we surely will want to discuss the violence of the established order as well as that of the insurgents. We shall adopt this definition as
a working model, however, and see how the other levels of analysis fall into
place.

What is it that Changes During a Revolution?

The second question locates the revolution and sets the object of study. What
is it that changes? This is a spatial question: where does the revolution
actually take place? Though it is tempting to glibly answer "society," by
which we most often mean the nation-state, the unit of analysis is a central
question to be addressed. Some of the definitions discussed above locate the
revolution within the government, or suggest that political transformation is the defining feature of revolution. To some social scientists, the forces
that shape revolutionary events lie outside the boundaries of the nation-
state. Revolutions, they argue, are shaped by the workings of transnational structures and institutions; international economic or international
geopolitical and military competition influence dramatically the direction
a revolution will take, the line-up of domestic forces, and the outcome of the
revolution. Some social scientists, such as Wallerstein, insist that revolutions
cannot be understood without reference to the world economic arena in
which all nations operate, and that a specific nation will reorganize its
internal structural arrangements to more profitably participate in that international economic arena. Others, such as Hintze and Skocpol, insist that
it is competition between military rivals that overextends financial resources
and weakens the state, making it vulnerable to revolutionary challenge.

By contrast, some social scientists argue that the analysis can remain purely
domestic, and that one particular sector of any society is the truly decisive one
in the analysis of revolutions. This view is summarized by Hagopian (1974: 1)
when he defines revolution as "an acute prolonged crisis in one or more of
the traditional systems of stratification (class, status, power) of a political
community, which involves a purposive, elite-directed attempt to abolish or
to reconstruct one or more of said systems by means of an intensification of
political power and recourse to violence."

Still others answer the question of what it is that changes in an ideological
way: what distinguishes revolution in their view is the ideas that it embodies.
Hegel, for example, wrote that "once the realm of the imagination has been
revolutionized, reality can no longer hold out" (cited in Zagorin, 1982, vol
1: 18). And Dr Johnson, writing after his tour of Scotland, reflected on the
Union of 1707 by declaring that "[e]stablished custom is not easily broken,
till some great event shakes the whole system of things, and life seems to

recommence upon new principles'' (cited in Kiernan, 1986: 121). In *The Rights of Man*, Thomas Paine also made this transformation its defining feature:

> What we formerly called Revolutions, were little more than a change of persons, or an alteration of the local circumstances. They rose and fell like things of course, and had nothing in their existence or their fate that could influence beyond the spot that produced them. But what we now see in the world, from the Revolutions of America and France, are a renovation of the natural order of things, a system of principles as universal as truth and the existence of man, and combining moral with political happiness and national prosperity.

Most recently, the philosopher Hannah Arendt has made this moral and ideational transformation the pivot around which the definition of revolution turned. She embraces a political and social understanding of the component elements of the phenomenon; she writes that a revolution does ''not end with the abolition of state and government, but, on the contrary, aims at the foundation of a new state and the establishment of a new form of government'' (Arendt, 1965: 265). On reflection, one realizes that this is not a structural but a moral analysis of the relationship between state and society. ''Only where change occurs in the sense of a new beginning, where violence is being used to constitute an altogether different form of government, to bring about the formation of a new body politic, where the liberation from oppression aim[s] at least at the constitution of freedom can we speak of revolution''(Arendt, 1965: 28). In its object, revolution differs from other forms of revolt since the goal of rebellion is ''liberation,'' but the goal of revolution is ''the foundation of freedom'' (Arendt, 1965: 140).

While the ideological goal of any revolutionary effort ought not be dismissed by social scientists, neither can it be the deciding mechanism in its definition. Revolutions are phenomena that involve large numbers of people acting collectively in the pursuit of both material (economic, political) and ideal (ideological, social) interests. An analysis of revolution, however morally compelling (as Arendt's is), must rest on more than the ideational objectives of the participants.

In this book, we will distinguish between several spatial levels of analysis, and later attempt to integrate an understanding of the role of ideology and visions of social reconstruction held by participants in revolution. First, we will place the revolutionary society within a larger context of international economic and geopolitical relationships with other actors. Thus framed within this context, the class-based forces that are mobilized in a revolution will come into sharper focus, and we will also stress the importance of the relationships among these class-based forces and the state. I will argue that an adequate model of revolution must analyze all three of these spatial relationships; the international context, class relations at the level of production, and political relationships among various classes and the state are the stuff of which revolutions are made, and hence the structural materials by which the social scientist can build a model of revolution.

What Causes Revolution?

An obviously central question concerns the causes of revolutions. A wide variety of economic, political, social, cultural, religious, and ideological forces can influence the revolution and the specific arrangement of these forces gives each revolution its unique historical shape. Yet some of these forces are more decisive in causing a revolution than others. Aristotle believed that inequality was the chief cause of revolution. "Everywhere," he wrote in *Politics* (cited in Pettee, 1938: 31), "inequality is a cause of revolution, but an inequality in which there is no proportion – for instance a perpetual monarchy among equals; and always it is the desire of equality which rises in rebellion." Other theorists have offered a wide range of combinations among these factors, assigning different determinant weights to each of these forces.

Just as the problem of the unit of analysis sets the spatial dimension of revolution, the problem of causation sets the temporal dimension. Revolutions do not simply happen because of an economic crisis, or because a religious leader urges his or her followers to rebel, or because a group of people suddenly find themselves discontented with political arrangements in society, or because a nation is defeated in a war and is therefore vulnerable to mass discontent – although each of these has been offered as a causal explanation of revolution. I will argue, however, that revolutions have their structural roots deeply embedded in the society's past. As nineteenth-century reformer Wendell Phillips once wrote, "Revolutions are not made, they come. A revolution is as natural a growth as an oak. It comes out of the past. Its foundations are laid far back" (cited in Ruiz, 1980: 406). The task of the social scientist is to sort out these long-run structural causes from the shorter-run events that set these structures in motion and the immediate historical events that ignite the conflict.

We will distinguish between the three temporal moments suggested in the last sentence, and between the *preconditions*, which include the longer-run, structural shifts in the social foundations of the society; the *precipitants*, which include the shorter-run historical events that allow these deeply seated structural forces to emerge as politically potent and begin to mobilize potential discontents; and the *triggers*, which are the immediate historical events that set the entire revolutionary process in motion. None of these levels is itself sufficient as an adequate analysis of revolution , although one cannot build such an analysis if anyone of them is missing.[2]

These temporal levels are easily grasped by metaphor. Imagine a revolution to be analogous to the outbreak of a fire in one's home. Preconditions might include the structural materials of which the house is constructed, its location in a cold climate in which furnaces are required for heat, the use of the basement as a storage area for home maintenance materials. Obviously, these by themselves do not cause a fire. Precipitants might include a series of very hot sunny, dry days in the summer, and additional oily rags placed haphazardly in the basement. Such a potentially explosive environment is vulnerable to a stray spark from a match or the hot-water heater, which might be sufficient to trigger the conflagration that could destroy the entire house. When the newspaper headline the next day cries that a stray match "caused" the fire, we are invited to mistake the trigger of an event for its long-run causes.

We might just as easily ask what motivates a student to take a course in political sociology, or the sociology of revolution or the like. We might explain such curious behavior by a host of factors, but I suggest that it is not immediately attributable to the presence of one's friends in a specific course, the reputation of the instructor, or the occurence of an empty slot in one's schedule at a convenient time. Rather, these individual biographical events are the products of a rather complex set of institutional forces that shape and mold immediate individual choices. To follow this example, the long-run preconditions might include the general structure of society – the need for a college education to secure a career with good chances of advancement, and the need to secure a career with good chances of advancement, and the need to receive the appro priate credentials to effect social mobility. Individuals – both students and teachers – end up at specific universities as a result of a number of social and economic factors. What precipitates a student's decision to take a particular class might be an interest in sociology in general or the belief that a sociology degree is a prerequisite for social mobility. Or the student might understand sociology courses to be the most interesting, or the least difficult, or the best taught, of all potential choices at this particular university at this particular time. With all these structural forces in place, we finally can determine whether the course fits our schedule, whether the professor has a good reputation, whether we have friends in the class. As we have seen, though, a serious problem with theories of revolution is the mistaking of the trigger for the structural cause. A stray match does not cause a fire; it creates the missing – often accidental – ingredient in the fire-prone situation. In our analysis of revolution, we shall distinguish between these three temporal levels in order to determine what causes revolutions.

Why Do People Participate in Revolutions?

Why do people rebel? What motivates people – either individually or in groups – to participate in a revolution in the first place? Every social scientific treatment of revolution must include a theory of motivation, a psychology of revolutionary behavior. Such theories may be based on an implicit set of psychological assumptions about what motivates human behavior in any case, or they may explain only the extraordinary behavior of people in a revolutionary situation. They may be based upon assumptions that people act rationally, calculating their interests and acting accordingly, or they may be based on theories that suggest a basic irrationality for human behavior, especially in the formation of, and behavior in, groups. They may stress the individual as the key historical actor, or understand individual behavior only in so far as the individual is a member of some group, whose "personality" he or she adopts.

Many of the scholars whose work we will consider also stress one social group – peasants, urban workers, disaffected intellectuals, and so on – as the key social group whose participation in some ways defines the revolution. I will argue for a more comprehensive structural model of participation, one which accounts for the participation of elites and non-elites, of peasants and workers, of loyal middle classes and dissident middle classes. I will argue that revolutions are made not by a politically disenfranchised class acting as a united front against another, politically empowered class, but that revolutions are made by a *coalition of political opposition* which brings together members from various social groups into a common cause against the existing political regime. I will also agrue that this coalition is brought together in part by the actions of the regime itself. Classes do not contend for the state, but rather coalitions form in opposition to the state and struggle with it.

The specific motivations that these participants may exhibit is also important. Many of the non-structural theories that we will discuss contain elaborate explanations of revolution in terms of these motivations. The sensitivity of these theorists is vital for us to retain, even if these theories are ultimately unsatisfactory, especially since many of the structural theories explain away participation by reference to other structural features. Here, however, it is imperative to continue to listen to Marx's famous line from his own historical analysis of the revolution of 1848. People, Marx wrote, "make their own history, but they do not do so just as they please; they do not make it under circumstances chosen by themselves, but under circumstances directly encountered, given, and transmitted from the past" (Marx, 1963 [1852]: 15).

Our analysis will attempt to understand the conditions under which people make their history, and the visions of the future that they develop when they do, in fact, make history. I believe that we can identify two sources of motivation, two emotions that combined, propel people into revolutionary activity and motivate their behavior. These two emotions are *despair* and *hope*. Although I argue that a structural explanation of revolution is the most essential, I believe it is important to constantly remind structuralists of the human factor in revolutionary events, the human experiences that drive some people and inspire others (or often inspire and drive the same people) to attempt to transform the society in which they live. Despair and hope motivate revolutionary activity in tandem; they are mutually reinforcing emotions in a society where structural conditions might produce a revolutionary situation. Neither alone captures my image of revolutionary motivation; it is neither the grinding misery of economic poverty and political repression nor the euphoric utopian "mad inspiration" of the visionary that alone can account for revolutionary participation (Trotsky, 1930: 320). Despair may make revolutionary activity necessary, but hope transforms a rebellion or revolt into a purposive and visionary movement, one capable of transforming the social foundations of political power.

What are the Consequences of Revolution?

Finally, every theory of revolution must examine the effect of the revolution on society. What are the outcomes of revolution? Are they always the same; that is, does the definition of revolution depend upon a certain outcome? Does a revolution actually change anything, or does it simply replace one set of rulers with another, who will eventually become corrupt and repressive, therefore sparking off another round of revolutionary upheavals? Social scientists have offered a variety of answers to this question, suggesting cyclical theories of revolution and restoration, historical processes with well-defined stages, or identifying specific results that define the nature of the revolution itself.

As we have seen, several social scientist have stressed the success of the revolution as a constituent element in its definition. Here, I shall follow Tilly, who suggests that we distinguish between *revolutionary situations* and *revolutionary outcomes*. By casting the outcome of the revolution as problematic, something to be explained, we remove the success or failure of the revolution as its defining feature, opening up an enormous number of empirical cases of revolutionary situations that may be fruitfully analysed.

A Method of Inquiry

How is one to study revolution in order to make sense of it? Political scientist Harry Eckstein (1965) has offered a suggestive program for research. Eckstein insists that the scholar make several strategic and analytic choices to pursue the study of revolution. Should one focus on insurgents or incumbents? Employ structural or behavioral hypotheses to explain participation? Stress particular conditions or general processes that structure the possibilities for revolutionary behavior? While I agree with Eckstein (1965: 152) that "studies have so far concentrated on precipitants rather than preconditions, insurgents rather than incumbents, and particular aspects of social structure rather than the effects of orientations on general social processes," I emphatically do not share his insistence that one choose between two items in each of three sets of variables. Instead of this false choice, I would argue that an adequate conceptual model of revolution should account for the participation of both incumbents and insurgents, and understand how the behavior of each conditions the possibilities for action of the other; employ both structural and behavioral hypotheses, to grasp the larger forces that ground specific behaviors; and examine the specific conditions for any one empirical case of revolution as well as the general processes common to all of these cases.

The questions posed in this introductory chapter demand that an adequate explanation of revolution be *both comparative and historical*. As Tocqueville reminded us (1970: 111) we must be comparative because "[w]hoever studies and looks only at France will never understand anything . . . of the French Revolution." And Otto Hintze argued that (1975: 23) "[y]ou can compare in order to find something general that underlies the things that are compared, and you can compare in order to grasp more clearly the singularity of the thing that is compared, and to distinguish it from others." The sociologist, Hintze claims, does the former and the historian performs the latter. Hobsbawm makes an even stronger historical case when he argues that to understand a revolution one needs to understand both the historical context of the revolution, and also of the person studying it. While the "historical study of revolution cannot usefully be separated from that of the specific historical periods in which they occur," the analysis of revolution can likewise "never be separated from the history of the period in which the scholar studies it, including the scholar's personal bias" (Hobsbawm, 1986: 17).

The study of revolutions must be historically sensitive and broadly comparative; we must, in the words of that masterful French historian Marc Bloch, "learn not to attach too much importance to local pseudo-causes; at the same time . . . learn to become sensitive to specific differences" (Bloch, 1967: 73). At the same time, we cannot remain dispassionately on the sidelines, studying revolutions without engaging ourselves in the process. Our own biases, our fears of change, or our pity for people's misery, will partially determine what elements we choose to study and the position we will take. ''Objective'' analysis is neither desirable nor possible. ''To 'let the facts speak for themselves'', Max Weber once wrote, (1958: 146) ''is the most unfair way of putting over a political position to the student.''

The study of revolution requires strategic analytic and intellectual choices and also the explication of our moral and political position. Although contemporary social scientists may have ignored or forgotten this important point, the historical founders of contemporary social science made it a prominent feature of their work. Tocqueville, Marx, Weber, and Durkheim were all passionately moral thinkers, whose political involvements often informed their choices about what to study and whose theories often impelled a reconsideration of easily accepted political truths. We will begin our inquiry into revolution then, with a look back at our forebears.

2

On the Shoulders of Giants: Classical Sociological Perspectives on Revolution

Although this book is primarily concerned with the ways in which contemporary social scientists have addressed the problem of revolution, such a discussion is impossible without first briefly examining the perspectives of the influential mid-and late-nineteenth-century European social theorists who are considered to be the classical social theorists. The issues raised by Marx, Weber, Tocqueville, Durkheim, and Freud have dominated social science theorizing; contemporary social scientists stand on the shoulders of these intellectual giants to gain any perspective at all on the terrain of revolution they seek to map.

Classical sociological theorists were preoccupied with the question of revolution.[1] For one thing, they all lived and wrote during eras of revolution, when revolutions made moral and political claims on Europeans' hearts and minds. Certain historical periods, such as the mid-seventeenth, late eighteenth, mid-nineteenth centuries, or the three years following the First World War, have been times when many societies on the European continent have been consumed with revolutionary upheavals. All of the theorists we will consider here lived during such times. Marx and Tocqueville wrote their major works in response to the calamitous upheavals of 1848, when no fewer than fifty revolutionary movements vied for political power in the major states and the smaller countries of western Europe. Weber and Freud were each deeply affected by the First World War (as well as the Russian Revolution to a lesser degree), and Durkheim responded directly to both socialist revolutionary organizing and the crisis in France precipitated by the Dreyfus affair.

Beyond the historical era in which they lived, and which they felt made moral claims upon them, classical theorists felt an intellectual need to deal with the problem of revolution because revolutions were extreme moments of social change, and to fail to explain them would indicate a failure to understand the dynamics of social change themselves, and hence the dynamics of social stability. Historically, morally, politically, and theoretically, then, classical social theorists were preoccupied with the problem of revolution. Their perspectives are not only theoretically compelling in their own terms, but they also set the intellectual agenda for contemporary theorizing, and so we will briefly discuss them here.

Karl Marx and Revolutionary Imperatives

Marx is, perhaps, the foremost theorist of revolution in all social science, "the greatest theorist . . . revolutions ever had" (Arendt, 1965: 55). Revolution forms the analytic core of his historical theory, and also dominates his prognosis of the future. As Tucker noted (1966: 218–19):

> The idea of revolution is present in nearly everything that Marx wrote. It is the theoretical axis of his early philosophical writings. It is the *leitmotif* of his great political pamphlets on the 1848 events, the *coup d'état* of Louis Bonaparte, and the Paris Commune. It informs almost all that he has to say on the strategy and tactics of the Communist movement. It is a favorite subject in the voluminous correspondence that he carried on with Engels and others. And his major work, *Capital*, together with his other economic writings, is essentially a political economy of revolution, an inquiry into the conditions of capitalism's revolutionary self destruction. In a basic sense, therefore, revolution was the master theme of Marx's thought and an exposition of the Marxian revolutionary idea in complete form would be nothing other than an exposition of Marxism itself as a theoretical system.

Revolution is, to Marx, not only the mechanism that brought us here, but it is also our ineluctable future. Marx's theory of revolution can be understood as composed of three separate parts, each linked to his overall model of the dynamics of society. First, we will need to discuss how revolutions are the inevitable outcome of the differential rates of development of the structural contradiction that defines any society. Second, we need to examine how revolutions have taken place through world history to establish the contemporary capitalist society and how Marx maintains that revolution is the inevitable outcome of the dynamics of this social formation. Finally, we will need to examine how these abstract theoretical claims are transformed or modified when Marx focuses his attention on concrete historical cases of revolution.

For Marx, revolutions happen when the objective conditions necessary for them have developed. Society, he argues, is held together by a dynamic

tension between the means (or forces) of production – the technical, material, natural, and human resources that are brought into play in the provision
of life's necessities, such as food, clothing, and shelter – and the relations of
production, which consist of those social arrangements that groups of men
and women develop by which to organize the provision of those necessities.
"[L]ife involves before everything else eating and drinking, a habitation,
clothing and many other things,' wrote Marx in *The German Ideology* (1978
[1846]: 156). "The first historical act is thus the production of the means to
satisfy these needs, the production of material life itself."

Historically, Marx observes, this process of production is social and yet the
means of production have been privately owned, thus dividing society into
two irreconcilable classes: those who own the means of production and those
who own nothing but their capacity to labor. The division of society into two
classes based on their relationship to the means of production is the central
objective fact of all societies that have ever existed; in the opening lines of *The
Communist Manifesto* (1848) Marx writes that "[t]he history of all hitherto
existing society is the history of class struggle" (Marx, 1978: 473).[2]

Although social dynamics differ within any particular mode of production
(the combination of the means and relations of production) the fact that
production is social and the means of production privately owned impels
their development to proceed at different rates. The means of production
always develop more rapidly than the relations of production. For example,
technological breakthroughs, new production techniques, the development
of new materials all occur within the existing relations of production, which
are then reorganized to accommodate these dramatic changes in the means of
production. Thus, the objective forces – technology, economics – develop
first, and social changes are efforts to keep pace with these changes in the
productive foundation of society. It is a form of "culture lag" in which
human relationships are constantly scrambling to keep pace with structural
changes. It is important to remember that these productive forces are
objective social facts to Marx; "the productive forces appear as a world for
themselves, quite independent of and divorced from the individuals,
alongside the individuals" (Marx, 1978 [1846]: 190).

At certain moments, the development of the means of production
proceeds so far that the existing relations of production can no longer
accommodate those changes within the existing social framework. At these
moments, Marx argues, an era of social revolution has arrived. The development of insoluble contradictions within society "prepares the way for *social
crises*, which burst out in *political revolutions*," Marx told a Cologne jury in
1849 (cited in Draper, 1978, vol. 2: 19). In his Preface to *A Contribution to
the Critique of Political Economy* (1978 [1859]: 4–5) Marx summarized his
position:

At a certain stage of their development, the material productive forces of society come in conflict with the existing relations of production, or – what is but a legal expression of the same thing – with the property relations within which they have been at work hitherto. From forms of development of the productive forces these relations turn into their fetters. Thus begins an epoch of social revolution. With the change of the economic foundation the entire immense superstructure is more or less rapidly transformed.

When Marx turns to capitalist society specifically in *The German Ideology* (1978 [1846]: 192–3), we can observe the application of this abstract model:

> In the development of productive forces there comes a stage when productive forces and means of intercourse are brought into being, which, under the existing relationships, only cause mischief, and are no longer productive but destructive forces (machinery and money); and connected with this a class is called forth, which has to bear all the burdens of society without enjoying its advantages, which, ousted from society, is forced into the most decided antagonism to all other classes; a class which forms the majority of all members of society, and from which emanates the consciousness of the necessity of a fundamental revolution, the communist consciousness, which may, of course, arise among the other classes too through the contemplation of the situation of this class.

Marx insists that the same mechanism that holds society together in dynamic tension – the conflict between the forces and relations of production – is also the force that will create the objective conditions for revolution. What is more, these objective conditions occur independently, and indeed are historically and logically prior to any psychological motivation towards revolution by any social groups. Revolutions may be made by discontented people, but they can only do so when the objective structural conditions are already conducive to revolution. "A radical social revolution is connected with certain historical conditions of economic development;" revolutions cannot be made, no matter how much people may struggle, in a non-revolutionary situation (Marx, 1978 [1875]: 543).

Thus far, then, we can say that Marx's theory of revolution is *structural*, in that it involves dynamics between objective structural forces; *economistic*, in that the development of a revolutionary situation, in the final analysis, depends upon the sharpening of contradictions in the sphere of economic production; *non-voluntaristic*, in that revolutions do not depend upon internal psychological states of members of any collectivity, but rather on the appearance of a revolutionary situation based on the differential rates of development of the means and relations of production; and *progressive*, in that revolutions are the culmination of historical processes and, by implication, should occur first in the most advanced societies as well as in the most advanced economic sectors within any one society. In addition, by allowing the relations of production to catch up with the economic capacity of the means of production, the revolution clears away those social obstacles to increased economic development.

The origins of revolution are structural, and its agents, those who make revolution, are also derived from economic relations. Classes make revolution in Marx's view, and they do so to capture political power, enabling the transformation of superstructural relations to facilitate their unfettered economic development. "If revolutions are the locomotives of history," writes Tucker (1966: 228), "class struggles are the locomotives of revolution." In feudalism, it is the bourgeoisie who become the revolutionary class; neither owners of the means of production (lords) nor those who labor (serfs), the bourgeoisie develop within feudalism only to overturn that system in the great bourgeois revolutions (such as the English, French, and American revolutions) and create the conditions for a new mode of production based on the economic and political power of the bourgeoisie. That system is called capitalism.

In such a model several themes are apparent. First, revolutions are the attempts of a revolutionary class to seize the political apparatus (the state) against the resistance of the class that currently holds political power. The state, in this model, is thus an institutional chameleon, able to adopt the class character of whatever class holds economic power. The bourgeois revolutions accomplish the transfer of political power from the aristocracy to the bourgeoisie, *because* economic power has already been transferred to the bourgeoisie. Revolution establishes in the superstructure what has already occurred within the economic base of society.

Second, as each revolution is the work of a particular class, we can see that the bourgeoisie was originally a revolutionary class that overturned the feudal mode of production. Only then did the bourgeoisie become the dominant and oppressive class, calling into being their own executioner, the proletariat. Political success transformed the bourgeoisie from revolutionaries into oppressors. Historically, then, the bourgeoisie has been a revolutionary force, simplifying the class antagonisms into two great class forces, and eliminating those non-economic, emotional connections that composed the oppressive coherence of the feudal community. "The bourgeoisie is here conceived as a revolutionary class – as the bearer of large-scale industry – relative to the feudal lords and the lower middle class, who desire to maintain all social positions that are the creation of obsolete modes of production," Marx wrote in *The Critique of the Gotha Program* (1978 [1875]: 532). In one of Marx's most eloquent passages in the *Manifesto* he recites some of these revolutionary changes:

> The bourgeoisie, wherever it has got the upper hand, has put an end to all
> feudal, patriarchal, idyllic relations. It has pitilessly torn asunder the motley

feudal ties that bound man to his "natural superiors", and has left remaining no other nexus between man and man than naked self-interest, than callous "cash payment". It has drowned the most heavenly ecstacies of religious fervour, of chivalrous enthusiasm, of philistine sentimentalism, in the icy water of egotistical calculation. (Marx, 1978: 475)

The emergence of the capitalist mode of production establishes the bourgeoisie not as the revolutionary class but as the dominant class, and this new form of production brings into existence the proletariat, who are the revolutionary class under capitalism. Capitalism is a historically unique mode of production for several reasons. Capitalism presents the first time in history when the forces of production are advanced and developed enough to provide for the material needs of all the members of a society. Thus capitalism eliminates scarcity as the basis for private property and private accumulation of wealth. Second, capitalism evidences the first time in history when the majority class is also the revolutionary class. In feudalism, you will recall, the majority class (serfs) and the revolutionary class (bourgeoisie) were different; in capitalism the proletariat are both the majority and the revolutionary class. Thus the revolution from capitalism to socialism provides the first historical possibility for genuine democracy, the political rule by the majority/revolutionary class; as Engels wrote in "The Tactics of Social Democracy":

All revolutions up to the present day have resulted in the displacement of one definite class rule by another; but all ruling classes up to now have only been small minorities in relation to the ruled mass of people. One ruling minoroty was thus overthrown; another minority seized the helm of state in its stead and refashioned the state institutions to suit its own interests. (Marx, 1978 [1895]: 560)

(Thus although capitalism may provide for *formal* democracy, as in elections, the choice is always between two capitalist candidates. *Substantive* democracy, the real majority rule, will have to await socialism, when the majority class will also be the class in power.)

The socialist revolution is the inevitable outgrowth of the dynamics of capitalist production, according to Marx. The contradictions that lie at the heart of capitalism are the structural sources of the revolution, with the proletariat as its agent. The contradictions within capitalism are several. First, production is oriented not towards meeting human needs but towards the generation of profits; thus the proletariat is not assured of material survival, and the bourgeoisie is trapped within an endless cycle of profit generation. Second, ownership and control are concentrated in private hands, although production is increasingly social. Third, although production in each individual factory is increasingly rational, disciplined, and planned, there is little or no planning within the system as a whole, and from factory to factory.

The consequences for the capitalist class and the proletariat flow directly from these structural contradictions. As competition for profits among capitalists increases, as each tries to maximize his or her position in the market and to undercut potential competitors, capitalists will attempt to innovate to gain market position, or will resort to suppressing wages and removing benefits given to the working class as a way to recoup potential drops in the ability to accumulate profits. (Thus capitalists will manipulate the two factors that compose capitalist production: the means of production (technological innovation) and human labor power (squeezing wages, eliminating social benefits) all in the name of maintaining profitability.)

This process has important consequences for both classes. First, the number of successful capitalists decreases while their wealth increases. Capital is increasingly concentrated into fewer and fewer hands, and those who are successful have greater shares of society's wealth. At the same time, the development of productive forces, in the pursuit of profits, is dramatically expedited. Among the proletariat, however, the consequences are the opposite. The number of proletarians increases as members of the middle classes and former capitalists lose out in the race for profits, and they are increasingly concentrated into larger and larger physical units as production is streamlined and factory production increases. But just as there are more proletarians and they are increasingly concentrated numerically, they are also increasingly impoverished by the squeezing of wages. Thus while capital is concentrated and the number of capitalists is reduced, the proletariat is numerically increased and physically concentrated, and its wealth decreases. The proletarians are *immiserated*: their lives are objectively worse than before.

The dynamics of capitalism have thus set the objective structural conditions for the socialist revolution. Yet the socialist revolution does not happen without the transformation of the proletariat into a revolutionary class, acting for itself as the active agent of historical transformation. In the concluding passage from Marx's *The Poverty of Philosophy* (1847), Marx explains the important transformation (1978: 218):

> Economic conditions first transformed the mass of the people of the country into workers. The combination of capital has created for this mass a common situation, common interests. This mass is thus already a class as against capital, but not yet for itself. In the struggle . . . this mass becomes united, and constitutes itself as a class for itself. The interests it defends become class interests. But the struggle of class against class is a political struggle.

Class-consciousness is thus the inevitable outcome of these structural developments, and the necessary condition for revolutionary action. The proletariat must recognize that it is a class *in itself*, a coherent entity opposed to capitalists, and then, through political struggle, organize itself as a class *for itself*, as an historical force capable of revolutionary transformation. The precise process of this transition is never clearly spelled out by Marx, and has been the subject of fierce political battles which the Marxist tradition. (I will return to this problem below.)

In the revolution, the proletariat first seizes political power, and then sets about the arduous task of social transformation through the socialization of the means of production. As Engels put it in *Socialism: Utopian and Scientific* (1978 [1892]: 717):

> The proletariat seizes the public power, and by means of this transforms the socialised means of production, slipping from the hands of the bourgeoisie, into public property. By this act, the proletariat frees the means of production from the character of capital they have thus far borne, and gives their socialised character complete freedom to work itself out. Socialised production upon a predetermined plan becomes henceforth possible. The development of production makes the existence of different classes of society thenceforth an anachronism. In proportion as anarchy in social production vanishes, the political authority of the state dies out. Man, at last the master of his own form of social organisation, becomes at the same time the lord over Nature, his own master – free.

Thus the socialist revolution produces the structural conditions for human freedom: by eliminating class struggle via the abolition of private property, by doing away with the role of the state as a regulator of anarchic competition, and by alleviating the scarcity of material goods that initially drives workers into the capitalist factories. By ushering in substantive democratic political control, political rule by the numerical majority, the need for the state as the political form of class rule is also diminished; the state no longer has to guarantee capitalists a safe and regulated arena in which to accumulate capital nor to enforce the exploitation of the proletariat.

We have seen how Marx's theory of revolution set two mobilized and conscious classes in opposition to one another, classes whose position and consciousness were sharpened in political struggle, a struggle for state power. And we have seen how the theory of revolution depended upon the sharpening of contradictions among structural forces, not on the subjective experiences of any individuals. Yet when Marx turned his attention away from theory, and examined the historical cases of revolution that erupted across the European continent in the mid-nineteenth century, his discussion of revolution took on far more nuances and shades. In these discussions allows for individual perception and for complex relations among the various social groups that compose any society. In his two best-known historical analyses of revolution, *The Eighteenth Brumaire of Louis Bonaparte* (1852) and *Class*

Struggles in France (1850), Marx modified some of his earlier rigid formulations.

In the 1848 revolution in France, Marx was confronted with historical situation that seems to disconfirm his abstract theory. The collapse of the July Monarchy in France in February 1848 ushered in a period of class struggles and political maneuvering that led to the establishment of the Second Republic, a parliamentary republic dominated by the bourgeoisie. This fits with Marx's model, in that a basically aristocratic system was replaced by a more bourgeois political form. However, the man who was elected president of this new republic was Louis Bonaparte, a rather unremarkable adventurer who was the nephew of Napoleon Bonaparte, and who confessed that he aspired to be an emperor, just as his uncle had been. In December 1851, Louis Bonaparte made good that promise and overturned the republic to establish a dictatorship, and in the process imprisoning many of the political representatives of the bourgeoisie. The Second Empire thus appeared entirely above society, and beyond the control of the dominant social class.

Marx contends, however, that this confirms his general model of revolutions because it demonstrates the ways in which political position and class position are connected, and because the only way to explain these events is by recourse to the social conditions that gave rise to Bonaparte's *coup d'état* and the class interests that underlay his action. Marx argues that in such a complex political situation, the bourgeoisie was threatened by class-based revolt from below, and thus was willing to abdicate political power in order to maintain and consolidate its economic power:

> [B]y now stigmatizing as "socialistic" what it had previously extolled as "liberal," the bourgeoisie confesses that its own interests dictate that it should be delivered from the danger of its *own rule*; that, in order to restore tranquillity [*sic*] in the country, its bourgeois parliament must, first of all, be given its quietus; that in order to preserve its social power intact, its political power must be broken; that the individual bourgeois can continue to exploit the other classes and to enjoy undisturbed property, family, religion and order only on condition that their class be condemned along with the other classes to like political nullity; that in order to save its purse, it must forfeit the crown, and the sword that is to safeguard it must at the same time be hung over its own head as a sword of Damocles.

Marx argues that the interests of a class are often at variance with the sum total of the interests of its members at any one time; thus to insure the social domination of a class, it may be necessary for certain of its members to be displeased or even displaced from positions of political power.

In a series of articles he wrote for the *New York Tribune* between 1851 and 1852, Marx also discussed the contemporaneous revolution in Germany.

Here he stressed the ways in which emotions and passions played a part in revolutionary motivation, arguing that the events "were not the work of single individuals, but spontaneous, irresistible manifestations of national wants and necessities" (1971: 2). Moreover, as in France, the revolutions of 1848 were not made by unified classes acting in concert, but by political coalitions – among classes, or among particular factions of classes. Although "this union of classes, which in some degree is always the necessary condition of any revolution, cannot subsist long," these class coalitions make the specification of the revolution's class character difficult to discern upon immediate inspection (1971: 31). In France, for example, the proletariat was socialist, whereas the lower middle class tended towards democratic republicanism, which also attracted a small number of bourgeois elements. The bourgeoisie was split between two parties of order, depending upon the source of capital: landed capitalists supported the Legitimist faction, and industrial and financial capitalists supported the Orleanist faction. Most significantly, the peasantry were solidly reactionary, supporting Louis Bonaparte, and hence the interests of capital. In one of the most memorable passages of *The Eighteenth Brumaire* (Marx, 1963 [1852]: 123–4), Marx insists that we should not look to the peasantry for revolutionary possibilities; they belong to a non-capitalist age and cannot see beyond it:

> The small-holding peasants form a vast mass, the members of which live in similar conditions but without entering into manifold relations with one another. Their mode of production isolates them from one another instead of bringing them into mutual intercourse . . . A small-holding, a peasant and his family; alongside them another small-holding, another peasant and another family. A few score of these make up a village, and a few score of villages make up a Department. In this way, the great mass of the French nation is formed by simple addition of homologous magnitudes, much as potatoes in a sack form a sack of potatoes . . . In so far as there is merely a local interconnection among these small-holding peasants, and the identity of their interests begets no community, no national bond and no political organization among them, they do not form a class. They are consequently incapable of enforcing their class interest in their own name, whether through a parliament or through a convention. They cannot represent themselves, they must be represented. Their representative must at the same time appear as their master, as an authority over them, as an unlimited governmental power that protects them against the other classes and sends them rain and sunshine from above. The political influence of the small-holding peasants, therefore, finds its final expression in the executive power subordinating society to itself.

I have quoted this passage from Marx at such length because I believe that it leads directly to a discussion of the problems in Marx's analysis of revolution. While Marx's structural logic of revolution is a brilliant formulation, and one that will inform the theory of revolution that I will develop in this volume, there are several historical developments that Marx's theory seems ill-equipped to confront. One of the most important of these has been the transformation of the peasantry in the twentieth century into the chief revolutionary actors in the development of socialist society. Marx predicted that the most industrially advanced societies would be the most susceptible to revolutions, since in these the structural contradictions of capitalism would result in the most highly polarized class struggle between bourgeoisie and proletariat. But the revolutions of the twentieth century – in Mexico, Russia, Cuba, Algeria, Angola, Vietnam, Nicaragua, and China – have all been characterized by the revolutionary mobilization of the peasantry; in fact it was the entry of the peasantry that allowed the revolutions to succeed (see Wolf, 1969).[3]

In addition, Marx seriously underestimated the linkages between classes, and the potential for inter-class solidarities to offset the structural tendency toward class polarization. In contemporary industrial society, revolution has failed to occur, in part, because of the powerful support of capitalist class rule by the industrial proletariat, precisely the sector that ought to be most revolutionary. In many ways, much of Marxist writing since Marx's own era has been an effort to salvage Marxism in the light of these significant problems with his predictions. Despite his insistence on the inevitability of revolution, the eruptions he predicted have failed to materialize in the places where he believed they would occur. In the chapters that follow, these post-Marxian elaborations will be discussed as we deal directly with the three structural elements that compose a theory of revolution – the international context, class struggle at the level of production, and the state – and the theory of political mobilization that we can derive from those elements.

Alexis de Tocqueville and Revolutionary Ambivalence

Alexis de Tocqueville observed the same revolutionary events as Marx, but came up with a decidedly different theoretical explanation, although there are many points on which the two agree. In briefly explaining Tocqueville's model we will employ the opposite strategy to that we used with Marx: first we shall look at Tocqueville's empirical and historical discussions of both the revolution of 1789 and the revolutions of 1848, and then we shall extract the elements that would compose his theoretical model of revolution in general.

Unlike Marx, who championed the cause of revolution, Tocqueville was profoundly ambivalent about it. While he understood that revolutions happened when aristocracies abandoned their traditional function of the preservation of liberty in the face of state centralization, he also believed that revolutions did not eliminate the state, as Marx had hoped, but cleared the path for further state centralization even as principles of equality were spread. This, for Tocqueville, was a mixed blessing.

His ambivalence can be observed in his classic treatment of the French Revolution of 1789, which Tocqueville distinguishes from other revolutions both by its objects and its results. Here was a decidedly *social* revolution, the object of which was "not merely to change an old form of government but to abolish the entire social structure of pre-revolutionary France;" "less the achievement of political rights than the destruction of privileges" (Tocqueville, 1955: 8; Tocqueville, 1959: 160). But the causes and consequences of the revolution as seen by Tocqueville were very different to those theorized by Marx. For one thing, the state was not simply the object of contention, but rather the centralization of state power was an important precondition of a revolutionary situation. And the outcome of the revolution was hardly the diminution of political power; if state centralization was a cause of the revolution, it was also a consequence. Thus, "the principle of the centralization of power did not perish in the Revolution [and] this very centralization was at once the Revolution's starting-off point and one of its guiding principles" (1955: 60). Finally, the various roles played by different classes differ from the roles assigned to those classes by Marx.

Tocqueville asserts that the origins of the revolution lay in the attempts by the state to centralize political power; "the monarchical government, after abolishing provincial independence and replacing local authorities by its nominees in three quarters of the country, had brought under its direct management all public business, even the most trivial" (1955: 204). As a consequence of this effort to centralize political power, the monarchy ran into conflict with the hereditary nobility, whose chief political function was to maintain the centrifugal tendencies to disperse political power to the localities and provinces. Over the centuries, however, Tocqueville points out, the monarchy was victorious, leaving no obstacles to state centralization. Thus, "the nobility, after having lost their political rights and ceased . . . to act as leaders of the people . . . ceasing to be a ruling class [and] remained a privileged, closed group" (1955: 204). Tocqueville locates the long-run structural preconditions of revolution not in the contradictions between two economic classes but in the political conflict between the state and its ruling class. Traditionally, the nobility were relentless critics of state centralization:

> They criticized the abuses of royal power; they censured its extravagance; they demanded an account of its expenditures; they spoke of the constitutional laws of the country, of the fundamental principles limiting the unlimited power of the Crown and, without exactly calling for national participation in the

government through the Estates-General, they continually kept suggesting the idea. (Tocqueville, 1959: 44)

But when the nobility permitted the king to impose a national tax, and offered no resistance, Tocqueville observes the pivotal moment in the transformation of the relationship between crown and aristocracy:

> It was on the day when the French people, weary of the chaos into which the kingdom had been plunged for so many years by the captivity of King John and the madness of Charles VI, permitted the King to impose a tax without their consent and the nobles showed so little public spirit as to connive at this, provided their own immunity was guaranteed – it was on that fateful day that the seeds were sown of almost all the vices and abuses which led to the violent downfall of the old regime. (1955: 98–9).

The function of the nobility is to preserve liberty in the face of the equalizing tendencies of the state; their abdication deprived the nation of its chief defenders.

The abdication of the nobility allowed state centralization to proceed without sustained and successful resistance, but over the long term, the divisions created in the wake of such centralization robbed French society of its social coherence. Thus the loosening of traditional bonds of social solidarity were precipitants of revolutionary transformation in old regime France:

> once the bourgeois had been completely severed from the noble, and the peasant from both alike, and when a similar differentiation had taken place within each of these three classes, with the result that each was split up into a number of small groups almost completely shut off from each other, the inevitable consequence was that, though the nation came to seem a homogenous whole, its parts no longer held together. (1955: 136–7).

France was coming apart at the seams.

But the revolution was not brought on by the increasing impoverishment of the lower classes; against Marxian ideas of immiseration, Tocqueville suggests that immediately before the revolution, economic and social conditions had actually improved. "I do not share the view that there was a continous decline in the prosperity of France during the first half of the eighteenth century," he writes (1955: 170). Indeed, Tocqueville points out that "the country did grow richer and living conditions improved throughout the land" although "this steadily increasing prosperity, far from tranquilizing the population, everywhere promoted a spirit of unrest" (1955: 174, 175).[4] This observation leads Tocqueville to one of his few theoretical statements (1955: 176–7):

> it is not always when things are going from bad to worse that revolutions break out. On the contrary, it oftener happens that when a people which has put up

with an oppressive rule over a long period without protest suddenly finds the government relaxing its pressure, it takes up arms against it. Thus the social order overthrown by a revolution is almost always better than the one immediately preceding it, and experience teaches us that, generally speaking, the most perilous moment for a bad government is one when it seeks to mend its ways.

State centralization and the abdication of their traditional role by the hereditary nobility were the long-run preconditions of the revolution; rising prosperity and the generation of revolutionary ideas were the precipitants. Unlike Marx, Tocqueville here assigns an important causal role to ideas, but only ideas in historical context, ideas set in motion by structural changes in the relationship between state and class. In the ten to fifteen years before the revolution, "the human mind was affected by strange, incoherent, irregular impulses, in a mood not seen for centuries" (Tocqueville, 1959: 33). The hatred of the old regime became the "passion dominating all others" and was "the *fundamental, essential, primordial* characteristics of the Revolution, *never* abandoned, *whatever* the circumstance" (1959: 109). When the revolution broke out, it was dominated and inspired by these ideas.

Although state centralization was a cause of the revolution, it was surely the most visible consequence of the revolution as well; the revolution "was essentially a movement for political and social reform and, as such, did not aim at creating a state of permanent disorder in the conduct of public affairs or at 'methodizing anarchy'. On the contrary, it sought to increase the power and jurisdiction of the central authority" (1955: 19). And so it happened; Tocqueville concludes that "the last word always rests with centralization, which grows deeper even when it seems less apparent on the surface, since the social movement, the *atomization* and the *isolation* of social elements, always continues during such times" (1959: 165). Here, Tocqueville echoes his conclusions from his masterful *Democracy in America* (1966). Yet he remains clear that the ideological underpinning of the society had shifted from the preservation of liberty (the dogma of the aristocracy) to the promotion of equality among the citizens (the ideology of the bourgeoisie).

Thus in a strange way, many of Tocqueville's conclusions on the causes and consequences of the French Revolution are actually consistent with Marxian principles. For one thing, both writers acknowledge that different social classes will promote different sets of ideas, that ideas have a class basis. Second, Tocqueville understands that although the immediate victor of the French Revolution was the state, whose centralization proceeded apace, the great losers were the aristocracy and the peasantry; the bourgeoisie gained while these other classes lost. As he wrote in 1852 (1980: 250):

Our history from 1789 to 1830, if viewed from a distance and as a whole, affords as it were the picture of a struggle to the death between the Ancien Regime, its traditions, memories, hopes, and men, as represented by the aristocracy, and the New France under the leadership of the middle class . . . In 1830 the triumph of the middle class had been definite.

Like Marx, Tocqueville's analysis of revolution is structural, relying on the shifting relations between the state and various social classes to establish the preconditions of revolution.[5] However, unlike Marx, Tocqueville assigns a secondary role to class struggle, which he sees as more a consequence of revolution than cause. For example, he writes that "violent and persistent class hatreds are not merely the products of unjust social conditions but of the struggles that upset these" (1959: 161). Revolution does not eliminate class struggle; it causes class struggle.

The fruits of Tocqueville's analysis of the revolution of 1789 are borne out when he recalls the events of 1848–51. Like Marx, Tocqueville was intimately involved in the mid-century revolutionary upheavals. But unlike Marx, he was an insider to the political maneuverings behind the peculiar twists and turns of those upheavals, first as a member of the National Assembly and later as the Minister for Foreign Affairs.[6] In his *Recollections* (1970 [1893]), Tocqueville weaves his immediate impressions of the mercurial events of those confusing days with an occasional analytic insight that stretches his earlier theoretical claims.

Early on in his recollections, for example, Tocqueville insists that the legacy of 1789 was the triumph of the middle class, which was most evident after the upheaval in 1830; then, the "triumph of the middle class was decisive and so complete that the narrow limits of the bourgeoisie encompassed all political powers, franchises, prerogatives, indeed the whole government, to the exclusion, in law, of all beneath it and, in fact, of all that had once been above it" (1970: 5). Class polarization and class struggle were the inevitable outcomes of this shift; in 1847, Tocqueville remembers saying that such developments portend potentially grave consequences (1970: 12–13):

> The time is coming when the country will again be divided between two great parties. The French Revolution, which abolished all privileges and destroyed all exclusive rights, did leave one, that of property. Property holders must not delude themselves about the strength of their position, or suppose that, because it has so far no where been surmounted, the right to property is an insurmountable barrier; for our age is not like any other . . . Soon the political struggle will be between the Haves and the Have-nots; property will be the great battlefield; and the main political questions will turn on the more or less profound modifications of the rights of property owners that are to be made. Then we shall again see great public agitations and great political parties.
>
> Why is everybody not struck by the signs that are the harbingers of this future? Do you think it is by chance, or by some passing caprice of the human

spirit, that on every side we see strange doctrines appearing, which have different names, but which all deny the right of property, or, at least, tend to limit, diminish, or weaken the exercise of that right? Who can fail to recognize in this the last symptom of the old democratic disease of the times, whose crisis is perhaps approaching?

Tocqueville continues his recollections by including a long passage from a speech he delivered to the Chamber of Deputies on January 29, 1848, in which he was "even more explicit and urgent" about the possibilities of revolution. In perhaps the most prescient analysis of the coming of revolution (1970: 13–14), Tocqueville exhorted his colleagues:

> It is said that there is no danger because there is no riot, and that because there is no visible disorder on the surface of society, we are far from revolution.
>
> Gentlemen, allow me to say that I think you are mistaken. True, there is no actual disorder, but disorder has penetrated far into men's minds. See what is happening among the working classes who are, I realize, quiet now. It is true that they are not now tormented by what may properly be called political passions to the extent they once were; but do you not see that their passions have changed from political to social? Do you not see that opinions and ideas are gradually spreading among then that tend not simply to the overthrow of such-and-such laws, such-and-such a minister, or even such-and-such a government, but rather to the overthrow of society, breaking down the bases on which it now rests? Do you not hear what is being said every day among them? Do you not hear them constantly repeating that all the people above them are incapable and unworthy to rule them? That the division of property in the world up to now is unjust? That property rests on bases of inequity? And do you not realize that when such opinions take root and spread, sinking deeply into the masses, they must sooner or later (I do not know when, I do not know how long) bring in their train the most terrifying of revolutions?
>
> Gentlemen, my profound conviction is that we are lulling ourselves to sleep over an active volcano . . .
>
> . . . I was saying just now that sooner or later (I do not know when or whence) this ill will bring into the land revolutions of the utmost seriousness: be assured that that is so.
>
> When I come to study what has been, at different times and epochs of history among different peoples, the effective reason why ruling classes have been ruined, I note the various events and men and accidental or superficial causes, but believe me, the real cause, the effective one, that makes men lose power is that they have become unworthy to exercise it.

Here, in these two passages we find a summary of most of the elements of Tocqueville's analysis of revolution: the abdication of the nobility from their traditional mediating function; the pivotal role given to the changes in the relationship between state and ruling class; the mobilization of ideational forces as motivating forces within a general context; the transformation of political discontent to social discontent; the historical development of class struggle as a consequence of the triumph of the middle classes; and, the slow-moving structural forces that lie dormant under a placid surface, but which, like a volcano, can erupt without warning and destroy the entire edifice of society.

Tocqueville amplifies these themes throughout his discussion of the events of 1848–51. The vicissitudes of political relationships remain both the cause of the revolution – the "prince's bad government had prepared the way for the catastrophe that threw him from the throne" – and the consequence: "when people say that we have nothing that is safe from revolutions, I tell them that they are wrong, that centralization is one thing. In France there is only one thing that we cannot make: a free government; and only one that we cannot destroy: centralization" (1970: 61, 170).

Tocqueville also distances himself from Marxian analysis, departing from Marx on several important issues. Again, Tocqueville notes that the revolutions of 1848 had been prepared for by general increases in prosperity:

> Had no one noticed that for a long time the people had been continually gaining ground and improving their condition, and that their importance, education, desires and power were all constantly growing? Their prosperity had also increased, but not so fast, and it was getting close to that limit which, in old societies, cannot be passed, when there are many candidates but few places . . . Inevitably, they were bound to discover sooner or later that what had held them back in their place was not the constitution of the government, but the unalterable laws that constitute society itself; and it was natural for them to ask whether they did not have the power and the right to change these too, as they had changed the others.

And Tocqueville assigns an important weight to accidental factors as well as structural ones. Although revolutions may be caused in the long run by structural shifts, such as industrial development, changes in political relationships, centralization, new ideas and theories, and social mobility, these alone did not cause the revolution to happen when it did and in the particular form it took. Accidental factors, such as the "clumsy passions of the dynastic opposition," "the mistakes and mental disorientation of [the] ministers," "the absence of the only members of the royal family who had either popularity or energy", and "above all, the senile imbecility of King Louis-Philippe" all contributed (1970: 63). Without accounting for these accidental factors, which go beyond those factors I labelled "triggers" in chapter 1, Tocqueville insists that the revolution would not have occurred in the ways that it did. These non-structural factors – individual personality, chance, and circumstance – must be given their role in the sociological analysis of revolution. "I believe . . . that many important historical facts can be explained only by accidental circumstances, while many others are inexplicable. [C]hance . . . is a very important element in all that we see taking place in the world's theatre." However, chance must be discussed in context; it "can do nothing unless the ground has been prepared in advance. Antecedent facts, the nature of institutions, turns of mind and the state of mores are the materials from which chance composes those impromptu events that surprise and terrify us" (1970: 62).

Politically, Tocqueville distances himself from Marx as well; he does not share Marx's enthusiasm for socialism, which, according to Tocqueville, attacks the very principles the French Revolution promoted. "Whereas the Revolution, fought in the name of liberty, broke the shackles of the old regime and thereby restored individuality, assuming responsibility for everything, socialism negates individuality and independence" (Pope, 1986: 97).

The institutionalization of democracy, suggested by the French Revolution and most fully expressed by the United States, Tocqueville argued, dampens revolutionary fervor and makes revolution increasingly rare. Revolutions, after all, threaten property and trade, whereas American democracy, Tocqueville reminds us, is based upon them. As a result, "the majority of citizens in a democracy do not see clearly what they could gain by a revolution, but they constantly see a thousand ways in which they could lose by one" (Tocqueville, 1966: 636–7). Thus Tocqueville notes that citizens will be increasingly afraid of a revolution.

But if revolutions are increasingly rare in democracy, there still exists the possibility of revolution, not in the equality which spreads through democratic systems, but from the inequality that lingers within it. (Here, his agreement with Marx stands out again.) In America, particularly, Tocqueville predicts that "[i]f there ever are great revolutions there, they will be caused by the presence of blacks on American soil. That is to say, it will not be the equality of social conditions but rather their inequality which may give rise thereto" (1966: 639). More generally, industrialization may lead to the potential for revolutionary upheaval, especially as the tension between employer and employee sharpens when contrasted to the general trend towards equality in democratic societies. This growing contradiction between spreading equality (political relations) and persisting inequality (economic relationships) may produce a revolutionary situation, and the concentration of the working class may facilitate collective action. Tocqueville notes (1966: 200):

> equality increasingly extends its dominion everywhere – except in industry, which is moving in a more aristocratic direction every day . . . Capital is concentrated in a few hands; the profits of those providing work is disproportionate to the worker's wage; the worker is in a position from which it is hard to escape, for he is situated at a great social distance from his employer, and is dependent on him.

Such shocking disparities cannot exist for too long in one society without producing a deep malaise.

Thus, although Tocqueville's route is more circuitous, departing from Marx on several key theoretical points – such as the assignment of weight to causal variables, the temporal sequencing of events, and the political side of the barricades that one should morally place oneself – as well as in their empirical analysis of specific historical events, he sides with Marx on the decisive structural features of the sociological analysis of revolution.[7] Ideas and passions must be seen in context; structural shifts provide the grounding for revolutionary behavior, which is therefore rational and explainable, and not the blind fury of an irrational mob.

Other Classical Perspectives

While our chief interest in this chapter has been a discussion of the theoretical positions of Marx and Tocqueville, other classical sociological theorists have provided more modest analyses of revolution that have informed contemporary analysis. In particular, the work of Max Weber, Emile Durkheim, and Sigmund Freud has made a lasting contribution to contemporary social scientific analysis of revolutionary events. While each of them offered valuable insights to contemporary analysis, their personal and theoretical postures as regards revolution tended to be more conducive to incremental reforms than sweeping transformations.

Max Weber

Weber's analysis of revolution is less concerned with the causes of revolution, which he believed to be structurally based but divided among political, economic, and social origins (he accepted many of Marx's analytic formulations but expanded the types of determinant structure), than with the outcomes of revolutionary upheaval. In this respect his analysis fits with that of Tocqueville. Weber notes that revolutionary breakthroughs are always followed by institutionalization and the strengthening of bureaucratic control; thus state centralization is the consequence of revolutionary change.

Weber locates his theory of revolutions within the larger frame of his typology of authority. For Weber, whose entire corpus is organized around the question of domination, revolution requires a dramatic rupture with relatively stable mechanisms of authority.[8] In fact, Weber suggests that historically, revolutions have had to break through the stability of either traditional, or legal rational forms of authority, in which domination is anchored by recourse to non-personal, historically transcendent forms of custom and legal codes, respectively. In traditional authority, domination is maintained because inherited custom demands obeisance, whereas in rational authority one obeys because of the rationality embedded by formal legal codes, which demand universal adherence. Both systems of domination are obviously stable and non-revolutionary. It is only through the vehicle of charismatic authority, Weber's third category, where domination is based upon the extraordinary characteristics of an individual person, that one could extract a theoretical analysis of revolutionary transformation in his work.

For the appeal of the charismatic leader is, by definition, revolutionary. "The legitimacy of their rule rests on the belief in and the devotion to the extraordinary, which is valued because it goes beyond the normal human qualities, and which was originally valued as supernatural. The legitimacy of charismatic rule thus rests upon the belief in magical powers, revelations and hero worship" (Weber, 1958: 296). Because charismatic authority is located in a person, and not in a system of customs or laws, the authority is, in a particular way, "irrational." Weber writes that charismatic rule "is not managed according to general norms, either traditional or rational, but, in principle, according to concrete revelations and inspirations, and in this sense, charismatic authority is 'irrational'." Further, it is revolutionary, Weber argues because it is not bound to the existing order. The classic statement of the charismatic leader reveals its revolutionary capacity: "It is written – but I say unto you . . .!" (Weber, 1958: 296).

But if charismatic authority is potentially revolutionary because it alone is capable of generating widespread collective action that will challenge the existing normative order, it is also ephemeral and transitory, since it is located in a person and not in a set of abstract principles. Human mortality insures this transitory quality. Unsuccessful charismatic leaders, in fact, are often executed, exiled, or otherwise excluded from the system of authority they challenged, which will allow the continuation of traditional or rational systems of authority, as well as the development of parallel institutions in which the diluted charisma of the absent leader is codified into a system of rituals. Over time, these rituals, designed to re-enact the immediate presence of the charismatic leader, become normative orders of their own, thus reducing the revolutionary quality of charismatic authority and creating instead a social institution in which domination is obtained not by personal qualities of the leader but through participation in a normative order. (Weber seems to think of the institutionalization of the early Christian church as an illustration of this process of institutionalization, thus locating the origins of legal rational authority in the historical outcomes of the disappearance of the charismatic leader.) Thus unsuccessful charismatic authority may return to the system that spawned it, or devolve into an institution which becomes, itself, a mechanism of legal rational authority. The revolutionary potential disappears through the process of institutionalization as easily as it does if the movement of followers is crushed politically or militarily.

This is equally true of successful charismatic leaders, who, after seizing political power, must face the task of rebuilding institutions to insure succession after they, themselves, leave the social order. Who is to take over from the leader? Who will succeed in future generations? The crisis of succession occurs regardless of the success of the movement, and Weber insists that even among irrational, revolutionary movements that succeed, the solution to the succession crisis will inevitably result in institutionalization, by which a set of normative regulations will replace the immediacy of the experience of the charismatic leader. Thus success leads to legal rational authority.

Weber's understanding of charisma as a revolutionary force leads him to a pessimistic conclusion about the potential of revolutionary change. In each case, "[e]motional revolutionism is followed by the traditionalist routine of everyday life; the crusading leader and the faith itself fade away, or, what is even more effective, the faith becomes part of the conventional phraseology of political Philistines and banausic technicians." In fact, he argues "one of the conditions for success is the depersonalization and routinization, in short, the psychic proletarianization, in the interests of the disciple. After coming to power, the following of a crusader usually degenerates very easily into a quite common stratum of spoilsmen" (Weber, 1958: 125).

Since revolutionary change always results in the development of larger, more pervasive normative institutions to replace the ones the revolutionaries have toppled, Weber is unimpressed with revolutionary claims made in the first few years of the twentieth century. He urges his followers not to engage in revolutionary movements, but to engage in politics, the cold, sober business of making political reforms within normative institutions. In the conclusion to his stunning essay "Politics as a Vocation" (1918), he faces the revolutionary world in which he lives and a reformer's zeal of the reader. Summarizing his position of the revolutionary intent of charisma, and the unlikelihood of success, Weber calls his reader to a less glamorous calling:

> Politics is a strong and slow boring of hard boards. It takes both passion and perspective. Certainly all historical experience confirms the truth – that man would not have attained the possible unless time and again he had reached out for the impossible. But to do that a man must be a leader, and not only a leader but a hero as well, in a very sober sense of the word. And even those who are neither leaders nor heroes must arm themselves with that steadfastness of heart, which can brave even the crumbling of all hopes. This is necessary right now, or else men will not be able to attain even that which is possible today. Only he has the calling for politics who is sure that he shall not crumble when the world from his point of view is too stupid or too base for what he wants to offer. Only

he who in the face of all this can say "In spite of all!" has the calling for politics. (Weber, 1958: 128).

Reforming bureaucracies is the only effective method of improving life and making it more meaningful. Reform may be less sweepingly exciting, but revolution only ends up strengthening precisely what needs to be changed.

Emile Durkheim

Durkheim's sociology was also non-revolutionary and reformist, but for strikingly different reasons from Weber's, and with, consequently, very different outcomes. Durkheim argued that the division of labor increased social solidarity, that individuals experienced increased levels of integration and regulation when they experienced themselves to be part of a larger normative order in which they played a small, but vital part. Solidarity was caused by the division of labor, but was experienced by members of society as a *moral* force, binding individuals together into a coherent whole that gave meaning to life. Through the division of labor, individuals could understand how all the component parts of a social system "contribute positively to the functioning of the whole", and how, therefore, "there was an enduring tendency towards equilibrium" within social systems (Fenton, 1984: 42).

Such assumptions lead Durkheim to understand hostility and conflict as the outcome of the incomplete integration or regulation within a society. If society functioned as smoothly as it could, there would be no conflict and certainly no revolution. (This departure from the theories of Marx, Tocqueville, and Weber sets the stage for later theories of revolution from the structural-functionalist school.) Against Marx, for example, Durkheim asserted that class conflict was the outcome of revolutionary efforts, not the cause of them, since revolutions tore apart existing mechanisms of integration and regulation.

Revolutions, themselves, sprang from insufficient integration and regulation of social life. Historically, Durkheim argues that the developing division of labor breaks apart traditional mechanisms of solidarity, so that the earlier experience of connectedness and the customary restraints on individual behavior are weakened. In a Rousseauian mode, Durkheim argues that social and technological progress has outpaced moral development, leaving society disorganized. It is the experience of anomie, the normless state that accompanies low levels of regulation, that leads to revolutionary outbursts, which erupt, like volcanoes, from the bubbling discontent of now disconnected masses.

Such a model assumes that modernization is the great destabilizing force, which produces widespread social dislocation, alienation, and economic hardship, as well as a quantum leap in the expectations that individuals have of what society can provide for them.

Time is required for the public conscience to reclassify men and things. So long as the social forces thus freed have not regained equilibrium, their respective values are unknown and so all regulation is lacking for a time . . . Consequently, there is no restraint upon aspirations . . . With increased prosperity desires increase. At the very moment when traditional rules have lost their authority, the richer prize offered these appetites stimulates them and makes them more exigent and impatient of control. The state of de-regulation or anomie is thus further heightened by passions being less disciplined, precisely when they need more disciplining. (Durkheim, 1951: 253)

Revolutions are like suicide to Durkheim; both are symptoms of social breakdown, the absence of sufficient levels of integration and regulation which could provide the moral coherence of solidarity that alone prevents social disorganization. As a process of economic transformation that loosens traditional bonds, modernization generates a cycle in which restraints on aspirations disappear. As Aya (1979: 51) summarized it:

the onrush of uncontrolled changes in the structure of society begets multiplex tensions, which, if unrelieved, erupt into mass violence where and when social controls relax or weaken. These tensions arise, in turn, from several sources: runaway expectations that outstrip gratifying achievements, producing frustration; disorientation suffered by simple folk recently wrenched from traditional milieux and subjected to the bewildering complexity, impersonality, and sheer novelty of modern life; and, concurrently, the trauma of integration into the alienating role structure of competitive, bureaucratic society. Whereas these discontents mount first in the hearts and minds of uncoordinated individuals, they find outlet sooner or later in collective behavior.

But revolutionary outbursts do not accomplish what they set out to do, which is to relieve tensions and provide new mechanisms of integration and regulation. Instead they plunge the population ever deeper into that anomic world from which they were trying to escape. In *Professional Ethics and Civic Morals*, Durkheim suggests that we "suppose that by a miracle the whole system of property is entirely transformed overnight and that on the collectivist formula the means of production are taken out of the hands of the individual and made over absolutely to collective ownership. All the problems around us that we are debating today will still persist in their entirety" (1957: 30). Revolutionaries, Durkheim argued, were utterly misguided, blaming the systems of rules for their woes, rather than understanding how those rules provided their only source of connectedness and anchored them in a moral community. In *Moral Education*, Durkheim chastized revolutionaries for this failure of moral logic:

Because the rules prevailing in their time offended them deeply, their sense of the evil led them to blame, not this or that particular and transient form of moral discipline, but the principle itself of all discipline. But it is precisely this that always vitiated their efforts; it is this that rendered so many revolutions fruitless, not yielding results corresponding to the effort expended. At the point when one is rising against the rules, their necessity must be felt more keenly than ever. It is just at the moment when one challenges them that he should always bear in mind that he cannot dispense with rules. (Durkheim, 1961: 53–4).

In a way, then, revolutions miss the point, blaming a symptom of unrest for the cause, and eliminating the very mechanisms that could provide emotional relief.

The consequences of revolutionary change are disastrous, Durkheim believes, destroying in a flash what has taken centuries to build. In a passionate argument, Durkheim warned of these dangers (cited in Fenton, 1984: 31):

Man's intelligence should precisely have, as its overriding aim, the taming and muzzling of these blind forces, instead of letting them wreak destruction. I am quite aware when people speak of destroying existing societies, they intend to reconstruct them. But these are the fantasies of children. One cannot in this way rebuild collective life: once our social organization is destroyed, centuries of history will be required to build another. In the intervening period, there will be a new Middle Ages, a transitional period, in which the old departed civilization will not be replaced by any other, or at least will only be replaced by a civilization that is incipient, uncertain and seeking to find itself. It will not be the sun of a new society that will rise, all resplendent over the ruins of the old; instead men will enter into a new period of darkness. Instead of our hastening the advent of that period, it is necessary to employ all our intelligence so as to forestall it, or, if that is impossible, to shorten it and render it less sombre. And to do that we must avoid acts of destruction that suspend the course of social life and civilization.

If revolution brings about precisely the results that gave rise to it in the first place, then the only logical course is to institute reforms to shore up those institutions that might provide integration and regulation of social life. Durkheim believes that this involves, above all else, the bringing of economic activities under increasingly legal, moral, and institutional control. Since the family and religion, the two traditional mechanisms of integration and regulation, can no longer provide the function in modern society that they provided in traditional society, then economic life, and especially the division of labor in the industrial organization, is the only possible source of integration and regulation, and thus the only hedge against revolution. Progressive reform will make society – the source of morality – stronger, which will eliminate the need for revolution and will allow members of the society to feel connected to one another and with the normative order.

Although I will elaborate the implications and contemporary resonances of

Durkheim's argument in the next chapter, it may be useful to note here some of the key themes he raises to foreshadow the appropriation of Durkheim by many of the non-structural contemporary models of revolution. First, revolutions are problematic departures from the normative order, in which all the parts of a system fit together to produce an equilibrated social system. Second, revolutions are the irrational outbursts of discontented groups, whose discontent derives from their disaffection from normative legitimate institutions. Third, these social dislocations stem, in part, from the variations in the rate of modernization among various subsystems of society; economic transformations precede, both logically and historically, the social institutions that will ameliorate their alienating, anomic qualities. Modernization, therefore, brings about a revolutionary situation. The political imperative for one concerned about social welfare is not revolution but reform, which entails strengthening normative institutions, not sweeping them aside in vague and vain efforts to create new ones. Unlike Weber, who argues that these new institutions will become even more rigidly authoritarian and more pervasively dominating, Durkheim argues that the rebuilding effort will take too long and that the new institutions will be neither strong nor pervasive enough to fully integrate the society; these revolutionary institutions will therefore create more social dislocation and anomie than shoring up existing ones would do.

Sigmund Freud

Freud fused elements raised by both Durkheim and Weber; for him, revolution was an irrational act, the dynamics of which were explained by the analogy of social development and individual personality development, and by Freud's characterization of all groups as "neurotic," and held together by irrational bonds between the leader and the followers. Freud's theory of revolution must be teased out of his work by implication, since Freud himself insisted that he was apolitical and that "psychoanalysis in its classic form is inherently ahistorical" (Weinstein and Platt, 1973: 1). When journalist Max Eastman asked Freud "[w]hat are you politically?" Freud replied "[p]olitically I am just nothing" (Eastman, 1936: 128).

Despite such caveats, Freud did observe the political events around him with a keen eye, commenting on the Russian Revolution on several occasions, and also on the European socialist movement. And theoretically, Freud's model of revolution can be discerned in his writings about the origins of society, the nature of groups, and his diagnosis of contemporary society. In these three areas, Freud makes an important contribution to the contemporary understanding of revolution by social scientists.

In a sense, the origins of society are revolutionary. Freud devises a mythic anthropological analog to the resolution of the Oedipal crisis for the young child. In the primal horde, the father prevents each of his sons from enacting his sexual desire for his mother. The sons then have two options, both of which ironically, produce similar results. They can abandon their sexual desire for the mother and identify with the father so as to symbolically develop the capacity to possess her; in this case they renounce the mother and develop mechanisms of cathexis with the father, which creates bonds among the brothers in a shared abstinence. (These are the original social bonds, since they arise out of the agreement among equal brothers and do not depend upon the material authority of the father, since it has become the symbolic means for their equality and obedience). As Freud wrote (1959: 58):

> the primal father had prevented his sons from satisfying their directly sexual impulsions; he forced them into abstinence and consequently into the emotional ties with him and with one another which could arise out of those of their impulsions that were inhibited in their sexual aim. He forced them, so to speak, into group psychology. His sexual jealousy and intolerance became in the last resort the causes of group psychology.

Conversely, the brothers may band together and commit the primal crime: parricide, slaying the father and devouring him, thus coming to possess his powers in the symbolic acts of ritual cannibalism. However, once the father is slain, there is no real authority, and therefore nothing that would prevent the band of brothers from attempting to act on their sexual impulses for mother, an act that would cause them to fight among themselves and eventually to kill each other as they had killed the father. Thus the brothers, symbolically possessing the power of the father, decide to renounce their desire for the mother so as to be reasonably certain that their lives will be spared. In this way, sexual desire for the mother brings the brothers together into a revolutionary social movement, parricide establishes their bonds as social, and their subsequent renunciation of that desire allows social order. The incest taboo, mutually agreed upon, is the first law, a contract entered into by the brothers to preserve the social organization they have created. Thus the brothers restore the authority of the father in a far more pervasive and permanent fashion than the father would have been capable of doing

Freud's mythic anthropological account of the origin of society implies several important themes for the sociology of revolution. First, although society is conceived by a revolutionary social movement overthrowing what is held to be illegitimate authority, it quickly becomes a repressive social order designed to keep the band of the brothers from slaughtering one another. Such an argument is based upon Freud's understanding that aggression is a basic human impulse, both pre-social and aimed precisely against society. Freud notes that ''the inclination to aggression is an original, self-subsisting instinctual disposition in man, and . . . it constitutes the greatest impediment to civilization" (Freud, 1961: 69). Counterposed to this aggressive instinct is civilization, whose mission it is to obtain "mastery over the individual's dangerous desire for aggression by weakening and disarming it and by setting up an agency within him to watch over it, like a garrison in a conquered city" (Freud, 1961: 70-1). This tension between the aggressive impulse and society is the key tension that underlies all human interactions in modern society; the "meaning of the evolution of civilization . . . present[s] the struggle between eros and Death, between the instinct of life and the instinct of destruction, as it works itself out in the human species" (Freud, 1961: 69).

A second implication of Freud's description of the origins of society in the primal horde is that groups themselves are formed through the neurotic experience of identification with the leader. Groups are problematic to Freud, since his whole theoretical model suggests that psychological health may be achieved only by shedding the need for others and achieving psychological autonomy and independence from those infantile and regressive needs for connectedness. "The great decisions in the realm of thought and momentous discoveries and solutions of problems are only possible to an individual working in solitude" (Freud, 1959: 15). Groups, by contrast, represent a regression to a pre-autonomous state. A certain kind of power holds a group together; "the mutual tie between members of a group is in the nature of an identification . . . based upon an important emotional common quality; and we may suspect that this common quality lies in the nature of the tie with the leader" (Freud, 1959: 40). Thus all groups re-enact the relationship of the child and his father.[9]

Groups are held together by irrational, regressive mechanisms of identification of the members with the leader; they are thus the product of the failure of the individual to become autonomous. What is more, the group acts as an irrational individual, the expression of irrational impulses that the members enact because of their incompleteness. Accepting many of the assumptions of Le Bon's notion of the "group mind," Freud writes (1959: 10):

> A group is extraordinarily credulous and open to influence, it has not critical faculty, and the improbable does not exist for it. It thinks in images, which call one another up by association . . . and whose agreement with reality is never checked by any reasonable agency. The feelings of a group are always very simple and very exaggerated. So that a group knows neither doubt nor uncertainty.

Since all groups are irrational and neurotic, so too are revolutionary social movements.

In his analysis of revolutionary motivations, Freud's discussion of the primal horde implies that the impulse towards social change derives from unsatisfied libidinal needs – those aggressive and sexual psychic impulses that cannot be met by society if the social order is to continue. But Freud also suggested another source of revolutionary motivation. If the super-ego demands more than the individual is capable of giving, that is, if social demands for instinctual renunciation are excessive, revolt may also follow; in his discussion of "the ethical demands of the super-ego" Freud writes (1961: 90):

> It . . . does not trouble itself enough about the facts of the mental constitution of human beings. It issues a command and does not ask whether it is possible for people to obey it. On the contrary, it assumes that a man's ego is psychologically capable of anything that is required of it, that his ego has unlimited mastery over his id. This is a mistake; and even in what are known as normal people the id cannot be controlled beyond certain limits. If more is demanded of a man, a revolt will be produced in him or a neurosis, or he will be made unhappy. The commandment "Love thy neighbor as thyself" is the strongest defense against human aggressiveness and an excellent example of the unpsychological proceedings of the cultural super-ego.

Either libidinal impulses will propel the irrational actor into a common bond with a group all following a leader or the demands of civilization will be so excessive that the hapless ego cannot possibly meet them.[10] No wonder Freud extends his compassion for the ego, who strives to maintain a rational balance among irrational forces: "The ego, driven by the id, confined by the super-ego, repulsed by reality, struggles to master its economic task of bringing about harmony among the forces and influences working in and upon it; we can scarce understand how it is that so often we cannot suppress a cry: 'Life is not easy!'" (Freud, 1965: 78).

If revolutions are the products of irrational actors mobilized for irrational reasons into groups, whose fundamental internal processes are irrational, then the ideologies that inspire revolutionary activity may also be understood as irrational. To Freud, all revolutionary ideologies are like religion, that is, they are designed to offer hope and illusory salvation to suffering people. And all groups are held together by ideologies that are, in form, religious ideologies, and which are as generous to insiders as they are cruel to outsiders. As Freud writes, "a religion, even if it calls itself a religion of love, must be hard and unloving to those who do not belong to it. Fundamentally, indeed every religion is in this same way a religion of love for all those whom it embraces while cruelty and intolerance towards those who do not belong to it are natural to every religion" (1959: 30). To Freud, socialism was simply another religion, one that will show "the same intolerance towards outsiders as in the age of the Wars of Religion" (1959: 31). What is more, socialists ignore the aggressiveness that lies at the center of human instincts; according to them, Freud writes (1961: 60):

> man is wholly good and is well-disposed to his neighbor; but the institution of private property has corrupted his nature . . . But I am able to recognize that the psychological premises on which the system is based are an untenable illusion. In abolishing private property we deprive the human love of aggression of one of its instruments, . . . but we have in no way altered the differences in power and influence which are misused by aggressiveness, nor have we altered anything in its nature. Aggressiveness was not created by property.

As a result of these theoretical arguments, Freud was unsure about the prospects of revolution. A political revolution "cannot succeed in emancipating humanity unless there is an independent effort to undo and modify pre-revolutionary character structures" (Gabriel, 1983: 174) – a prospect that made Freud skeptical and uncomfortable. Nor was he comfortable with actual historical cases of revolution. When he thought about the French Revolution, for example, he was more impressed with the dying aristocracy than he was with the claims of the revolutionaries themselves. "Who," he asked (1965: 535), "could fail to be gripped by narratives of the Reign of Terror, when the men and women of the aristocracy, the flower of the nation, showed that they could die with a cheerful mind and could retain the liveliness of their wit and the elegance of their manners till the very moment of the fatal summons?" And he was profoundly skeptical of the Russian Revolution. Freud did admire "the grandeur of the plan and its importance for the future of human civilization" (cited in Roazen, 1968: 243) and he was impressed by the leaders of the revolution as well:

> [They] are men of action, unshakable in their convictions, inaccessible to doubt, without feeling for the sufferings of others if they stand in the way of their intentions. We have to thank men of this kind for the fact that the tremendous experiment of producing a new order of this kind is now actually being carried out in Russia. At a time when the great nations announce that they expect salvation only from the maintenance of Christian piety, the revolution in Russia – in spite of its disagreeable details – seems none the less like the message for a better future (cited in Gabriel, 1983: 155–6).

Yet Freud also believed that communism was another false god that promised deliverance to suffering people, whose psychological health required ego autonomy not collectivized production. "Communism and psychoanalysis go ill together," he said (cited in Roazen, 1968: 243).

Despite the illusion of socialist revolution, Freud believed in instituting reforms to make life more bearable. "If we cannot remove all suffering, we can remove some, and we can mitigate some," he wrote (Freud, 1961: 33).

He was sympathetic to the poor and underprivileged: "[a]nyone who has lived through the misery of poverty in his youth, and has endured the indifference and arrogance of those who have possessions, should be exempt from any suspicion of having no understanding of or goodwill toward the endeavors made to combat the economic inequality of men and all that it leads to" (cited in Roazen, 1968: 244). His sympathy with the downtrodden also derived from his analysis that seething hostility was the natural outcome of frustrated impulses:

> If we turn to those restrictions that apply only to certain classes of society, we meet with a state of things which is flagrant and which has always been recognized. It is to be expected that these underprivileged classes will envy the favoured ones their privileges and will do all they can to free themselves from their own surplus of privation. Where this is not possible, a permanent measure of discontent will persist within the culture concerned and this can lead to dangerous revolts (cited in Gabriel, 1983: 155).

Notice here how classes are not characterized as irrational groups in the same way as others are in Freud's analysis. Perhaps the revolt of the underclass might be thought of as a rational response to irrational – and unbearable – conditions. If there are grounds for a synthesis of Marxian and Freudian perspectives on revolution they may lie here.

For other post-Freudian radicals, the synthesis of Marx and Freud has lain in the recognition of sexual repression as "one of the principal mechanisms of political domination" (Robinson, 1969: 5). But even here they disagree about what might be accomplished by linking political revolution to sexual revolution. For example, Wilhelm Reich argues that the political revolution was doomed to failure unless it was accompanied by the abolition of repressive morality, a sexual revolution: "to define freedom is the same as to define sexual health," Reich wrote (in Robinson, 1969: 52).

But Herbert Marcuse believed that sexual revolution was ultimately illusory, encouraging passivity and conformity instead of political rebellion. Sexual revolution, Marcuse believed, was not necessarily liberatory but accommodationist. In a sense, sexual liberation might be offered as a substitute for political liberation – a case, he believed, of "repressive de-sublimation," the freeing of instincts (de-sublimation) in an ultimately regressive, and hence repressive, direction. Marcuse therefore supported a sublimation of sexual instincts towards political ends. "Today, the fight for life, the fight for Eros, is the *political* fight," Marcuse wrote (cited in Robinson, 1969: 243).

In this chapter, we have explored the theories of revolution of several of the classical sociological thinkers. In the chapters that follow we shall explore the ways in which parts of their theories were adopted by contemporary theorists and other parts dropped. These classical theorists set the stage for subsequent models of revolution, which were shaped in different historical eras and for different historical reasons. As we examine these contemporary theories, it will be important to recall the ways in which they employ categories derived from the classical thinkers, and the ways in which they attempt to move beyond the limitations of their nineteenth-and early-twentieth-century forebears.

3

Stages, Systems, and Deprivation: Non-Structural Theories of Revolution

Classical sociological theorists fashioned their explanations of revolutions during historical eras when revolutions were of immediate importance. Marx and Tocqueville wrestled with the consequences of the French Revolution as they observed the series of contemporaneous revolutions across Europe in 1848. While revolution was less immediately salient for Durkheim and Weber, each responded to important and potentially revolutionary historical events in France and Germany, and in Europe generally, such as the Dreyfus affair, and the abortive 1905 revolution and the 1917 revolution in Russia. More important than living in a revolutionary era, though, was the experience of living in a revolutionary, or potentially revolutionary, society, in which the elements of a revolutionary upheaval were already in motion.

While some might contend that living within a revolutionary moment inevitably distorted their visions and fatally compromised their analytic skills with partisanship, I believe that it may have provided both an analytic advantage as well as a moral imperative towards partisanship. Since none of the classical theorists could know the outcome of the revolution beforehand, they were forced to leave open several possibilities for those outcomes. That is not to say that they did not *predict* the outcomes of these revolutionary upheavals; they certainly did. But they literally predicted them, basing their predictions on the historical sequences unfolding beforehand and the analytic weight that each gave to particular sociological variables. They were historically unable to fall into a teleological trap of reading the causes backwards in time from the historical outcomes. Forced to reason from beginning to end, they remained intellectually honest. (This is one reason why I believe Marx's historical analyses of revolutions, such as *Class Struggles in France* and

The Eighteenth Brumaire of Louis Bonaparte are among his finest theoretical as well as historical works.)

Successive generations of sociological theorists of revolution have certainly lived in an era of revolution; the twentieth century has witnessed more revolutionary upheavals than any previous century, and more, perhaps, than all other centuries combined. But most of the best-known sociological theorists of revolution – especially between the end of the First World War and the outbreak of the Vietnamese revolution – were Americans, who generalized from an observed stability in American society to stability as a normative condition of modern society. Revolutions were seen as disruptive, destructive, and regressive; they were anachronistic moments when the legitimacy of political institutions was challenged by angry malcontents. And they were unnecessary, especially when society was functioning properly.

Four types of non-structural sociological explanations of revolution developed in the United States. One school attempted to chart the *natural history of revolutions* from their earliest stirrings to the consolidation of the new regime. Another school cast revolutions as the collapse of a *social system* normally in an equilibrium that promotes evolutionary change. The final two schools emphasize the psychological factors that lead to revolutions. One stresses the *psychological development of individual leaders* of revolutions, searching for the origins of their discontent as well as their ability to mobilize others. Finally, a more sociological tradition stresses the *aggregate social psychology* of mass discontent that leads to revolutionary mobilization. While these traditions often draw on similar metaphoric devices and overlap considerably, I will treat them separately first, and suggest some of these particular commonalities at the end of the chapter.

The "Natural History" of Revolution

Some social scientists have attempted to analytically elaborate the stages that a revolution takes as it courses through its tumultuous events. The most influential works by these theorists – Crane Brinton's *The Anatomy of Revolution* (1965 [1938]), Lyford Edward's *The Natural History of Revolution* (1972 [1927]), and George Pettee's *The Process of Revolution* (1938) – as well as others, propose a sequential model that allows the observer to track a revolution through its "natural history."[1] As in classical tragedy, different social groups take various unalterable parts in the unfolding drama, which moves through a vicious cathartic bloodbath before the orderly passing on to a new regime. More accurately, these theorists often treat revolution as a disease infecting an otherwise healthy body. The disease develops slowly, manifesting confusing symptoms at first, and culminating in a cathartic fever, after which it subsides and the body returns to normal, perhaps even strengthened by new immunities to the disease. Edwards, for example, argues that a "country in revolution is like a person suffering from a deadly cancer," and that after the disease has run its course, there will normally follow "a fairly long period of peace and quiet" since "the revolutionary society requires time for recuperation" (Edwards, 1972: 149, 202). Brinton is more elaborate, casting revolution as a form of "fever" which

> works up, not regularly but with advances and retreats, to a crisis, frequently accompanied by delirium, the rule of the most violent revolutionaries, the Reign of Terror. After the crisis comes a period of convalescence, usually marked by a relapse or two. Finally the fever is over, and the patient is himself again, perhaps in some respects actually strengthened by the experience, immunized at least for a while from a similar attack, but certainly not wholly made over into a new man.

Since the "patient emerges stronger in some respects from the conquered fever, immunized . . . from attacks that might be more serious," Brinton concludes that revolutions may be "a sign of strength and youth in societies" (Brinton, 1965: 17, 263).

According to the natural history school, revolutions pass through a number of successive stages.[2] All agree that the single pivotal event is the transfer of allegiance of the intellectuals from support to criticism of the old regime. Revolutions begin, Schwartz writes (1972: 59) "with the attempted withdrawal from politics of individual (and especially intellectuals') attention, affection, and involvement" with the existing system. Interestingly, all agree that the alienation of the intellectuals is caused less by economic distress than by thwarted upward mobility in relatively prosperous conditions. Edwards takes perhaps the most Marxian-informed position of this school; he argues that:

> [r]evolutions do not occur when the repressed classes are forced down to the depths of misery. Revolutions occur after the repressed classes, for a considerable time, have been in the enjoyment of increasing prosperity. A marked increase of power, intelligence, and wealth in the repressed portion of society is a phenomenon invariably found in the period preceding any great revolution.

At the same time, he understands that the alienation of the intellectuals is caused by this fermenting lower-class discontent, as "those whose function it is to form and guide public opinion become infected with the discontent of the repressed classes of society" (Edwards, 1972: 36, 38). Curiously, for a theory that makes the alienation of the intellectuals such a centerpiece, Edwards downplays the role of ideology in revolution. For example, he argues that Russian communism "was not the result of theory; it was the result of crisis." He continues, as if to illustrate, that "[s]hipwrecked sailors in an

open boat with an insufficient supply of food always institute communism''
(Edwards, 1972: 203).

Brinton and Pettee, by contrast, ignore entirely this lower-class discontent
and play up the role of ideology, hinging the outbreak of revolution entirely
on the thwarted mobility of intellectuals. Brinton (1965: 33) notes that
among these groups the pivotal moment arrives with the ''feeling that prevailing conditions limit or hinder their economic activity'' and Pettee (1938: 11)
locates revolutionary sentiment in ''lack of social mobility [which] leaves a
large portion of the intrinsic elite barred from the use of their talents, or
denied appropriate rewards.'' Potential elites who are prevented from
realizing political aspirations experience ''cramp'' according to Pettee: ''the
cramped individual is one who not only finds that his basic impulses are inter-
fered with, or that he is threatened by various ills, but not also feels that his
repression is unnecessary and avoidable, and therefore unjustified'' (Pettee,
1938: 33).

The withdrawal of intellectual support for the old regime and the articulation of political criticism prompts the old regime to attempt to implement
badly needed reforms, but these prove too little too late, as the structural
weaknesses of the system are revealed. ''The governmental machinery is
clearly inefficient,'' writes Brinton (1965: 251–2), ''partly through neglect,
through a failure to make changes in old institutions, partly because new
conditions . . . laid an intolerable strain on governmental machinery
adapted to simpler, more primitive conditions.'' For one thing, the old
ruling class no longer maintains the same moral claim to political power as it
once did, and its crisis of confidence prevents the implementation of reforms.
This class ''come[s] to distrust themselves, or lose faith in the traditions and
habits of their class'' and becomes ''politically inept'' (Brinton, 1965: 252).
Brinton quotes Lucy Hutchinson's description of the court of James I in
England (in Brinton, 1965: 57–8):

> The court of the King was a nursery of lust and intemperance . . . the nobility
> of the land was utterly debased . . . The generality of the gentry of the land
> soon learned the court fashion, and every great house in the country soon
> became a sty of uncleanliness. Then began murder, incest, adultery, drunken-
> ness, swearing, fornication, and all sorts of ribaldry to be countenanced vices
> because they held such conformity to the court example.

These efforts at reform are futile, and the next stage of the revolutionary
sequence is the collapse of the old regime. Old regime breakdown is brought
about by an acute crisis, such as bankruptcy. The actual event is often
insigificant in itself, but it provides the signal that the ruling class is unable
and unwilling to rule and that the repressive machinery of the state is incapable of suppressing revolt (Edwards, 1972: 98).

However, the collapse of the old regime also reveals deep rifts in the coalition of political opposition that has developed in opposition to state policies. Although the revolution itself follows the metaphoric course of a feverish body, the social groups that comprise the revolutionary coalition are hardly "fevered," but rather a loosely held coalition of various *déclassé* intellectuals, lower middle classes, and the poor; in fact, "the important part of any mob playing a decisive revolutionary role is always made up of decent, self-respecting common people, mechanics and laborers, butchers and bakers and candlestick makers" (Edwards, 1972: 102). These were "quite ordinary men and women" who were "not in general afflicted with anything the psychiatrist could be called in about" (Brinton, 1965: 119–20). (Not all natural history theorists agree with this assessment. Hopper (1950: 274), for example, relies on "social contagion" to explain increasingly radical behaviors among crowds, "an intense form of milling and collective excitement in which rapport is established.")

A group of moderate reformers, led by many of the alienated intellectuals, come to power as a result of the disorganization among the revolutionary coalition and the collapse of the old regime. These moderates immediately set about implementing badly needed structural reforms, and eliminating formerly autonomous pockets of old regime privilege. They thus extend the purview of the state and raise the expectations of the popular classes that these reforms are also undertaken in their interests. However, the mobilization of these lower-class elements signals a new stage in the revolutionary sequence.

The mass mobilization of the urban popular classes and the rural peasantry pushes the revolution decisively to the left, instituting widespread reforms that are far more dramatic than any envisioned by the moderate reformers. It is at this stage that utopian visions of revolutionary possibilities are most urgently articulated, because it is at this point that the revolution has decidedly destroyed the old regime, and the outlines of the future social structure are not yet in place. In these optimistic moments, all is possible; with the revolution, one observer believed, "poverty would vanish, the lowliest would begin the struggles of life on equal terms with the mightiest, with equal arms, on equal ground." Or, as Wordsworth observed France: "standing on the top of golden hours / And human nature seeming born again" (cited in Brinton, 1965: 90–1).

It is this optimism that fuels the moral self-righteousness of the revolution's next stage. The radicals inevitably meet with difficulties in immediately implementing their utopian visions, as external military challenges drain revolutionary resources (nations undergoing revolutions are especially vulnerable to military aggression from other competitors) or as internal divisions weaken the assumed unanimity of the revolutionary impulse. As

Hopper notes, "collective excitement and social contagion are not adequate to serve as the processual foundation for enduring social change" (1950: 275). Thus the radicals impose a coercive form of social order on the society, instituting a Reign of Terror. This stage of the revolution replaces the random and sporadic violence of revolutionary upheaval with systematic and repressivd violence of revolutionaries in power. Revolutionary violence always accompanies revolution; there can be non-violent revolutions. Revolutions ?
"weaken laws, customs, habits, beliefs which bind men together in society; and when laws, customs, habits, beliefs tie men together insufficiently, force must be used to remedy that insufficiency" (Brinton, 1965: 208).

The extreme forms of violence employed by the revolutionaries however, and the ruthlessness with which they are applied, may prefigure the consolidation of a revolutionary regime, but they also alienate significant former moderates, who had earlier joined the radicals in a revolutionary coalition. The ensuing struggle between the reformers and the radicals often allows new leaders to emerge, leaders who are capable of confronting and defeating the radicals in power. These are often military leaders, who have excelled in the protection of national boundaries against external threats, and who return to the nation's capital as popular heroes and in the service of the moderate reformist faction. These military leaders institute a political reaction against the radicals, who are themselves purged from the revolutionary coalition in the "Thermidorian reaction" stage of the revolution.

It is this reaction that permits the successful consolidation of the new regime on the twin pillars of the collapse of the old regime and the suppression of the extreme radical wing of the revolutionary movement. Within the new regime, pragmatic reforms are instituted by cooler-headed politicians. The "restoration" is therefore incomplete: the post-revolutionary society is radically different from pre-revolutionary society in both its governing ideologies (which are often inclusive, incorporating and based on ideals of popular sovereignty) and its ruling elites (who are composed of precisely the urban professionals and intellectuals whose career trajectories had been blocked by corruption and the decadence of the old regime). The restoration provides the stability and order necessary for long-term reforms.

After the revolution has been consolidated, the natural history school again using an anatomical metaphor, observes, "a fairly long period of peace and quiet. The revolutionary society requires time for recuperation" (Edwards, 1972: 202). Ironically, the power and purview of the state, against which the revolution was originally aimed, is increased by the process of revolution, and especially during the moments of extreme revolutionary violence, when the means of repression are centralized on a scale never before achieved. "A revolution does not diminish the power of a central government in any essential particular; it rather increases it" (Edwards, 1972: 205).

The natural history school of explanation presents several important and useful issues in the study of revolution. For example, the description of the coalition of revolutionary opposition as a loosely held together amalgam of different class elements is an important corrective to the traditional Marxian notion of two monolithic class fronts squaring off against one another. In addition, the understanding of the activation of utopian visions by the popular classes places human agency in the center of one of the revolution's pivotal moments, even if this emphasis is later undermined by the school's positing particular outcomes from these non-determined moments. When revolutions occur, one does not know exactly how they will turn out, since one believes (and experiences one's actions as consistent with these beliefs) that the future is an open book awaiting new authors.

Yet the natural history school of revolution is also open to serious criticism. First, the model overemphasizes the role of intellectuals in revolutions, especially in their earliest stages. The alienation of the intellectuals may seem important in the analysis of the French or English Revolutions, but is hardly the central variable in the twentieth-century revolutions, such as those of Mexico, China, Vietnam, Angola, or Nicaragua. Second, the model has a tendency to overemphasize the French case as the template for all revolutionary events. The names of the stages that all revolutions must pass through are very often the names given to particular moments in the French Revolution. In a sense, the French Revolution is all revolutions, crystallized and distilled, in which the process of revolution unfolded in its purest form. Such a perspective, however, overgeneralizes from the particular case, so that all historical events are judged in terms of how well they fit the model, while it simultaneously underplays the historical particularity of the French model, removing it from its specific socio-historical circumstances and forcing it to stand as the ahistorical model for all revolutions.

This suggests a third problem with the natural history approach, namely that the outcome of the revolution is part of the definition of the revolution itself. (This is certainly a problem that the approach shares with many others, as we shall see in succeeding chapters.) This negates the importance of human agency during the revolutionary process itself, suggesting that if a revolution does not go through all the specific stages leading to the inevitable conclusion of restoration and consolidation, then it can not really be regarded as a revolution. But surely one can imagine dozens of revolutionary situations that follow a different trajectory – are these not revolutions? And what of revolutions that fail – do these not count as revolutions? I will argue in this book for a wider definition of revolution that does not presuppose any particular outcome, leaving open the possibility for people to shape their own destinies, although not entirely out of thin air.

Finally, there are two related methodological problems that weigh heaviest on the natural history approach. For one thing, typological sequences are notoriously inaccurate, doing grave injustice to the historical record in order to demonstrate the validity of a particular model. Even Edwards was aware of this danger when he wrote (1972: 140) that ''[i]t is the easiest thing imaginable to draw up an arbitrary series of stages and then twist and torture the data to fit this Procrustean bed.'' And perhaps most important, narrative sequences of revolutionary stages are not the same thing as theoretical explanations of revolutions. The narrative quality of the natural history approach brings us no closer to the sociological variables that cause revolutions in the first place, that structure the parameters for human action within those revolutionary events, and that structure the potential transformations that revolutions promise. We may understand sequences of revolution better as a result of the natural history approach, but we are no closer to an adequate theoretical explanation of revolutions.

The Disequilibrated Social System

The natural history approach to revolutions was articulated largely in the United States in the period between the two world wars, a period that was relatively non-revolutionary. During this time the consolidation of post-revolutionary regimes in Mexico, Russia, and Turkey indicated future political stability, and the tremendous increase in revolutionary challenges in the years following the Second World War was still to come. The efforts of a number of American social scientists to elaborate a paradigm for an integrated social science produced a new theory of revolution. In contrast to natural history narratives of revolutionary sequences, the social systems model developed by structural-functionalist theorists developed a causal view of revolution as resulting from the disruptive character of modernization and the generation of various forms of collective behavior. The model responded to the tremendous interest in the development of the non-western nations in the post-war era, and in explaining their proclivity for revolutionary challenges to established political elites.

The functionalist model, in brief, assumed that social order was both normal and normative, that functional societies were societies in which all components fitted together to produce stability and equilibrium. ''A social system is always founded on a consensus, itself based on interests and convictions;'' therefore, ''all social systems are conservative'' (Baecheler, 1975: 107). In part, this formulation borrowed from Vilfredo Pareto's understanding that a functional system institutionalized a mechanism to insure the circulation of elites – the absorption into the legitimate social order of potential contenders which allowed the social system to maintain itself. In his *Treatise of General Sociology* Pareto wrote (cited in Baecheler, 1975: 132):

> Revolutions occur because elements of inferior quality accumulate in the upper strata of society, either because of a slowing down of the tempo at which the elite circulates, or for some other cause. These elements do not possess the resources capable of maintaining them in power, and they avoid the the use of force; whereas in the lower strata superior elements are developing, with the resources needed to govern, and the desire to use force if need be.

Pareto continued this analysis by explaining that it is not only the "accumulation of inferior elements in a social stratum" that leads to a revolutionary situation, "but also the accumulation in the lower strata of elite elements which are prevented from rising." A revolutionary situation brings these two together. "When simultaneously the upper strata are full of decadent elements and the lower strata are full of elite elements, the social equilibrium becomes highly unstable and a violent revolution is imminent" (cited in Hagopian, 1974: 53).

Conflict and change are not the elements of a functional social system, and therefore all conflicts, revolutionary or otherwise, are problems that need to be explained. As Eisenstadt says (1978: 334): "the emergence of modern revolutions . . . should not be seen as a natural, inevitable development but rather as a unique development or mutation." The implication is that the impetus towards social change is most often the result of exogenous factors, such as the transformation of economic activity to participate more fully in the international market, which may destabilize the functional social system. As Ellwood wrote (1905: 51):

> revolutions are disturbances in the social order due to the sudden breakdown of those habits under conditions which make difficult the reconstruction of those habits, that is, the formation of a new social order. In other words, revolutions arise through certain interferences or disturbances in the normal process of the readjustment of social habits.

Such disequilibrating changes lead inevitably to anomic social behavior, from random normless violence to purposive revolutionary movements.

In this sense, revolutions are cast as a special case of collective behavior; revolutionary movements are those movements whose aim is an entire transformation of the organizing values of a social system. The revolutionary movement, according to Talcott Parsons, the most influential structural-functionalist theorist, "organizes a set of alienative motivational orientations relative to the main institutionalized order" which results from strains on the existing social equilibrium (Parsons, 1955: 520).

Parsons based his model of the functional social system on earlier theoretical traditions that sought to replace conflict as the essential feature of social life with a more benign model of consensus. Concretely, this involved using a particular reading of Weber along with Durkheim, Pareto, and Marshall as theoretical weapons against the Marxian view of social organization as the constantly changing tensions created by the omnipresent struggle between social classes. Although Parsons himself only hinted at a theoretical explanation of revolutions, his students and followers – especially Chalmers Johnson, Neil J. Smelser, S. N. Eisenstadt, and Samuel Huntington – have fully articulated it.

Chalmers Johnson's theoretical works on revolutions, *Revolution and the Social System* (1964) and *Revolutionary Change* (1966), develop the systems model of revolution at the level of the disequilibrated social system. He argues that to understand the breakdown of value consensus, one must first understand the functional society, "a system whose members cooperate with each other by 'playing' various 'roles' that, taken together, permit the whole system to 'function' " (1964: 4). Drawing an analogy between the sociology of revolutions and physiology, Johnson claims that the "sociology of functional societies comes logically before the sociology of revolution" (1966: 3).

Social systems manifest two distinct characteristics: the component parts are "mutually influencing" and "they tend to maintain the relationship they have with each other over time" (Johnson, 1966: 40). Though social systems would therefore tend towards static equilibrium, there are several destabilizing sources of change, according to Johnson. Exogenous value changes are changes introduced from outside the system, such as the "demonstration effect" of other revolutions on the populations of other countries. Endogenous value changes are internally induced changes in a society's value system, such as the efforts to separate church and state during the process of modernization. Exogenous environmental changes occur in response to external factors, such as technological inventions imported from other countries, while endogenous environmental changes indicate the indigenous origin of these technological innovations which exert an impact on economic organization and social structure (see Taylor, 1984: 14).

These changes, whether exogenous or endogenous, disequilibrate a functional social system, allowing certain subsystems to progress more rapidly than others, and disrupting the process by which the system returns to its normal state of equilibrium. Specific dysfunction-inducing phenomena, such as rapid industrialization, relative deprivation, incoherence in the myths which underlie a society's value system, or the dysynchronization between societal values and the social division of labor are the long-run causes of revolutions, precisely because they disrupt traditional and legitimate patterns of institutionalized behaviors. The first necessary condition for a revolution is the gradual development of the disequilibrating impact of these forces, or what Johnson calls "multiple dysfunction."

The disequilibrated social system, a result of the accumulation of multiple dysfunctions, must be accompanied by the incapacity or unwillingness of the ruling elite to continue to exert its authority during the crisis. If the elite "reacts to changes in the environment to maintain the synchronization between values and the division of labor" it is possible thereby to "maintain the values of the essential variables within their limits" (Salert, 1976: 85). If the elite retains its legitimate authority, it can adapt to changing conditions, and thus a potentially revolutionary situation may be avoided. "Elite intransigence" is thus a second necessary condition for revolution in Johnson's model. "Revolution is the preferred method of change when (a) the level of dysfunctions exceeds the capacities of traditional or accepted methods of problem solving; and when (b) the system's elite, in effect, opposes change" (Johnson, 1964: 10).

And yet still revolution may not occur, even with multiple dysfunctions and elite intransigence. Revolution requires the infusion of some indefinable ingredient, which propels the dysfunctions towards a revolutionary outcome. These "accelerators" usually consist of "some ingredient, usually contributed by fortune, which deprives the elite of its chief weapon for enforcing social behavior . . . or which leads a group of revolutionaries to believe that they have the means to deprive the elite of its weapons of coercion" (Johnson, 1966: 91). Drawing on the metaphor of pathology, Johnson likens the accelerator to a case of pneumonia unexpectedly contracted by a patient with heart disease; although a healthy man can normally survive this new illness, the combined effects of the two are fatal. Thus defeat in a foreign war, the rise of a charismatic leader, or the effective organization of a revolutionary party are all examples of accelerators that, although insufficient by themselves to cause revolution, can nevertheless determine its occurrence.

Multiple dysfunction plus elite intransigence plus an accelerator provides a revolutionary situation, and yet still revolution may or may not occur. The personal sense of dislocation and disruption may not lead to revolutionary eruptions, although it may over time:

> As the disequilibrium of a social system becomes more acute, personal tensions are generated in all statuses. These tensions may be controlled by some people through internal psychological defense mechanisms, and the alienative [?] sentiments of others may be dissipated through deviant behavior (e.g. fantasies, crime, mental disease, and psychosomatic illnesses). However, with the passage of time, these mechanisms tend to lose their efficacy, and persons subject to highly diverse status protests will begin to combine with each other and with deviants generally to form a deviant subcultural group or movement. (Johnson, 1966: 81)

This suggests that power-holders should be wary of such "deviant subcultural groups'', because these people are angry and crazy enough to think that revolution might solve their problems!

But revolution is more than this; revolution also involves purposive, intentional behavior on the part of a significant movement. Revolution is not the same thing as rebellion, which is the "violent, spontaneous act of 'ordinary people' saying no! to conditions as they are;" revolution is "the act of rebuilding the society shattered by rebellion in accordance with a plan or vision (an 'ideology') of a more nearly perfect, or equitable, or at least tolerable society" (Johnson, 1973: 8). Here Johnson develops a typology of rebellious behaviors and therefore a typology of revolutions; this typology distinguishes between the target of the movement, its social composition, the goals and ideology of the movement, and its level of organization. From this set of criteria, Johnson distinguishes six forms of insurrection. As we can see from table 3.1, only two of these movements, the "Jacobin communist revolution" and the "mass militarized insurrection," fall into the category of revolution that earlier theorists have employed, and Johnson's typology is thus capable of differentiating the earlier historical revolutions (the "great" revolutions, which were Jacobin communist) from contemporary peasant revolutions (which are examples of mass militarized insurrections). While all revolutions aim at changing the community, the essential difference between these two examples of revolution consists in the level of organization and calculatedness of the movement. Millenarian movements differ from *coups d'état* in that the former develop revolutionary ideologies but lack revolutionary organization, while the latter develop revolutionary organization but lack revolutionary ideology.

Revolutionary social movements respond to social dysfunctions which are set in motion by social changes, according to Johnson. This position is also articulated by Smelser, in his theoretical work *Theory of Collective Behavior* (1962) and also in his historical study *Social Change and the Industrial Revolution* (1959). Like Johnson, Smelser takes the functional social system as his point of departure: "all systems are governed by the principle of equilibrium" (Smelser, 1959: 10). All social change is "set in motion by specific disequilibrating conditions" (Smelser, 1959: 2). Revolutions are simply a possible set of responses to the disequilibrated social system. After all, he writes "people enter episodes of such behavior because something is wrong in their social environment" (Smelser, 1962: 47).

Smelser specifies six necessary structural conditions for the development of social movements, which, while not necessarily progressive, do suggest a certain sequential organization. First, "structural conduciveness" indicates the structural cleavages which make a social system more or less vulnerable to different forms of collective behavior. Thus a racially stratified system will be more prone to racial social movements, and a free market economy might be

Table 3.1 *Johnson's typology of revolutions*

Type of revolution	Aim	Composition	Ideology	Organization
Jacquerie	Government (restore regime)	Masses, peasants	Legitimist/reform 'primitive rebels'	Spontaneous
Millenarian	Community	Masses, followers	Eschatological, revolutionary (heaven on earth)	Charismatic individuals
Anarchist	Restore idealized version of old regime	Coalitions of *déclassés*, peasants, and rural aristocracy	Utopian, anti-nationalist, nostalgic	Coalitions/ spontaneous
Jacobin communist ("great" revolution)	Community	Masses under elite guidance	Nation-forming (citizenship)	Simultaneous, unconnected, spontaneous
Coup d'état	Regime	Conspiratorial revolutionary brotherhood, secret societies	Elitist, tutelary	Calculated/ highly organized
Mass militarized insurrection	Community	Mass under elite guidance, guerrilla armies	Nationalistic	Calculated/ highly organized

Source: Adapted from Johnson (1964 and 1966).

more prone to panics and social movements aimed at stabilizing the business cycles. Second, "structural strains" indicate the various social tensions that emerge in response to the cleavages suggested by the existing social organization. Strains are based less on structural factors than upon the perceptions and experiences of members of the social order. Structural strains are thus inversely related to the perception of legitimacy, and facilitate collective behavior when they become shared. The third condition is the "growth of a generalized belief system," that is, the development of ideology, which galvanizes widespread strains into an ongoing movement. The fourth structural condition is that of "precipitating factors," which are present when "events confirm or justify the fears or hatreds in a generalized belief; they may initiate or exaggerate a condition of strain; or they may redefine sharply the conditions of conduciveness" (Smelser, 1962: 17). Fifth is the mobilization of participants for action, which is the actual eruption of collective behavior, the "onset of panic, outbreak of hostility, or beginning of agitation for reform or revolution" (Smelser, 1962: 17). This leads to the final structural condition, in which social control mechanisms – those "counter-determinants which prevent, interrupt, deflect or inhibit the accumulation of the determinants" – are brought into play (Smelser, 1962: 17). These forces can be mobilized before the episode to prevent collective behavior by minimizing the strain or the structural conduciveness to behavior, or they can be mobilized after the episode has begun, and determine the extent, scope, and intensity of the behavior. The police, courts, press, and religious authorities can all serve as such counter-determinants.

These structural conditions establish the possibilities for various forms of collective behavior. These forms differ on criteria such as their goals, means, and levels of organization, but the central determinate feature of different forms of collective behavior is the ideology of the movement, or the type of "belief" it expresses. Smelser lists, in ascending order of seriousness, several forms of collective behavior. The most primitive forms are distinguished precisely by the type of ideological impulse each reveals, and the direction in which such an impulse drives the participants. A *panic* is a "collective flight based on a hysterical belief," while a *craze* is the "mobilization for action based on a positive wish-fulfillment belief," and a *hostile outburst* is the "mobilization for action under a hostile belief" (Smelser 1962: 131, 171, 226).

The last two forms of collective behavior, in Smelser's scheme, differ on the level of the social system that each seeks to transform and the methods that each will utilize to effect such change. A *norm-oriented movement* is "an attempt to restore, protect, modify, or create norms in the name of a generalized belief" (1962: 270); this reform-oriented movement's object is to create new institutions or laws within an existing framework. For example,

Smelser lists the labor, peace, and feminist movements as examples of norm-oriented movement. These are not the same as a *value-oriented movement*, a "collective attempt to restore, protect, modify, or create values in the name of a generalized belief" (1962: 313). These are revolutionary social movements, and under this rubric Smelser lists religious cults (such as the Father Divine movement), nativistic movements (the Ghost Dance), contemporary nationalistic movements in underdeveloped countries, and internal revolutionary movements (such as Nazism).

Even value-oriented movements, the most complex and sustained of all forms of collective behavior, are neither rational nor purposive in this model. Conflict and revolt are always the "disturbed *reactions* to specific structural pressures rather than . . . the manifestations of a permanent state of war between them" (Smelser, 1959: 394). Collective behavior is the social manifestation of psychological states of unrest such as anxiety, aggression, and fantasy. Defined as a form of social "disturbance" an episode of collective behavior such as a social movement is defined by the fact that "it be sufficiently undirected or misdirected to be considered unrealistic" (Smelser, 1959: 39; see also p. 402). All social movements are "characterized by a deep pessimism about the present, unrealistic blame heaped upon one individual or class" (Smelser, 1959: 38).

When Smelser turns directly to revolutionary social movements, therefore, he notes their inherent irrationality and weaknesses rather than their articulation of a new vision or the resources they are able to mobilize. For example, he writes that the "[i]nadequacy of knowledge or techniques to grapple with new situations sets the stage for value-oriented movements." He argues that value-oriented beliefs "arise when alternative means for reconstituting the social situation are perceived as unavailable" because either (a) the aggrieved group does not possess facilities whereby they may reconstitute the social situation, or (b) the aggrieved group is prevented from expressing hostility that will punish some person or group considered responsible for this disturbing state of affairs, or (c) the aggrieved group cannot modify the normative structure or cannot influence those who have the power to do so (1962: 338, 325).[3] In addition, the success or failure of the revolutionary movement has little to do with structural relationships among groups mobilizing resources in political struggle; instead success "depends largely on the choice of appropriate tactics at the right time by the leaders" (1962: 358–9). Happily, in most historical cases, "through police activity, governmental investigation, public debate, and journalistic controversy, these disturbances were brought into line" (Smelser, 1959: 407).

In another example of social systems theory, S. N. Eisenstadt reasserts many of Johnson's and Smelser's arguments. In his dense theoretical tome,

Revolution and the Transformation of Societies, Eisenstadt argues that functional social systems manifest several potential sources of change: (1) the disequilibrating tendencies that exist in any relationship between a social system and its environment; (2) the strain that exists between the normative and the structural elements of any social system; and (3) the generation of new resources, which leads to more structural differentiation, which leads to changes in value orientations, which can lead to strain (Eisenstadt, 1978: 25). In Eisenstadt's model, revolutions depend on the conjunction of several structural features that hinge on the capacity of the social system, and especially its elites, to meet the challenges of structural strain brought about by the onset of modernization. Serious inter-elite or intra-elite competition, the interweaving of dissident elites with broader social movements, and the articulation of sentiments of political discontent must be handled (1978: 204). Thus, the "crucial intervening variable that explains the relations between the structure of centers and the outcomes of revolutions is the ability of the center, first, to mobilize the resources needed for coping with the problems attendant on the transition to modernity; second, to incorporate new or potential claimants to participation in it; and third, to establish links with the broader strata in order to attempt institution building" (1978: 240).

In such a model, Eisenstadt argues, the great historical revolutions have been only one type of potential revolutionary event. "They have emerged from imperial and imperial–feudal orders in which, traditionally, there were tendencies toward coalescence among heterodox protest movements, social revolts, and central political struggles, and tendencies toward the interlocking of transformations in social hierarchies and political institutions" (Skocpol, 1979b: 452).

This insistence on the historical specificity of societies vulnerable to revolutionary transformation is an important corrective to the seeming ahistoricity of much systems theory. But Eisenstadt remains squarely within systems theory when he turns to the outcomes of revolutions, which are uniformly the stabilization and re-equilibration of the social system.

> The modern revolutions pushed the societies in which they took place in the direction of modernization in its organizational and symbolic aspects alike. All postrevolutionary societies experienced growing structural differentiation and specialization; the establishment of international organizational frameworks and markets; the development of market economies and of modern institutional frameworks (industrial or semi-industrial ones in the economic field); the elaboration of relatively open, nontraditional systems of stratification and mobility in which criteria of achievement – specifically, economic, occupational, and educational criteria – became relatively predominant; and the

weakening of traditional strata formation and its replacement by more open class formation in the structuring of social hierarchies and political systems. (Eisenstadt, 1978: 215–6).[4]

In a sense, modernization is both the cause and consequence of revolution.

In the work of Samuel Huntington, especially *Political Order in Changing Societies* (1968), modernizaion is surely both cause and consequence of revolution: "[i]t is not the absence of modernity but the efforts to achieve it which produce political disorder" (1968: 41). Huntington develops a specifically political version of structural-functionalism that depends upon the capacity of political institutions to meet new demands for incorporation by groups mobilized during the process of modernization.

In Huntington's model, modernization is a disequilibrating process which places new strains on existing political institutions. As he writes (1968: 5):

> Social and economic change – urbanization, increases in literacy and educa-tion, industralization, mass media expansion – extend political consciousness, multiply political demands, broaden political participation. These changes undermine traditional sources of political authority and traditional political institutions; they enormously complicate the problems of creating new bases of political association and new political institutions combining legitimacy and effectiveness. The rates of social mobilization and expansion of political parti-cipation are high; the rates of political organization and institutionalization are low. The result is political instability and disorder. The primary problem of politics is the lag in the development of political institutions behind social and economic change.

If, as Huntington argues, a revolutionary situation is potentially created as the process of modernization creates a gap between mobilization and the capacity of traditional political institutions to absorb these new demands, then revolutions are the failure of political institutions to contain these new demands and to absorb potential challengers. "The political essence of revolution is the rapid expansion of political consciousess and the rapid mobilization of new groups into politics at a speed which makes it impossible for existing political institutions to assimilate them" (Huntington, 1968: 266). Revolution depends therefore on a high level of modernization and mobilization combined with a low level of political institutionalization. This can be observed in figure 3.1.

Huntington disaggregates political mobilization by reference to a rural-urban split. Opposition by urban intellectuals is important, but not decisive, because the city's role is constant: "it is the permanent source of opposition. The role of the countryside is variable: it is either the source of stability or the source of revolution. For the political system, opposition within the city is disturbing, but not lethal. Opposition within the countryside, however, is

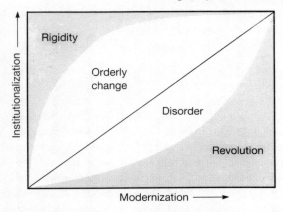

Figure 3.1 Huntington's model of revolution as related to levels of modernization institutionalization. *Source*: Tilly (1978: 20).

fatal. He who controls the countryside controls the country'' (1968: 292). Revolutions thus require the conjuncture of opposition by urban intellectuals and the peasantry; these two forces may combine and seize power after the collapse of decaying political institutions (the ''western-style'' revolution) or defeat militarily a regime whose political institutions have only partially developed in response to political modernization (the ''eastern-style'' revolution). (Note here the difference between Huntington's analysis of west and east and Johnson's analysis, which rested on the different levels of organization of the oppositional coalition, and not differences in the types of political institution and their relationship to modernity.)

In developing countries currently undergoing the enormous social and economic dislocations attendant upon modernization, Huntington offers a sequential model that begins and ends with political stability and equilibrium. In table 3.2 one can observe a sequence that is not especially different from the natural history model, in which the alienation of the intellectuals derives from earlier social dislocations, and they are eventually joined in coalition by the mass mobilization of the rural peasantry, who steer the revolution decidedly to the left. Despite the participation of the peasantry, and the fact that the revolution is made in their name, they are the victims of the eventual reforms instituted by the revolutionaries, who consolidate political power and re-establish political institutions by imposing them upon the peasants. Functionalist models of revolution point to several important features of the phenomenon, but are also open to serious criticisms on theoretical, methodological, and historical grounds. For one thing, the functionalists' insistence on value consensus as the essential ingredient of social stability blinds them to

Table 3.2 Political modernization: changes in urban–rural power and stability

Phase	City	Countryside	Comments
1 Traditional stability	Stable, subordinate	Stable, dominant	Rural elite rules; middle class absent; peasants dormant
2 Modernization take-off	Unstable, subordinate	Stable, dominant	Urban middle class appears and begins struggle against rural elite; peasants still dormant
3 Urban breakthrough	Unstable, dominant	Stable, subordinate	Urban middle class displaces rural elite; peasants still dormant
A4 Green uprising: containment	Unstable, subordinate	Stable, dominant	Peasant mobilization within system re-establishes stability and rural dominance
A5 Fundamentalist reaction	Stable, dominant	Unstable, subordinate	Middle class grows and becomes more conservative; working class appears; shift of dominance to city produces rural fundamentalist reaction
B4 Green uprising: revolution	Unstable, subordinate	Unstable, dominant	Peasant mobilization against system overthrows old structures
B5 Modernizing consolidation	Stable, dominant	Unstable, subordinate	Revolutionaries in power impose modernizing reforms on peasantry
6 Modern stability	Stable, dominant	Stable, subordinate	Countryside accepts modern values and city rule

Source: Huntington (1968: 76), *Political Order in Changing Societies*, Yale University Press.

other structural factors, such as the economy or polity, which may be determinants. "In a stable social system," Johnson writes, for example, "the members share values which permit them, through mutual expectations, to orient their behavior" (1966: 28). Despite his explication of political variables as central, even Huntington relies on value consensus, assuming that "political stability could be maintained only if there was a high degree of voluntary consensus among the members of any collectivity both as to the values and goals of the social organization and also as to the legitimacy of the social institutions created to achieve those goals" (Taylor, 1984: 127).

This overvaluation of cultural values at the expense of structural analysis leads systems theorists to identify legitimacy with political power, no matter how it is constituted and exercised. Both power and authority refer to relationships of legitimacy, "the first being a generalized kind of legitimate relationship and the second being a highly specific institution charged with regulating tests of legitimacy when they occur and exercising physical coercion in order to preserve the division of labor" (Johnson, 1966: 28). It is therefore *authority* that is both specific and coercive, and *power* that is diffuse and non-repressive! Huntington's assumption is less bizarre, but is unable to distinguish the mechanisms by which stability is achieved, and, like Johnson and Smelser, casts the existing political regime as the legitimate agent of social consensus and cohesion (see also Bell, 1973: 72). Huntington's model does not "give due weight to the ability of regimes to maintain themselves by coercion and oppression" (Taylor, 1984: 150). Systems theories generally overestimate the degree of cohesion and consensus within any society, and underestimate the level of coercive and repressive behavior on the part of any government in maintaining what stability is achieved.

All systems theorists share, to a greater or lesser extent, a metaphorical understanding of revolution as the eruption of a volcano: discontent smolders for years, while the pressure below builds and builds, until, unable to contain it any longer, the volcano erupts, destroying the stable mountain underneath and sweeping away all that was beautiful in the traditional landscape. This derives directly from Durkheim (and, to a lesser degree, Freud); these systems theorists tend to see "revolutions and popular violence as unfortunate concomitants of 'modernization' processes that set expectations soaring faster than incumbent governments could coopt, crush, or liquidate the groups that harbor them" (Aya, 1979: 76). The oppressive weight of the metaphoric mountain, its repressive capacities, are ignored in favor of legitimacy and stability in the equilibrated social system.

Systems theorists differ as regards the degree of rationality and organization that exists in revolutionary behavior. Johnson and Huntington imply a formal rational model of revolutionary behavior; Johnson writes that revolution is "the purposive implementation of a strategy of violence in order to effect a change in social structure" (1966: 57). Without again raising the issue that many political regimes, such as military distatorships, exemplify "the purposive implementation of a strategy of violence" far better than do revolutionary coalitions, one can easily see a form of psychological voluntarism in this model. Revolutionary situations are those in which two purposive, organized groups, manifesting antithetical ideological assumptions and expressing mutually exclusive cultural values, square off against one another, with the winner stabilizing the social system back to equilibrium.

While Smelser's model of social change in the eighteenth-century English textile industry follows this general pattern of disequilibrating social changes leading to new structural arrangements and a re-establishment of equilibrium, his model of revolutionary social movements departs significantly from the others in terms of rationality and levels of organization. He lumps together under the heading of value-oriented movements religious cults, nativistic movements, Third World nationalist movements, and internal revolutionary movements such as Nazism; these are the only "revolutionary" movements he discusses. His model leaves us little room to distinguish among these movements, and no grounds to assume that any revolutionary social movement contains rational responses to intolerable social conditions. This is compounded by Smelser's collective behavior approach, which insists that revolutionary behavior is a non-institutionalized response to social strain, a non-institutionalized mobilization of discontents which ignores established mechanisms for responding to social dislocations and change. Collective behavior, he writes, is "the action of the impatient" (Smelser, 1962: 72).

But what may appear to be spontaneous and irrational outbursts may also evince a deeper logic and rationality:

> To the discerning eye, even the most "spontaneous" and seemingly anarchic forms of collective violence – food riots, tax revolts, jacqueries, *journées* – reveal, each of them, not only implicit theories of right and justice, as well as practical objectives . . . but a political anatomy, a standard operating procedure, even . . . a veritable customary script which police and people knew by heart. (Aya, 1979: 71)

Finally, systems theory is vulnerable to another, more historically based criticism. By defining revolution as a large-scale ideological movement aimed at violently transforming the underlying cultural basis of society, these theorists "define out of existence those types of revolutionary events that do not conform to the totality demanded" (Zagorin, 1976: 156). Moreover, even within that definition, large-scale ideological movements have occurred far more frequently than revolutions, and the model is incapable of explaining why some movements lead to full-scale revolutions and why some do not (Goldfrank, 1979: 140), especially without recourse to an explanation that stresses the repressive capacity of the state, not as an actor whose legitimacy is assumed, but as a contender for legitimate political power in sustained conflict with other contenders.

The Psychology of Revolutionary Behavior

The natural history theorists and structural-functionalists understand revolutionary behavior as non-rational, non-normative behavior, episodes of "collective behavior" when traditional normative constraints on irrational actions are dissolved. But their theoretical models have not been developed from a psychological understanding of human motivation, as attempted by both individual and aggregate social psychological theorists. All might agree with Platt, who insists (1980: 69) that "a theory of revolution must take as its point of departure the subjectivities of revolutionary participants," or with French historian Roland Mousnier, who writes that

> [t]here is no strict determinism in the matter of revolt and revolution, no logical sequence, no direct link between the set of circumstances explaining and justifying revolt and the act of revolt itself. The link is a psychological one, a very complex psychological one, and in the most cases, the historian is unable to enter into the psychology, conscious or subconscious, of the men he studies. (Mousnier, 1970: 157–8)

But psychological theorists do differ about which subjectivities are more decisive. For some it is the particular configuration of characteristics that brings some individuals to the center of the stage: why do some people become revolutionary *leaders*? For others it is the combination of social trends and group psychological characteristics that brings about revolutionary movements: why do large groups of people *follow* revolutionary leaders at any particular time?

Interestingly, both sets of social scientists, those who follow the trajectory of the individual leader and those who explain the mobilization of aggregates, trace their origins from Freudian notions about personality development. What characterized all groups, Freud claimed, was the neurotic relationship between the followers and the leader. In *Group Psychology and the Analysis of the Ego*, for example, Freud defines all collectivities as pathological. "A group is an obedient herd, which could never live without a master. It has such a thirst for obedience that it submits instinctively to anyone who appoints himself its master" (Freud, 1959: 13). What characterize groups are the strong, quasi-erotic bonds, first between each member and the leader and, second, between the individual members of the group. Group cohesion is itself a product of simultaneous identification on the part of all group members with the leader; the object of this identification "serves as a substitute for some unattained ego ideal of our own" (1959: 44). Had individuals fully developed an autonomous ego, Freud suggests, there would be no need for collective behavior, since individuals would need neither obedience nor solidarity to feel complete. Thus, to Freud, all psychological dispositions to collective action are themselves the product of neurotic needs on the part of individuals.

Some modern writers have also followed the perspective of Freud's contemporary, Gustave Le Bon, whose books *The Crowd* (1960 [1895]) and *The Psychology of Revolution* (1913), expanded the argument about the irrationality of collective action. Le Bon's antipathy to the French Revolution led him to exaggerate the violence, irrationality, and destructiveness of crowds, and to ignore the ways in which crowds interact with existing political institutions (see Hagopian, 1974: 308). While individual behavior may or may not be rational, Le Bon argues, group behavior is always irrational. "Whoever be the individuals that compose it . . . the fact that they have been transformed into a group puts them in possession of a sort of collective mind which makes them feel, think, and act in a manner quite different from that in which each individual of them would feel, think, and act were he in a state of isolation" (cited in Freud, 1959: 5).

Writers who follow Le Bon invariably stress the pathology of revolutionary action. Le Bon's contemporaries, such as William McDougall, in *The Group Mind* (1920), and Everett Dean Martin, in *The Behavior of Crowds* (1920), also portrayed the revolutionary crowd as blindly irrational, and open to suggestion to commit unspeakable acts of collective atrocity. Modern writers such as Leiden and Schmitt write (1968: 16) of the "initial frenzied efforts to overhaul the whole fabric of society." Goodspeed insists that (1962: 234–5) rebels live "perpetually in a realm of phantasy;" the leaders of the Irish Rebellion were "mystic, dreamers, men exalted, but they were not completely sane. It is the same with the Bolsheviks . . . Mussolini, of the bulging eyes and the timid disposition, was clearly psychopathic."

Not all contemporary social scientists concerned with the psychological underpinnings of individual participation stress the irrationality of collective action. Several authors adopt a utilitarian model of individual calculation, in which individuals rationally choose from among several alternatives. This sober and rational "Millian" calculator is a sharp contrast to the frenzied "Le Bonnian" psychopaths, lashing out blindly against forces they do not understand. Olson (1965), for example, applies a market model to individual psychology; it is this form of calculation, not collective interests, that motivates individual behavior. The "common interests in collective goods is insufficient to bring a large group of actors together for collective action," he writes.

In fact, "common interests are *unnecessary* to collective action as well as insufficient – in fact they are irrelevant" (cited in Gamson et al., 1982: 11). Similarly, Downs (1957) and Ireland (1967) rely on economic models of individual decision-making to explain revolutionary psychology. Individuals participated, Ireland argued, only when "they perceived that their participation could exert a significant effect on the outcome" (Taylor, 1984: 97).

Few social scientists employ strictly rational models of individual decision-making to explain collective behavior, since those models reduce social life to simple aggregates of individuals. Many, however, have transformed these models for their analyses of collective mobilization and revolutionary behavior. As we shall see in a subsequent chapter, Tilly develops a model of collective rationality – of the collective calculations of group interests, resources, and possible outcomes of strategic action – that avoids the problems inherent in psychological approaches that cast individuals as the chief actors in the revolutionary drama or that cast collective action as pathological or disturbed.

Perhaps the most sophisticated attempt to apply rational utilitarian models of individual calculation to a theory of revolution is contained in Granovetter's threshold models of collective action (Granovetter, 1978). Granovetter assumes rational calculation, but also argues that these calculations vary. While he assumes that one can account for "collective action by simple principles of aggregation," Granovetter also argues that individual participation varies from one situation to another.

The threshold indicates the moment when an individual will decide to participate in collective action. This decision is based on the number of other people who are already participating. If one would participate in some action alone, without any other participants, that person could be said to have a threshold of zero. If one would only join after everyone else had already begun, one would have a threshold of over 99 percent. Thus any particular collective action will depend on the distribution of these thresholds within a population. Where they are distributed at the low end, the likelihood of mass participation is higher; where they are distributed at the high end, there is a lower likelihood of participation.

Unlike other rational individual models, Granovetter's stresses how an individual's threshold varies not only according to individual calculation but also according to historically specific circumstances. This, then, is a model of individual rationality *and* historical contingency. "Thresholds are situation specific. An individual's riot threshold is not a number he carries within him from one riot to another but rather results from the configuration of costs and benefits to him, of different behaviors in one particular riot situation" (Granovetter, 1978: 1436).

Thus, while Granovetter's model may "take the 'strangeness' often associated with collective behavior out of the heads of actors and put it into the dynamics of situations,'' it still relies on additive models of collective action, assuming that the collective is the sum of the thresholds within a population (Granovetter, 1978: 1441). Although Granovetter allows for historical contingency in the distribution of thresholds, there is no structure or group whose behavior is greater than the sum of its parts.

The Revolutionary Personality

Most writers who have employed psychological variables in their analyses have discussed either the psychological characteristics of revolutionary leaders or the relationships between leaders and followers. Hopper (1950: 277) argued that the latter cannot arise without the former; since followers must have someone to follow, the leader is both logically and historically prior to the follower. A revolutionary movement, he writes,

> needs the iron will, daring and vision of an exceptional leader to concert and mobilize existing attitudes and impulses into the collective drive of a mass movement. The leader personifies the certitude of the creed and the defiance and grandeur of power. He articulates and justifies the resentment dammed up in the souls of the frustrated. He kindles the vision of a breathtaking future so as to justify the sacrifice of a transitory present. He stages the world of make believe so indispensable for the realization of self-sacrifice and united action. He evokes the enthusiasm of communion – the sense of liberation from a petty and meaningless individual existence.

As Leiden and Schmitt (1968: 81) write: "only authoritarian personalities have the drive and the conviction to carry out revolutions successfully."

E. Victor Wolfenstein makes the psychodynamic characteristics of the revolutionary leader the centerpiece of his study, *The Revolutionary Personality* (1971). In this "comparative psychopolitical biography" of Lenin, Trotsky, and Gandhi, Wolfenstein investigates "why a man becomes a revolutionist," ignoring the leader–follower relationship, and searching instead for common elements in the child socialization, adolescence, and young manhood of these future leaders (Wolfenstein, 1971: 17, 31–2). What Wolfenstein discovers is that each man had a complex and "unusually ambivalent relationship with his father" which became decisive in his personality and predisposed him toward revolutionary activity (1971: 306).

That the father–son relationship should be decisive in the development of the revolutionary personality depends upon two assumptions. First, Wolfenstein assumes the irrationality of revolutionary behavior, that revolution is defined psychologically by the "expression of aggression towards authority" (Wolfenstein, 1971: 236). Second, Wolfenstein assumes that this difficulty with authority is especially intense for those who eventually become revolutionaries, who project on to governmental authority their own problematic relationship with parental authority. The revolutionary "views the authority against which he fights as a powerful and evil father figure" (1971: 234–5). Such a position also assumes the legitimacy of governmental authority as constituted, locating the source of the problem not in a repressive political institution which denies full humanity to specific groups of citizens, but in the personality configurations of specific individuals' inabilities to fully resolve authority relations within the family. (Whether certain political systems are more or less conducive to this psychological resolution of familial authority is not addressed by Wolfenstein.) Revolutions are, therefore, not problems of the relationship between state and society, or between classes, but the opportunity for partially developed, psychologically wounded individuals to act out their problems on a larger historical stage.

We can see then the basic attributes of the revolutionary personality:

> it is based on opposition to governmental authority; this is the result of the individual's continuing need to express his aggressive impulses vis-a-vis his father and the repressive action of governmental officials. The latter permits the individual to externalize his feelings of hatred – previously he had been tormenting himself because his feelings of antipathy toward his father were balanced by feelings of love, respect, and the desire to emulate him. (Wolfenstein, 1971: 308)

The developmental trajectory of this personality is evident through Wolfenstein's work. The future revolutionary experiences the early childhood trauma of the Oedipal complex in an especially powerful form. His adolescent development is prolonged, and the resolution of the father–son ambivalence is stymied by a complex of rage and guilt. Thus each revolutionary "carried with him into his adult life unfinished business with his parental generation. Each carried a burden of guilt he had been unable to relieve in the context of the family" (1971: 100). Even into early adulthood, the revolutionary individual "still feels himself to be a rebellious son against a very strong father" (1971: 226). For each, therefore, "the issue was, at root, how to deal with paternal authority and the strong feelings of guilt that attached to the relationship of father and son" (1971: 100).

The potential revolutionary leader resolves this crisis temporarily by sublimating his instinctual rage, beginning to find an outlet for his murderous aggressive urges through the articulation of a revolutionary ideology that blames an unresponsive governmental authority for failing to meet the needs that were psychologically unmet within the family. "The aggression which had been directed against the self is partially redirected against an external authority, onto which the revolutionist also projects this aggressive feeling" (1971: 225). The ideological goal of the revolutionary is always the overthrow of existing authority and the reconstitution of power along the lines preferred by the revolutionary. Thus the original Oedipal aggression is displaced from the real father and projected outward to the symbolic father, the state.

Once in power, however, the revolutionary leader will be unable to completely resolve the unresolved psychological issues that propelled him into revolutionary activity in the first place; he becomes fanatic, authoritarian, and incurably suspicious of others. "They have built up their personalities in terms of rebellion against the father; once they take up the father's role, they suddenly find themselves guilty of the same acts which for so long provided the aim of their opposition" (1971: 296). Thus the cycle is maintained, and soon new revolutionary leaders will emerge from identical psychodynamic origins to challenge the once-rebellious actor who has become an entrenched authoritarian father figure.

A psychological approach to revolutions that focuses exclusively on the psychodynamic elements in the developmental process of individual revolutionary leaders is bound to suffer from important drawbacks. Although it may provide some insights into why one person and not another may become a revolutionary leader, it fails to suggest why some historical moments are more conducive to revolutionary movements than others, or how the interactions between existing political authority and significant social groups may produce revolutionary situations. But it is not even clear that this model explains why one person and not another participates in revolutionary behavior, let alone becomes a revolutionary leader. Recall that, for Wolfenstein, revolutionary leadership hinges on an unresolved relationship between father and son. "[A]ll people who have their psychic configuration as adolescence draws to a close will have a propensity or tendency to become involved in political protest in general and revolutionary activity in particular" (Wolfenstein, 1971: 101). (Of course, this means that such a model is, by definition, uninterested in and incapable of explaining revolutionary activity and leadership by women, such as Rosa Luxembourg, Emma Goldman, or Alexandra Kollentai – at least without recourse to a different set of psychoanalytic principles.) But there are few models of a "resolved" relationship between father and son; in fact, the incomplete resolution of the father–son relationship is often used to explain every kind of psychological behavior. Most importantly, psychologists have used the same pivotal variable – incomplete resolution of the Oedipal relationship fueling rage, aggression, and guilt – to explain *both* extraordinary individual deviance, such as revolutionary behavior, and extraordinary obedience, the attempted merging of the conflicted self into the larger mass. Studies of blind obedience in Nazi Germany, for example, have stressed precisely this issue (see Adorno et al., 1950). It is difficult to imagine how the central causal dynamic can be used to explain both extreme forms of behavior – rebellion against authority and blind obedience to it – when that same dynamic is found in a large number of non-extreme cases as well. The causal mechanism for revolutionary behavior must lie elsewhere.

Within the problematic of participation in revolutionary movements, the relationship between the leader and followers must be addressed, and the same causal principle is unlikely to satisfy our theoretical requirements. It is not, after all, individuals who rebel, but collectivities, and the ways in which these collectivities mobilize their resources and the claims that they make cannot be reduced to variables which center only on individual leaders. The aggregate social psychological models of revolutionary behavior, to which I shall now turn, address this issue, even if their answers are also ultimately less than satisfactory.

Aggregate Social Psychological Models

Some social scientists have located the origin of revolution not in the relationship between leaders and followers, nor in the psychological characteristics of the leaders themselves, but in the relationship between what people want and what they receive. Such an approach permits us to understand how groups respond to structural conditions, and more specifically, how revolutions are always the outcome of frustrated collective expectations or desires. This approach centers on the frustration–aggression hypothesis in social psychology, a model that understands human aggression as the consequence of frustration (Dollard et al., 1967: 1). Politically, this model predicts that "the higher the level of systemic frustration . . . the greater the political instability" and the higher the likelihood of revolutionary activity (Feierabend and Feierabend, 1972: 137).

Some accounts relied on theories of cognitive dissonance, by which revolutions were attempts on the part of some groups to bring social realities into line with their expectations, motivated by the psychological discomfort which is the result of the disparity between such realities and potentialities (Geschwender, 1968). Thus "discrepancies would lead to dissonance between normative and reality-based cognitions; this would engender psychic tension, and ultimately motivate changes in behavior to bring the real world into line with expectations and hence achieve cognitive consonance and the consequent reduction or elimination of tension" (Taylor, 1984: 55). And although Geschwender offered a model that might explain the political direction that such a movement could take, he examined only the cognitive dispositions of the actors, and not the historical development of the possibility for such cognitive dissonance.

Other theorists have relied on a collective understanding of Freud's theory of neurosis and anxiety. Social, economic, and technological changes bring changes in the individual psyche, which may result in revolutionary behavior. Platt and Weinstein's *The Wish to be Free* (1969) and *Psychoanalytic Sociology* (1973) represents the most articulate effort to synthesize Freudian and Parsonian perspectives on the psychological disruption attendant upon modernization:

> Revolutionary demands for change occur when standards and expectations are rendered ineffective or dysfunctional as a result of social-structural change. Personality is thus affected on all levels, not only in terms of morality, but also in that the ego's capacity to master internal and external reality is disrupted. In this instance, the basis for stability no longer exists and must be dropped. (Platt and Weinstein, 1973: 99)

In the absence of the functional basis for emotional stability as well as social stability, the revolutionary becomes "emotionally commited and oriented to another course of action, whatever that may be" (Platt and Weinstein, 1973: 94). (Notice that the *content* of revolutionary doctrine matters not at all – "whatever that may be" – but simply that it is different.) In an interesting twist, Platt and Weinstein suggest that in those circumstances, the problem to be explained is the absence of revolutionary activity:

> If a group of people hitherto excluded from participation in decision-making processes develops . . . areas of competence and novel forms of expertise, and if the sources and symbols of prestige do not then become systematically available, and the social structure does not change to account for changed emotional relationships, including changed perceptions of self, it may become too anxiety provoking for people *not* to revolt. (Platt and Weinstein. 1973: 109–10)

In such circumstances, revolutions may not be irrational responses to rational social conditions (the functionalist argument) but rather rational responses to irrational social conditions. At least Platt and Weinstein do not problematize the revolutionary participants, but locate the source of the revolution in changing social conditions.

This position is also taken up by Feierabend and Feierabend, who locate the source of revolutionary activity in the social dislocation produced by social changes outside the individual's control. Their large-scale aggregate study of political stability leads them to the conclusion that "modern and traditional nations tend toward stability, while transition leads to turmoil and violence;" what is more, "the faster the rate of socio-economic change, the higher the level of political unrest" (cited in Aya, 1979: 55).

But the Feierabends argue that revolution is irrational, the result of the confusion wrought by disruptive social changes:

Change, especially extensive, rapid, and abrupt change, is an unsettling and bewildering human experience. It is likely to create strain in the psyche of the individual and crisis in the social order. Old ways, familiar environments, deep-seated habits, and social roles become obsolescent, while a new way of life and a new routine are not yet clearly established. (Cited in Aya, 1979: 56)

(Of course, if this were true, once a revolution began there would be no way to stop it, and it could, at least in theory, go on forever, for what could be more "extensive, rapid, and abrupt" than revolutionary change? Without any foothold, there would be no basis for stability and therefore no way to turn off the revolutionary faucet.)

Revolution, then, is the result of confusion; as Durkheim suggested, individual experiences of anomie may lead to suicide, and collective anomie to revolution. The Feierabends write that "massive change that moves people physically into new environments, exposes their minds to new ideas, and casts them in new and unfamiliar roles is very likely to create collective bewilderment. This bewilderment may find expression in turmoil and social violence" (cited in Aya, 1979: 56). Or, then again, it may not. Or it may be expressed in individual "acting out", like crime and deliquency. But from the Feierabend's portrait, it is impossible to tell when it might result in any of those actions, and when it might result in something as *purposive* and *coordinated* as a revolution.

Other social scientists have tried to explain precisely why revolution happens rather than some other irrational behavior. James Davies and Ted Robert Gurr elaborated a theory of relative deprivation, in part inspired by Tocqueville's observation that the origins of the French Revolution lay not in intensified repression under the Old Regime, but in the slight lifting of repression through political reforms. Davies suggests the structural origins of revolutions:

> Revolutions are most likely to occur when a prolonged period of objective economic and social development is followed by a short period of sharp reversal. The all-important effect on the minds of people in a particular society is to produce, during the former period, an expectation of continued ability to satisfy needs – which continue to rise – and then, during the latter, a mental state of anxiety and frustration when manifest reality breaks away from anticipated reality. The actual state of socio-economic development is such that past progress, now blocked, can and must continue for the future. (1962: 5)[5]

Davies thus reverses the Marxian model that increasing misery and poverty will eventually provoke a revolutionary response, and argues that short-term downturns during longer-term increases in material well-being constitute the revolutionary situation, since people's expectations do not decrease when the capacity of the system to satisfy them does. Graphically, such a model

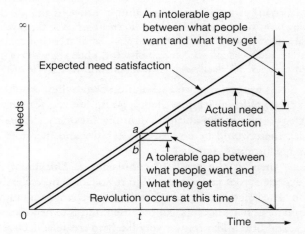

Figure 3.2 The J-curve model of revolution. *Source*: Davies (1969: 548).

produces a J-curve of rising expectations and declining satisfactions in which the gap between expectations and performance generates frustration which builds to a level that leads to aggressive behavior (see figure 3.2).

Davies applied his model to several disparate cases, including Dorr's Rebellion, as well as revolutions in Egypt (1952), Russia (1917), France (1789), and the United States (1776). (In subsequent articles he added the Nazi movement, the American Civil War, and the black movement in the United States.)

But Davies leaves several areas unexplored, rendering his theory less than adequate for our purposes. For one thing, Davies does not explain how the "revolutionary state of mind" can be transformed into an organizational weapon capable of toppling a government. Instead, he seems to assume that this transformation happens automatically (Aya, 1979: 54). In addition, Davies fails to identify which groups experience the declining gratification, which ones feel frustrated, and which ones rebel. He assumes that they are the same, but offers little evidence of this (see Aya, 1979: 54).

Gurr takes up where Davies leaves off, and attempts to formalize this model into a predictive theory capable of explaining historical outbursts as well as predicting their likelihood. Gurr claims that relative deprivation (RD) is "the basic condition for civil strife of any kind" (Gurr, 1968a: 1105). In *Why Men Rebel* (1971) and other works (Gurr, 1968a, 1968b, 1970, 1976), Gurr operationalizes RD as the "perceived discrepancy between men's value expectations and value capabilities," that is, the perceived difference between what people expect of society and what it appears society will be able to provide (1971: 13).

Gurr argues that the intensity and scope of political violence is a direct function of the level of RD. ''The more widespread and intense deprivation is among members of a population, the greater is the magnitude of strife in one or another form'' (Gurr, 1968a: 1105). And ''the greater the intensity and scope of discontent in a population, the greater the magnitude of strife'' (Gurr, 1970: 129). Gurr thus proposes a simple additive model of the causes of revolution; incremental building of RD increases the likelihood and eventual intensity of the revolution.

Gurr does differentiate between types of RD. ''Decremental deprivation'' results when value expectations remain constant but the institutional capacity to meet them declines (figure 3.3). This approximates to the Marxian model of immiseration. By contrast, ''aspirational deprivation'' is the result of the opposite movement, in which the institutional capabilities remain constant while value expectations increase (figure 3.4). Aspirational deprivation is the likely outcome of societies undergoing rapid economic and social change.

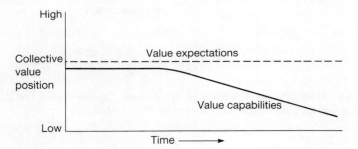

Figure 3.3   Gurr's model of decremental deprivation.   *Source*: Gurr, Ted Robert, *Why Men Rebel*. © 1970 Princeton University Press. (1971: 47).

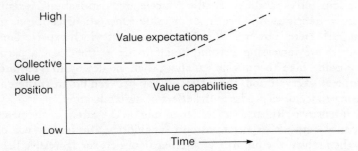

Figure 3.4   Gurr's model of aspirational deprivation.   *Source*: Gurr, Ted Robert, *Why Men Rebel*. © 1970 Princeton University Press. (1971: 51).

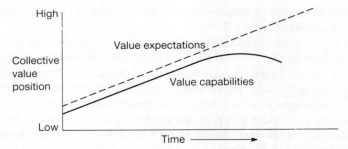

Figure 3.5   Gurr's model of progressive deprivation.   *Source*: Gurr, Ted Robert, *Why Men Rebel.* © 1970 Princeton University Press. (1971: 53).

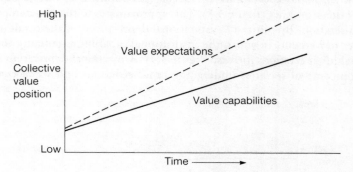

Figure 3.6   Gurr's model of accelerated deprivation.   *Source*: Gurr, Ted Robert, *Why Men Rebel.* © 1970 Princeton University Press. (1971: 56).

''Progressive deprivation'' illustrates the J-curve model proposed by Davies (figure 3.5). While rising expectations are matched by rising capabilities for a time, a short-term setback dramatically increases the gap between expectations and capabilities. Finally, ''accelerated deprivation'' is similar to progressive deprivation, since in both value expectations continue to rise (figure 3.6). Here, however, the different rates at which expectations and capabilities are increasing become destabilizing as they pass a particular tipping-point. Like Tocqueville's analysis, then, no downturn is required for the outbreak of revolution; the increasing gap between the two differentially increasing trajectories produces the effect of destabilization.

The intensity of RD also varies, depending on the extent of the perceived discrepancy between expectations and capabilities; the importance of the values themselves; the number of alternative outlets for aggressive behavior besides political violence; the number of satisfactions that might depress the level of frustration; the time frame during which the RD is experienced; and, the effectiveness of aggression in reducing frustration and achieving goals. Deprivation is more intense "the greater the gap between expectations and capabilities, the more salient were the values in question, the fewer the number of non-violent outlets, the fewer the number of offsetting deprivations, the longer the time period over which deprivation was perceived to have been present, and the greater the effectiveness of the expression of aggression in stimulating improvements in performances" (Taylor, 1984: 73).

Gurr also differentiates between types of civil violence. These depend upon the mix of RD among elites and masses, as well as the level of institutionalized dominance. Turmoil is the product of high RD among the masses and low RD among elites; limited scope of RD; a high level of political dominance; and a low level of support for dissidents. Conspiracy is likely when RD is high among elites and low among the masses; the scope of RD is large, extending over a large number of values; the regime is strong, but elites can develop closely knit counter-institutions. Thus the dissident elites can launch a short-term focused attack against the regime with no mass mobilization. Finally, internal war is likely where there is a high level of RD among both masses and elites that extends over a wide range of values; the institutional power of the existing regime has been weakened; and dissidents are concentrated beyond the control of the regime's repressive apparatus.

After all the analysis of the types of deprivation, its scope and intensity, and its historical trajectories, what have Gurr and Davies, and the other aggregate social psychological theorists actually accomplished, and how much closer does it bring us to understanding revolutions? First, their analyses take us beyond the facile reductionism of collective action to individual psychological states: RD must depend upon a set of collective perceptions about value expectations and capabilities. Second, while aggregate psychological theorists understand revolutionary behavior as non-normative, they do not insist that it is the behavior of pathologically disturbed individuals. Even at the collective level, RD theorists do not succumb to the view of revolutionaries as irrational "riff-raff" blindly led by forces they do not understand and by leaders that they cannot help but follow.

But aggregate social psychological models also fall short of explaining revolutions; this mode of analysis reveals three levels of problem: theoretical, historical, and political. Theoretically, the model is "inadequate," according to Hobsbawm, because it "tells us nothing about what may cause 'deprivation,' or about the significantly different reactions of different groups to it in particular historical contexts, or the different consequences of their reactions" (Hobsbawm, 1986: 7, 15). And Hagopian adds (1974: 104) that Davies

did not compare his supposedly confirming cases with other similar cases in which revolutions failed to occur. With the exception of the American Depression, he did not look for instances in which J-curves appeared without revolution. He provided no rule for deciding which satisfactions are crucial when some are being frustrated and others not. Nor did he specify, much less verify, the presumed links from the J-curve of satisfactions to the necessary discontent, or from the discontent to the seizure of power . . . In a universalizing mood, he compared a number of instances to a model and claimed to have discovered a correspondence.

Part of the theoretical problem may lie in terminology; terms such as "deprivation," "frustration," "aggression," frame the theoretical discourse in such a way that empirical research will only confirm the irrationality of revolutionary behavior. One writer suggests that "indignation" might be more appropriate than "frustration" as the emotional impulse:

> Indignation is a culturally grounded and relational concept recognizing the actor to make some contextual positioning of the act in terms of . . . what is right and proper . . . To be frustrated assumed no relational aspect vis-à-vis other actors or learned norms, except the existence of some blocking agent or agency. Thus, while the concept of indignation moves one immediately into questions of legitimacy and the "rightness" of actions, frustration remains outside any such normative framework. (Lupsha, 1971: 102)

Such theoretical inadequacy points to some historical issues as well. The model is ill-prepared to explain revolutionary outcomes, even if we accept its explanation of their origins. But the fact that similar gaps between expectations and capabilities occur all the time without provoking revolution make us suspicious of RD as the decisive element in the historical trajectory. In addition, the location of revolutionary change is historically suspect. To Gurr, revolutions are decidedly urban phenomena, since "a 'critical mass of' disaffected citizenry is more often to be found in cities than elsewhere, which means also that cities are promising places to organize agitational politics . . . People are more readily organizable in cities" (Gurr, 1976: 81–2). Such an assertion is difficult to reconcile with an important characteristic of revolutions, especially in the twentieth century, which is their decidedly rural character. Revolutions, when not made exclusively by peasants, must include them in a decisive role. Peasant participation transforms an urban revolt or a political revolution into a social revolution, a transformation of the society (see Skocpol, 1979a).

Perhaps one way to rescue the model, at least in terms of its historical time frame, might be to simply expand the temporal frame. While Davies and Gurr might see general upswings followed by immediate declines that trigger revolutionary outbreaks, perhaps we can see these two trends as shorter-term trends within a larger frame. The preconditions for revolution are longer-run structural transformations that significantly worsen the quality of daily life. A shorter-run (several years) upswing might lead to increased value expectations, as groups begin to believe that their needs might be met. The immediate cyclical decline is thus a *return* to the longer-run downward structural trend.

But even this reframing of the temporal dimension does not answer the political critique of aggregate social psychological theories. Political violence is directed towards the state by the groups whose expectations have not been frustrated by the institutional inability to meet them; for these theorists, though, political violence is never directed by the state against those groups. Thus the repressive capacity of the state is not seen as a cause of revolution; rather political repression can only be seen as a guarantor of social order. Such a view articulates easily with systems theory as both assume that a stable polity is one without political violence, and therefore that political violence is problematic only when it is generated from below. What is more, this model makes the satisfaction of members of a polity the chief criterion of political stability, again ignoring the repressive capacity of the state, and, like functionalism, assuming the legitimacy of any exiting polity. "The fundamental precondition for public order is congruence between the cultural values of the ordinary members of a society and the operating codes of order and opportunity maintained by political elites" (Gurr, 1976: 183). In this model the state is struggled *over* when it fails to deliver the goods; it is not struggled *with* over the foundations of political legitimacy.

Moreover, this model assumes that the source of frustration lies in the demands made by consumers on the state. But "[i]t is man as frustrated producer rather than as dissatisfied consumer who makes a revolution, and the need of man as producer is freely to develop and express his manifold powers of productive activity, his creative potentialities in material life" (Tucker, 1966: 228).

The voluntarism implicit in aggregate social psychological models has also been criticized by a number of contemporary analysts (see, for example, Skocpol, 1976a, 1979a; Aya, 1979; Goldfrank, 1979). These critics point out the inadequacy of assuming that revolutionary movements are "made" in the first place. In fact, they argue, revolutions *happen*. Never has a revolutionary movement, or even a vanguard party or a mass movement, singlehandedly made a revolutionary situation that catapulted them to political power. The situation is structural, and the behavior of individuals or groups can only be comprehensible in those terms.

Although Gurr claims that his model "is not a reductionist argument that analysis of social systems or collective behavior can or should be reduced to analysis of component individual behaviors," he casts institutional factors as the mediations and individual psychological states as ultimately causal of revolutionary events (Gurr, 1971: 20). In a sense, this confuses the motivations with determinant causes, inverting sociological logic that would explain individual behavior by reference to larger structural and cultural factors, and understanding the behavior of individuals as mediating factors.

A far more effective theoretical analysis will cast the existing polity as a significant political contender, along with potentially mobilized groups. These groups will mobilize for revolutionary behavior not simply by becoming increasingly frustrated that the state fails to meet their needs, but by the collective assessment of the types of resources and organizational capacity they have at their disposal, and a calculation of the likelihood of success of any effort to transform existing political relationships. Such a model cannot assume the legitimacy of the existing polity, nor can it regard the behaviors of revolutionary participants as the irrational explosions of disordered personalities. Such a model must account for revolutions by reference to long-term structural shifts in the relationships among classes, between classes and the state, and between the state and the international arenas (geopolitical and economic) in which it is institutionally located. Only in that context can the motivations of specific actors or the social system as a whole be comprehended. In succeeding chapters, I shall turn to explicitly structural theories of revolution, theories which focus precisely on these structural relationships as determinant of both the causes and consequences of revolution.

4

Revolution in an International Context: Geopolitical Competition and the Capitalist World Economy

The Need for Structural Analysis

Non-structural theorists of revolution have attempted to build models of revolution that are applicable across a wide variety of cases, and can explain a large number of phenomena – from riots and spontaneous collective outbursts to organized and planned revolutionary social movements. But as we have seen, these models are incapable of distinguishing between those situations in which revolutions occur and those in which all the necessary elements are present but revolutions do not occur. Further, they are often notoriously insensitive to specific historical circumstances within particular cultures. It seems that in their effort to create a theory of global applicability they often ignore what is unique about any particular revolutionary situation.

For this reason I have argued that an adequate social scientific explanation of revolution must be *historical*; we must study the historical particularity of any revolution, paying attention to its articulation with local cultural traditions, religious values and ideologies, and the sense of national identity that people might possess. The study of revolution must also be *comparative*, so that in building an explanation of what is truly decisive about any revolution, we remain sensitive to these historical differences and particularities, but we do not let them blind us to the commonalities among different revolutionary situations.

It is also crucial that any explanation of revolution locates the revolutionary society within a larger framework. Revolutions do not take place in countries that are disconnected from one another, but in countries that maintain economic and political relationship with other countries, both immediate neighbors and distant nations. To study revolution in a specific country and to fail to locate that country in this larger field of vision will produce an explanation that is decontextualized and distorted.

But the interrelationships among nations are important for historical as well as theoretical reasons. Revolution, as we have come to understand it, is a relatively modern phenomenon, a phenomenon that is specific to the last three centuries. Most of the models of revolution that we have examined were developed by studying a limited number of empirical cases and generalizing from them: England (1640–60 and 1688), France (1789), Russia (1917), China (1949), and a host of less celebrated cases such as Mexico, Vietnam, Angola, Nicaragua, Iran, Turkey, Egypt, and Cuba. In a sense, there really were no "revolutions," in the sense that social scientists use the term, before that of England in the mid-seventeenth century. If we are to explain revolutions from the mid-seventeenth century in England to the present day, then we must discuss revolution in relationship to the two central transformations of social structure that have been occurring throughout the world in the past three centuries. These two processes are: capitalist industrialization and state centralization.

Revolutions occur in different societies at different times, and for somewhat different reasons – but revolutions always have something to do with a set of responses to the dynamics of industrialization and the process of state centralization. These two forces exert a tremendous, perhaps even decisive, influence over us, shaping our sense of ourselves and providing the context in which we develop a personal and national identity. Thus Charles Tilly writes (1985b: 147) that "it is hard to imagine the construction of any valid analysis of long-term structural change that does not connect particular alterations, directly or indirectly, to the two interdependent master processes of the era: the creation of a system of national states and the formation of a worldwide capitalist system."

Industrialization involves more than a transformation of technology, or the types of product produced or the machinery used to produce them; industrialization's human consequences include the social transformation of peasants, farmers, artisans, and small shopkeepers – the traditional petit-bourgeoisie – into workers. The process of *proletarianization* is one of the single most significant contemporary social processes. Even today, close to one-half of the world is composed of peasants. But this number is probably half of the number of peasants in the world in 1910, and that number is probably less than one-half of the number in 1880. The transformation of relatively independent peasants into proletarians is one of the central processes of global industrialization, and it remains a pivotal theme in any adequate explanation of revolution.

The location of the revolution within the international economic sphere is essential in building an adequate theory of revolution. As political scientist John Dunn (1972: 249) writes of revolutions that have taken place in this century, "[a]ll successful twentieth century revolutions have taken place in countries which were integrated into the international capitalist economy . . . in a way which disrupted traditional economic adaptations or made future economic progress excessively difficult to achieve." Integration into the global economy transforms domestic economic relationships and distorts indigenous national development strategies.

Similarly, integration into the global political arena transforms national political arrangements. Just as the past three centuries have witnessed the global transformation of the peasantry into proletarians, they have also witnessed the political incorporation of many different groups whose identities lay in their political independence from the central political authority. The gradual centralization of political power has transformed these previously independent peoples into *citizens*, all subject to the same centralized political authority. Formerly independent subcultures (such as the Basques, Bretons, Corsicans, Québécois, Tyrolians, Welsh, and Scottish) have all become subject to central political authority in France, Spain, Canada, England, and other nation-states. The process of nation-building involves the suppression of these independent ethnic, geographic, linguistic, and cultural enclaves, and their incorporation within the national whole. The process of transformation of, for example, an independent Breton fisherman or a Basque shepherd into a French citizen working for a large fishing fleet or a Spaniard working in a privately owned factory generates a significant amount of political and economic resentment, which can easily be tapped to fuel a revolutionary social movement.

Here, readers will already sense one of my points of departure from Marxist theory – one that will become significant in later chapters. Whereas Marx argued that revolutions occur in those countries in which the contradictions between the forces and relations of production have proceeded to such a level as to have resulted in widespread immiseration of an already oppressed proletariat, I believe that revolutions really take place at the *beginning* of the process of proletarianization rather than at its end. Revolutionary resistance more often stems from people's efforts to resist the process of industrialization and state-building; revolutionaries oppose becoming citizens and workers, because this involves a loss of economic autonomy and political community, therefore poses a serious threat to their sense of themselves as full human beings. Revolutions are not made by a desperate people, a working class with "nothing left to lose but their chains" as Marx put it in that famous last line of the *Manifesto*, but by people who believe that they have a great deal to lose if these twin processes of capitalist industrialization and state centralization are allowed to proceed unchecked. (This may also explain why so many social movements around the world today are the results of these unincorporated ethnic groups resisting both political incorporation and the gradual erosion of their economic autonomy. This is true both in the west – for example Bretons, Corsicans, Basques, Québécois, Welsh – and the east – where *perestroika* has unleashed seething resentments on the part of the Estonians, Latvians, Lithuanians, and Armenians, precisely those ethnic nationalities whose cultural particularities were suppressed by Stalin, who was, among many other things, perhaps the greatest state centralizer in Russian history since Ivan the Terrible.)

The decisive importance of capitalist industrialization and state-building forms the centerpiece for structural theories of revolution in the social sciences. Revolutions are, at their core, *about* capitalist industrialization and state centralization, and these processes provide the framework for structural theories. In the next three chapters, we will examine these structural theories, and explore the different weights that they give to the three structural elements that compose the processes of industrialization and state-building: global interdependence, the transformation of class relations, and the transformation of political relationships.

In this chapter we shall examine the various theories that stress the international context for revolution. If capitalist industrialization and state centralization are the twin processes that shape the dynamics of revolution, then any adequate explanation of revolution must go beyond the individual national state and discuss the dynamics of the international context in which revolution takes place. Industrialization surely takes place within a global context, a context of international competition, trade relationships, banking, and financial transactions, all of which occur increasingly at a global level. Economies are increasingly linked through a global network of bank, financial institutions, stocks and bond trading. Revolutions are, in part, responses to this increasing globalization of the national economy, the integration of the particular national economy into the capitalist world economy.

At the same time, state centralization also occurs in an international context, a context of global political competition among nation-states. Most often this competition takes the shape of military rivalries, geopolitical competition for colonies and allies, and, when all else fails, war between and among national political rivals. The sequence of revolutions – so many revolutionary outbreaks occurring immediately after wars, for example – is directly effected by this international level of analysis. More than this, however, the types of strategy adopted by political regimes to incorporate internal groups are often responses to increased geopolitical competition. For example, since most autonomous ethnic groups live in geographically marginal areas, the drive to incorporate those marginal frontiers may be simultaneously prompted by a desire to shore up potentially vulnerable geographic outposts and to insure political loyalty from those areas should they be invaded by a hostile neighbor. State-building, both internally, with one's own citizens, and externally, in the face of a world of armed and potentially dangerous nation-states, sets the other structural parameter for the development of revolutionary opposition.

The international economy and global geopolitical competition form a central structural feature that must be analysed if we are to build an adequate explanation of revolution. In the remainder of this chapter we shall explore the works of several theorists who emphasize different facets of the international system and assign different weights to it, from viewing it as the context in which revolutionary events are staged to regarding it as the single unit of analysis for all explanations of social change.

The Marxist Background

Marx recognized the centrality of the international economic arena in the transition from feudalism to capitalism. Although later in his career Marx stressed the centrality of class relations at the level of production, his earlier works reveal an interest in the framing properties of the international market as an external force that propels domestic economic developments. Capital knows no geographic boundaries, Marx argues, and therefore transforms economic relationships in roughly similar ways wherever it goes. In *The German Ideology*, for example, Marx discusses the overarching power of the market when he asks how it can happen that "trade, which after all is nothing more than the exchange of products of various individuals and countries, rules the whole world through the relation of supply and demand" (Marx, 197: 162).

Similarly, in *The Communist Manifesto*, Marx argues that the historical transition of feudalism to capitalism can be accounted for by the transformative power of capitalist trade:

> The discovery of America, the rounding of the Cape, opened up fresh ground for the rising bourgeoisie. The East-Indian and Chinese markets, the colonisation of America, trade with the colonies, the increase in the means of exchange and in commodities generally, gave to commerce, to navigation, to industry, impulse never before before known, and thereby to the revolutionary element in the tottering feudal society, a rapid development. (Marx, 1978: 474)

The world market, therefore, is posited as a cause of the development of capitalism, not just a consequence.

The causal power of the market extends to its effect on individuals. Marx notes that capital creates "a *universal* intercourse between men," which, in turn, "produces in all nations simultaneously the phenomenon of the 'propertyless' mass (universal competition), makes each nation dependent on the revolutions of the others, and finally has put *world-historical* empirically universal individuals in place of local ones" (Marx, 1978: 162). Thus capitalism has the ironic effect of creating "individuals" and simultaneously makes all individuals the same. Ideologically, capitalism creates the conditions for the ideology of individualism as it creates the material conditions that undermine the possibility of individual autonomy. And yet at the same time this destruction of individual autonomy, even though accompanied by the illusion of individualism, is a prerequisite for the development of a revolutionary proletariat, a class more aware of their similarities than their differences, and thus capable of uniting for revolutionary collective action.

Thus it appears that Marx believed that the world market's impact was more profound than merely setting the parameters for national political events; indeed, the world market exerted a decisive causal influence, setting processes in motion, pulling national political structures and traditional locally based identities along with it. Marx believed that the historical moment of the emergence of the world market, the sixteenth century in Europe, set various processes in motion that transformed trade relations and consequently gave rise to industrial capitalism at the national level.

Lenin modified Marx's position by asserting that the decisive causal impact of the world market was not truly experienced until the late nineteenth century, when imperialism came to transform the domestic political economy of both colonizer and colonized. Traditionally, social scientists understand Lenin's theory of revolution to grow out of an unadulterated assertion of the primacy of class struggle at the level of production. As we shall see in the next two chapters, this understanding is largely correct. But Lenin also asserted the centrality of imperialism in shaping the experiences of European nations as well as transforming the structure of revolutionary opposition in the countries colonized by Europeans. Here, Lenin shares with Marx a conception of the historically specific emergence of determinant transnational structures, although he disagrees about the exact date of its arrival. After the late-nineteenth-century scramble for colonies among European powers, Lenin suggests, revolutions would never be the same.

Trotsky more carefully explicated the processes by which the world system transforms the industrialization schemes of specific countries. Trotsky's massive *History of the Russian Revolution* remains one of the most historically detailed and theoretically compelling accounts of any revolution. In this work, written during and immediately after the events of 1917, Trotsky was faced with a theoretical puzzle, which he answered in a manner more sociologically satisfying than almost any other Marxist analyst of revolution: why did revolution occur in Russia when it did, and not in any of the several more economically developed countries in Europe at the time? After all, Marxism predicted that proletarian revolution would occur first in the most highly developed societies, those countries in which the contradictions between private ownership and collective production, between owners' profits and workers' miseries, were most fully developed. But early-twentieth-century Russia lagged far behind the other European powers. Industrialization was proceeding rapidly in some quarters, as the tsarist state attempted to compensate for the absence of a strong, independent class of entrepreneurs who would press an agenda for capitalist industrialization. In other areas, however, Russia was still an agrarian society, in which a mass of unorganized peasants were dominated by a backward, arrogant, and politically immobile aristocracy.

Trotsky found the solution to this puzzle in the concept of "combined and uneven development," one of the most useful sociological tools for understanding the development of revolutionary tensions in any one society. This principle holds, as Trotsky saw it, a revolutionary transformative role for capitalism as a world system. "Capitalism . . . prepares and in a certain sense realizes the universality and permanence of man's development. By this a repetition of the forms of development by different nations is ruled out. Although compelled to follow after the advanced countries, a backward country does not take things in the same order" (cited in Edwards, 1982: 87).

Proletarian revolution, Trotsky asserted, will often occur in backward countries, not just in the most economically advanced ones. It is in the backward countries that the contradictions of capitalism are most fully revealed. What makes combined and uneven development potentially revolutionary is the fact that industrial capitalism is a world system, and events in any particular country are shaped by that country's relationship to the rest of the economic picture. Trotsky writes (cited in Lowy, 1982: 48):

> Binding all countries together with its mode of production and its commerce, capitalism has converted the whole world into a single economic and political organism . . . This immediately gives the events now unfolding an international character, and opens up a wide horizon. The political emancipation of Russia led by the working class . . . will make it the initiator of the liquidation of world capitalism, for which history has created all the objective conditions.

In such a situation, individual societies may "skip" the theoretically necessary stages that Marx had postulated, and still make proletarian revolution. "Savages throw away their bows and arrows for rifles all at once, without travelling the road which lay between those two weapons in the past," Trotsky writes (in Edwards, 1982: 87); "the development of historically backward nations leads necessarily to a peculiar combination of different stages in the historic process.''

To Trotsky, ''Tsarist Russia's involvement with this developing world capitalist system had significant domestic consequences. Politically, Trotsky writes, the 'pressure from richer Europe' pressed down hard on the Russian state, which then ''swallowed up a far greater relative part of the people's wealth than in the West, and thereby not only condemned the people to a twofold poverty, but also weakened the foundations of the possessing classes'' (Trotsky, 1959 [1932]: 4). Economically, as Stinchcombe describes it, ''the cumulative insertion of Russia into the international capitalist system, with the consequent commercialization of her feudalism and colonization of her commerce . . . inserts tensions into the social system which are difficult to resolve with the mechanisms of that ''system'' (Stinchcombe, 1978: 67). As a result, he continues, Russia was faced with a ''specific kind of cumulation of incapacity, in which the new problems are inserted into the system by powerful outside forces; and the incapacity has to do in part with conflicts within the upper classes about how to get the poor to work for them and how to provide the political preconditions for that work'' (Stinchcombe, 1978: 67–8).

Thus Trotsky appears to rescue Marxism from the error of assuming that revolution will only occur in the most advanced nations by positing two simultaneous claims: (1) that the objective conditions for revolution, the sharpening of contradictions to a revolutionary moment, *have* in fact taken place in system of capitalism *taken as a whole*, that is as an international economic system, and (2) within that world economic system, revolutions will move not from the most advanced to the less advanced countries but from those countries squeezed in the middle between full industrialization and complete economic backwardness. In fact, Trotsky's argument suggests that

> [a] proletarian revolution may take place sooner in a backward than in an advanced country; this proletarian revolution, moreover, will not *follow* the completion of the democratic revolution, but *precede* it and/or combine with it. Under proletarian (communist) leadership and with the support of the peasantry the democratic revolution will grow over into a socialist revolution. (Edwards, 1982: 98–9)

Thus Trotsky moves the geographic location of revolution within the world system of capitalism from the economic center to the backward, but industrializing, countries, those trapped by the contradictions of world capitalism.

It is in this context that Trotsky can revise Marx's famous, but flawed, thesis on immiseration, which held that revolution depended upon the sharpening of contradictions in the most highly developed nations, and the progressive worsening of the conditions of the proletariat. As he writes (1959, vol. 2: vii):

> the mere existence of privations is not enough to cause an insurrection; if it were, the masses would be always in revolt. It is necessary that the bankruptcy of the social regime, being conclusively revealed, should make these privations intolerable, and that new conditions and new ideas should open the prospect of a revolutionary way out. Then in the cause of the great aims conceived by them, those same masses will prove capable of enduring doubled and tripled privations.

Trotsky thus modifies Marx's economic absolutes with a sociological analysis that posits not the absolute misery of the proletariat but that class's *experience* of it within a particular context. Economic processes only become motivations for action within a context that is social and political; privations do not prompt revolutionary behaviour until the incapacity of the regime to resolve them becomes evident.

Within the context of the world system of capitalism, Trotsky argues that a revolutionary situation is the political outcome of the economic processes of combined and uneven development. Combined and uneven development implies multiple sources of economic authority: traditional elites in those areas where industrialization lags behind; urban entrepreneurs who contend for economic power with traditional agrarian elites; political bureaucrats who develop state-sponsored industrialization schemes that bypass traditional agrarian elites and "create" new economic entrepreneurs. Combined and uneven development creates a politics of "multiple sovereignties" as a variety of political groups – old elites, new elites, and the state itself – contend for political power.[1] This context of multiple sovereignties thus defines a revolutionary situation, because it indicates a power vacuum at the political center of the society, in which a variety of political forces can begin to mobilize. The appearance of the working class and the peasantry on the political stage in Russia depended upon the breakdown of political hegemony of the traditional ruling class and its alliance with the Tsarist regime, and the possibility of political transformation in the resulting vacuum.

In this sense, multiple sovereignties provide the opportunity for revolutionary organization. In addition, the revolutionary situation is also defined by a political vacuum or multiple sovereignties, as the old regime and the oppositional coalitions set themselves up as political rivals contending for state power. Thus Trotsky modifies the terms but accepts the basic Marxian principle that the new regime is born within the contradictions of the old regime. Even as it is attempting to shore itself up and reconstitute itself, the old regime groans under the weight of its own contradictions and creates the conditions for the emergence of alternative centers of political power.

Political Competition Among States

The global arena is, of course, an arena of multiple sovereignties, as nations struggle with one another, sometimes openly, as in warfare and sometimes covertly, as in diplomacy and mercantilist policies, to edge out or conquer other states. State-building is a process that occurs within the boundaries of a nation-state, an effort to organize domestic resources under a central political administration, but state-building is also structured by the larger competition among states within the world geopolitical arena.

Although I will discuss the relationship between state-building and revolution in chapter 6, it is important to understand how this process has both national and international dimensions. The internal processes that bring outlying geographic areas into the central administrative purview, or that suppress potential domestic opposition are also processes that facilitate competition in the global political arena of diplomacy and war. For example, state-building requires the intensification of taxation, the building of a powerful centralized administrative bureaucracy, and the rationalization of the law, so that isolated pockets of the nation are assured that they are treated in the same way as those who are in the political center. These three processes are all affected by the ways in which the state seeks to compete with other states in the global arena.

Rulers often increase the burden of taxation to build the administrative bureaucracy and the military forces to allow them to compete successfully in the global arena; conversely, these rulers may need to increase the burden of taxation to build up military and administrative strength because they are threatened by other states. Rationalization of the law allows for the pursuit of state interests in the global arena in diplomatic negotiations, which is often a way of pursuing war without arms. Thus, the relationship between internal state centralization and geopolitical competition is closely connected. Tilly argues that the motor behind state centralization is geopolitical competition among states – political competition forces states to centralize or be conquered. Thus "war-making and preparations for war created the major structures of the national state" (Tilly, 1985a: 75).

If competition among states – war and diplomacy – leads to domestic efforts at state centralization, then revolutions can be understood as movements of resistance against those domestic efforts to centralize. "Great rebellions occurred chiefly either when rulers sought major increases in the contributions of theri subject populations for war or when war and its aftermath weakened the repressive capacity of rulers" (Tilly, 1985a: 75).

Historically, this notion of revolution as a form of resistance to state centralization can be seen in a number of different cases. It was the international over-involvement of the Spanish state in the early seventeenth century that led to repressive measures designed to intensify the centralization of Castilian hegemony over various outlying territories. And it was these territories – Catalonia, Naples, Palermo, Portugal – that revolted against Madrid in mid-century. Similarly, the French Revolution displays elements of geopolitical competition structuring the dynamics and timing of revolution: "it was the costs of Bourbon intervention in the War of American Independence which forced on the ultimate fiscal crisis of French Absolutism at home" (Anderson, 1974: 111). In Russia, throughout the nineteenth century, the "government wavered between the determination to modernize Russian society in order that the Russian state should be able to compete effectively with the other great world powers and the conflicting determination to maintain intact the autocratic structure of social control" (Dunn, 1972: 29).

In these examples, we can see how larger political considerations and involvements shape the possibilities of revolution at home by creating potential opposition of state-building policies which eliminate local political autonomy and intensify the burden of taxation, often on the lower classes. Global military competition – diplomacy and war – raise the stakes for political regimes, and these regimes must either compete successfully with other states or face an uncertain future as client state or also-ran. As global competition intensifies, so too does the pressure the regime puts on its domestic population for increased revenues to build bureaucracies and armies. (Often, the development of the bureaucracy is a consequence of the increasingly rational efforts to extract resources from a recalcitrant population.)

This sequence partially explains the reason why there are so-called "eras of revolution" in which revolutions appear to break out in many different countries at the same time. For example, the mid-seventeenth century witnessed revolutionary outbreaks in Spain, France, and England; and the late eighteenth century witnessed revolutions in France, Belgium, tne United States, and several other countries. The year 1848 stands as the great year of revolution, when

> [a]lmost simultaneously revolution broke out and (temporarily) won in France, the whole of Italy, the German States, most of the Hapsburg Empire and Switzerland (1847). In a less acute form the unrest also affected Spain, Denmark and Rumania, in a sporadic form Ireland, Greece and Britain. There has never been anything closer to the world-revolution of which the insurrectionaries of the period dreamed than this spontaneous and general conflagration . . . What had been in 1789 the spontaneous rising of a single nation was now, it seemed, "the springtime of peoples" of an entire continent. (Hobsbawm, 1962: 112)

The years 1917–20 were also an era of revolution, when Russia, Turkey,

Mexico, and China all experienced revolutionary upheavals. As one can see, these eras of revolution often occur immediately following the end of a major international war, when domestic opposition galvanizes against a regime that drained the national economy of resources to pursue its military designs.

Revolutions can also occur after countries fail to implement their grand designs in the international political arena. Specifically, several revolutions have occurred immediately after a nation has attempted to expand geographically through military adventure and has failed. The regime having drained national resources for what is now perceived as useless military adventurism, the earlier nationalist sentiments are turned against it. Groups that have experienced such intensified financial pressures and have lost local and regional autonomy are often likely to throw in their lots with a revolutionary coalition of political opposition, as we might have observed in Russia (1905 and 1917), England (post-1588), and France (post-1763).

Competition among states, therefore, can serve as a long-term structural cause of revolution, by generating domestic political opposition to a centralizing regime. The global arena of geopolitical and military competition of therefore one structural dimension that transcends national boudaries.[2] Effort to explain revolution must locate the revolutionary society within this larger complex of competing states, and observe the ways in which domestic political efforts are prompted by increased military competition.

Polanyi and the World Market

The other critical structural dimension of international activity is, of course, international economic activity. The writings of Karl Polanyi and Immanuel Wallerstein use the international market as the locus of analysis, the generative force in creating the possibilities of revolution. Polanyi's work places the international capitalist system squarely in the center of his analysis of historical social change. In his masterful treatise, *The Great Transformation* (1957), Polanyi traces the rise and fall of the world market as the crucial analytic variable in historical development. However, Polanyi makes several significant departures from a simple theoretical assertion that the market is the overarching cause of social change or revolution within any particular society. In fact, Polanyi is careful to avoid such assertions; his analysis is decidedly historical. He traces the mechanisms by which the market came to be the dominant force shaping human endeavor in eighteenth and nineteenth century Europe, and then discusses the political transformations of the early twentieth century that challenged and ultimately toppled the market from its decisive position. Thus Polanyi argues that it was not inevitable that the market came to dominate human life – its ascendence was a historical process. Neither was the market's centrality a permanent phenomenon once it did become the dominant force – its decline was also a historical process.

Historically, Polanyi traces the rise and fall of market society by examining European economic and political history from the eighteenth through the early twentieth century. The market, he argues, becomes the historical engine of social change, transforming labor into a commodity, and irrecoverably transforming the old classes of the old regime. Finance comes to replace political or religious authorities in its capacity to organize social life; finance becomes "an undisclosed powerful social instrumentality . . . which could play the role of dynasties and episcopacies under the old regime" (Polanyi, 1957: 9). The impact of the market dislodges traditional political and ideological authority, leaving behind what Polanyi calls the "double movement" of two organizing principles in society. These two principles, economic liberalism and social protectionism, describe in summary fashion the consequences of the rise of market society to a dominant position in the world.

The principle of economic liberalism defines the economic trajectory of the market; the principle aims "at the establishment of a self-regulating market, relying on the support of the trading classes, and using a largely laissez-faire and free trade as its methods" (Polanyi, 1957: 132). The second principle is self-protection, which describes the social consequences of unrestricted economic liberalism, and social and political efforts to constrain economic liberalism; this principle aims "at the conservation of man and nature as well as productive organization, relying on the varying support of those most immediately affected by the deleterious action of the market – primarily, but not exclusively, the working and the landed classes – and using protective legislation, restrictive associations, and other instruments of intervention as its methods" (Polanyi, 1957: 132).

These twin principles describe the continuing contradictions between the economic sphere on the one hand, and the social and political spheres on the other. The market requires freedom of movement, but social order and political balance among classes require some constraints on that freedom. This is the origin of the conflict between "liberty" – the ability to pursue one's interests in the market without social or political constraints – and "democracy" – the capacity of the social and political institutions to constrain individual liberty for the common good. The market disrupts traditional arrangements and distorts human interactions; as a consequence people seek political redress. As Polanyi asks, "if market economy was a threat to the human and natural components of the social fabric . . . what else would one expect than an urge on the part of a great variety of people to press for some sort of protection?" (1957: 150).

Although Polanyi believed that the dominance of the market was decisive in the eighteenth, nineteenth, and early twentieth centuries, he did not believe that its origins were solely economic. The power of the market derived not from its superior capacity for organization of human activity, but was brought into being by non-economic forces. The emergence of the market "did not result from the gradual extension of local or long-distance trading, but from deliberate mercantilist state policy," write Block and Somers (1984: 53–4). "The creation of national markets was the by-product of state building strategies that saw economic development as a foundation for state strength" (Block and Somers, 1984: 53–4). The emphasis on the role of the state in the development of the market marks Polanyi's decisive break with Marxian models that locate the origins of the capitalist market in the capitalist market itself. For Polanyi, though, the "road to the free market was paved with continuous political manipulation, whether the state was actively involved in removing old restrictive regulations . . . or building new political administrative bodies to bolster the factors of production in the new market economy" (Block and Somers, 1984: 56).

Not only are the origins of the market political for Polanyi, but the mechanisms that keep it in place are also political. "[P]olitical instruments had to be used in order to maintain equilibrium in the world economy" as a whole, he writes, and political instruments were also imperative domestically to protect individual nations from the instability and unpredictability of the world market (Polanyi, 1957: 208). For example, Polanyi discusses the development of central banking as a method of protecting individual nations from the vagaries of the market. But central banking also had political consequences, as it "tended to solidify the nation as a cohesive unit whose economic interests were in conflict with those of other nations. The effort to protect the national market from the world market led directly to efforts to manipulate that market in one nation's favor" (Block and Somers, 1984: 60). Domestic political protection from the market – itself the product of political efforts to dominate economic trade – thus forms the basis for geopolitical competition among nation-states who all seek to maximize their position in the market they created. Even imperialism is thus a consequence of these domestic political arrangements, writ economically and then projected on the world screen. "The import tariffs of one country hampered the exports of another and forced it to seek for markets in politically unprotected regions" (Polanyi, 1957: 217).

In the twentieth century, Polanyi argues, the primacy of the market has been dislodged by new political forces that have emerged on the world scene. Both fascism and socialism replace the economic with the political as the determinant factors shaping human life. Each transforms the economic level, reducing the possibility of individual freedom in the name of some larger collective social good. Of course, fascism and socialism are not synonymous, and clearly fascism is a far greater danger to Polanyi than is socialism. For socialism is merely the consequence of the political origins and maintenance of the market and the inherent conflict between the market and the social world that gave it rise. Socialism, Polanyi argues, is the "tendency inherent in an industrial civilization to transcend the self-regulating market by consciously subordinating it to a democratic society" (Polanyi, 1957: 234). Fascism, by contrast, subsumes both economic liberalism and democratic politics to an authoritarian political strategy to dominate the world market and promote and protect national economic institutions. In its effort to dominate the political sphere, however, fascism destroys the dominance of the market that it seeks to dominate.

Theoretically, Polanyi's work is important for our analysis of revolution in several ways. While he points to the decisiveness of the international capitalist market, he does so in historically specific ways. Historically, the international economic arena is decisive in our sociological understanding of revolutions that occurred in the eighteenth or nineteenth century – that is, for the "classic" revolutions. The chief error that Marx made, being a product of the nineteenth-century dominance of the market and the chief prophet of its demise, was the ahistorical belief that because the market was dominant in the nineteenth century, it had always been dominant and would always continue to be so. Thus Marx assumed that all revolutions would follow a similar trajectory. This Polanyi labelled the "economistic fallacy," a fallacy that projected backwards and forwards through history the historically specific dominance of the market in the nineteenth century. Polanyi was more interested in the power of the social to generate economic and political institutions; he was, at heart, a sociologist of the market. He wrote (1957: 154–5):

> Once we are rid of the obsession that only sectional, never general, interest can become effective, as well as of the twin prejudice of restricting the interests of human groups to the monetary income, the breadth and comprehensiveness of the protectionist movement lose their mystery. While monetary interests are necessarily voiced solely by the persons to whom they pertain, other interests have a wider constituency. They affect individuals in innumerable ways as neighbors, professional persons, consumers, pedestrians, commuters, sportsmen, hikers, gardeners, patients, mothers, or lovers – and are accordingly capable of representation by almost any type of territorial or functional association such as churches, townships, fraternal lodges, clubs, trade unions, or most commonly, political parties based on broad principles of adherence. An all too narrow conception of interests must in effect lead to a warped vision of social and political history, and no purely monetary definition of interests can leave room for that vital need for social protection, the representation of which commonly falls to the persons in charge of the general interests of the community – under modern conditions, the governments of the day. Precisely because not the economic but the social interests of different cross sections of the

population were threatened by the market, persons belonging to various economic strata unconsciously joined forces to meet the danger.

Clearly, for Polanyi, classes are among the active agents in history; but they
do not form entirely for economic reasons; they are the residual coalitions of
the myriad social groups to which one belongs as a way of asserting a positive
identity in the face of the levelling market mechanisms. "Class interests offer
only a limited explanation of long-run movements in society," Polanyi wrote
(1957: 152). "The fate of classes is much more often determined by the needs
of society than the fate of society is determined by the needs of classes."

Polanyi's work indicates that we must remain especially historically
sensitive if we are to understand the sociological problem of revolution.
Indeed, it implies that there are two types of revolution: classic revolutions,
which occurred in Europe when the market was dominant, and contemporary
revolutions, which occur in reaction to the fall of the market from its
dominant position. If we extend Polanyi's analysis through to the end of the
twentieth century, contemporary revolutions occur in the absence of the
determining force of the market, and in the vacuum created by the failure of
the market to reassert its dominance after the appearance of fascism and
socialism. Thus any analysis of revolution must understand the crucial role of
the world market, but not its singularly decisive role. Analytic weight must
equally apply to the role of the state and to class relations in order to fully
explain any revolutionary phenomenon. The market came into being as
various nations tried to secure dominant positions relative to other nations; it
fell from dominance as other nations sought to protect themselves from the
market's capacity to incorporate them as less-powerful actors and still other
nations sought to re-establish political primacy over the market by geopolitical and military means. Revolution takes place within this historical context
of the dominance of the market in the eighteenth and nineteenth centuries,
but in the twentieth century, it is no longer solely determined by it.

Wallerstein's World System Theory

Immanuel Wallerstein's theory of the world system is perhaps the most
ambitious reorientation of theories of social change in recent years.
Wallerstein focuses his attention almost entirely on the international level of
social change, arguing that the world system is not simply the context in
which national-level events must be situated, but the prime mover of social
change, the single unit of analysis of social change. In the first three volumes
of *The Modern World System* (Wallerstein, 1974, 1980, 1989), and in inter-
mittent collections of essays (Wallerstein, 1979 and 1984), Wallerstein has

sketched in bold strokes the contours of world system theory and taken on the remarkable task of rewriting the history of capitalism from a world system perspective. The enormous size of his analytic canvas and the sweep of his historical brush has meant that Wallerstein's work has generated a significant amount of debate among historians, sociologists, and political activists.

The emphasis on the casual properties of a transnational arena – what Wallerstein calls the world system – has important implications for the building of an adequate sociological explanation of revolution. For Wallerstein has attempted to recast the entire landscape of revolution, insisting that a particular nation's political boundaries are, in many ways, artificial boundaries which serve to spatially locate a collection of classes, ethnicities, and political actors within a larger geographic field. Focusing on the topography of capitalist circulation, Wallerstein makes a strong case that revolution cannot be understood by reference to the internal dynamics of any one national unit within the world system, but must be seen as the political response by economic actors, mobilized by their activities within the world system, to redirect their national unit's policies to better facilitate their world systematic activities.

In order to fully understand the implications of world systems theory for our study of the sociology of revolutions, I will explore Wallerstein's work conceptually, historically, analytically, and politically. What exactly is the world system? How does it work? How has it developed historically? What are the sociological properties of the world system? How does social change happen within it? Why did the classical revolutions occur where and when they did? What are the explanations for contemporary revolutionary movements? What are the political implications of such a theory? What kinds of problems develop as a result of the world system perspective?

To Wallerstein, the world system is the unit of analysis of social change. All other units of analysis – class, nationality, ethnicity, region – are simply sub-units that cohere within the context of, and in response to, the dynamics of the world system as a whole. Wallerstein uses the metaphor of astronomy to explain his sociology. "I was inspired," he writes, "by the analogy with astronomy which purports to explain the laws governing the universe, although (as far as we know) only one universe has ever existed" (Wallerstein, 1974: 7). The world system is a single, integrated unit, divided into zones based on the method of surplus extraction, to which individual nation-states orient themselves. Until the emergence of capitalism in the sixteenth century in Europe, the world system was often composed of competing "world empires," political efforts to force a symmetry between economic and political domination by one political unit. World empires dominated both production and politics; military strength facilitated a single dominant polity as well as the political domination of commerce and trade. But the emergence of capitalism ended the era of world empires (even though there have been several notable attempts to re-create them). Capitalism is a "world economy," a system composed of a single economy and multiple polities. Capitalism establishes the contradiction between economics and politics; "economic decisions are oriented primarily to the arena of the world economy, while political decisions are oriented to the smaller structures that have legal control," that is, the nation-state.

The capitalist world economy is the unit of analysis for social change. It is, Wallerstein asserts, "a totality – its structure, its historical evolution, its contradictions – is the arena of social action. The fundamental political reality of that world-economy is a class struggle which however takes constantly changing forms: over class consciousness versus ethno-national consciousness, classes within nations versus classes across nations" (Wallerstein, 1979: 230).

The world system is composed of three zones, which depend upon the individual subunit's relation to the world economy, the method of appropriation of surplus from laborers, the strength of state institutions to maintain order and promote the interests of economically mobilized classes, and the ideologies that bind inhabitants into coherent groups. At one end, the *core* countries dominate the world market; they are characterized by advanced forms of wage-labor, strong states, and secular ideologies of rationality and progress. At the other end, the *periphery* countries are dominated by the world economy; these countries use extra-economic methods of control over workers in mostly manual labor, and are characterized by states too weak to adequately promote the interests of less-highly mobilized entrepreneurial classes, and more doctrinal theologies to create national unity in the absence of progress. Between these two poles are the countries of the *semi-periphery*, an intermediate zone that is both dominated by core countries and capable of dominating some periphery countries. The semi-periphery countries are often regional, but not international powers, in which older, more coercive, forms of labor control spring up side by side with newer wage-labor mechanisms, states become powerful administrative bureaucracies strong enough to promote growth in the absence of economically mobilized classes, and secular ideologies compete with traditional religion for people's allegiance.

Wallerstein's division of the world into these three zones finds a parallel in the class composition of any capitalist nation. Core countries function as the capitalist class, and periphery countries function as a disorganized proletariat. Between the two is the middle class – part buffer zone that eases the weight of oppression on the periphery and part subimperial exploiter of the more easily dominated periphery. The semi-periphery is characterized internally by the "combined and uneven development" that Trotsky identified as a precursor to revolution in Russia – this dual society makes the semi-periphery far more susceptible to revolution within the capitalist world economy than either the core or the periphery, where reformist class struggle or movements of national liberation are, respectively, the more dominant forms of social change.

The symmetry between Wallerstein's concepts of core, semi-periphery, and periphery and Marxian categories of class is more than conceptually coincidental. At both geographic levels, national and international, capitalism is, from its moment of origin, a system of unequal exchange among national units and between producing and owning classes. The inevitable tension created by this unequal exchange is the engine that drives the system forward at both the national and international level. Revolutions are among the possible political processes that occur within any subunit situated within the larger capitalist world economy. In this way, although Wallerstein focuses on the world system as a unit of analysis, he also remains faithful to the Marxian claim that class struggle is the central dynamic of social life. Within the capitalist world economy, nations act toward one another as classes within any one nation.

Capitalism as History

Much of Wallerstein's work describes the origins and history of the capitalist world economy, and he situates his analysis of specific revolutionary events within the larger, grander, historical sweep. Wallerstein traces the historical development of the capitalist world economy, sketching the mechanisms by which this overarching totality came to dominate the various national and regional modes of production. Methodologically, Wallerstein's argument depends on the application of Kondratieff waves – regular cycles of economic expansion and contradiction endemic to capitalist accumulation – to pre-capitalist economic formations. Each roughly 300-year wave is composed of two symmetrical 150-year phases of expansion and contraction. Chronologically, Wallerstein divides his historical account into these 150-year eras of expansion and contraction. At the apex of feudalism, roughly 1150–1300, Europe expanded demographically (a significant population increase), commercially (the revival of Mediterranean and Baltic trade routes), and geographically (as eastern Europe and the Balkans were brought into western feudal markets through the trade revival).

From 1300 to 1450, "what had expanded now contracted" (1974: 37), which led to a prolonged set of crises within feudalism. Demographic, geopolitical, economic, and cultural crises all converged in this era of wars, plagues, and religious persecution. The eventual solutions that were employed to resolve these crises took three forms. First, "the expansion of the geographical size of the world in question'' expressed a deepening need for expansion as a means of offsetting the crisis (Wallerstein, 1974: 38). New productive areas with higher soil content allowed for higher agricultural yields that could compensate for the declining production of European manors. The dramatic age of exploration also opened new markets for consumption, which further fueled the increases in prices. Second, the ''development of variegated methods of labor control for different products and different zones of the world economy'' can be seen as an attempt to assuage the crisis by patching up some of the feudal relations of production, by again going outside the western European zone for the intensification of feudal bonds (Wallerstein, 1974: 38). Some areas within western Europe fundamentally altered the types of commodities they produced, which meant that they were then in need of certain staples which they had formerly produced themselves, as in England's dramatic conversion from cereal production to sheep-rearing. Thus the trade between these developing zones was becoming a trade between unequals, between producers of primary products and producers of finished, higher-priced goods. Finally, the solution to the feudal crisis was the development of the state, ''the creation of relatively strong state machineries . . . served to develop new internal political arrangements by which individual nations might better integrate into the world market so that particular royal monarchies might partake of the economic advantages of a dominance in trade relations'' (Wallerstein, 1974: 38).

Wallerstein takes this model and reinterprets historical events in their light. He discusses European expansion into both North and South America, as well as parts of Africa; the ''price revolution'' and the attendant wage lag; changes in the patterns of rural labor in western Europe (the rise of the yeoman farmer and the enclosure movement) and eastern Europe (the introduction of ''coerced cash crop labor'' and the ''second serfdom''); and the simultaneous availability of free wage-labor derived from the transition to money rents, the leasing of the demesne and the development of wage-labor methods (Wallerstein, 1974: 128). The end of this historical epoch is symbolically signalled by the Netherlands Revolution in the last decade of the sixteenth century. The appearance of the first relatively strong state structure in the Netherlands coupled with the tailing off of the immediate cyclical crisis and its inflationary spiral (price reversal, fall in importation demand for bullion, and devaluation of various currencies) marked for Wallerstein the emergence of a new and historically unique era, an economic order qualitatively different from the one that had begun the crisis. This was the genesis of the capitalist world economy: conceived as an effort to shore up a failing feudal Europe, capitalism was ushered in through the back door. And capitalism's first revolution, the Dutch Revolution of the late sixteenth century, is explained entirely by its relation to the nascent capitalist world economy.

The first era of contraction for the capitalist world economy is the subject of the second volume of Wallerstein's historical account. This B-phase contraction from 1600 to 1750 is marked by a market downturn, the contraction of the global economic network, and the efforts of states to consolidate and stabilize their positions in the world economy. It was also an era of revolution, as the mid-seventeenth century witnessed efforts at revolutionary transformation in virtually every country in Europe – particularly the English Revolution, the Frondes in France, revolts by Naples, Palermo, Portugal, and Catalonia against Castilian domination. Wallerstein explains these events in the context of the world economy; these were political realignments to facilitate expanded participation and control in the world market. What dominate this era are ''the efforts of England and France first to destroy Dutch hegemony and then to succeed to the top position'' (Wallerstein, 1980: 241).

Within the core countries, Wallerstein chronicles the ways in which France and England attempted to dislodge the Netherlands from hegemony within the capitalist world economy and then subsequently turned their attention to one another. Although both France and England were thriving industrial and agricultural centers, France was actually better situated and more self-sufficient to make the move into the dominant position. England's ''relative backwardness'' during this era was paradoxically advantageous, as it spurred the English to innovate, to invite Dutch investment, to search for alternative fuel sources (from timber to coal) and for foreign sources of supply and distribution, all of which allowed the English to gradually outdistance the French. Thus after 1673, the French state became paralyzed between agricultural crises and languishing overseas trade, and their industry lagged behind England's. Louis XIV's continental ambitions siphoned potentially productive capital into unproductive military adventures. French finances were chaotic, and the crown limped from one fiscal expedient to another. By contrast, after the Civil War in England, the ruling class was reunited, the state captured by entrepreneurs, the Celtic fringe easily incorporated, and a national bank founded. Earlier slight differences had become crucial; the advantages of the French were eclipsed by the innovations of the English. The signing of the Treaty of Paris in 1763 ''marked Britain's definitive achievement of superiority in the 100 years struggle with France'' (Wallerstein, 1980: 257).

In such a tale, Wallerstein poses a theoretical paradox that is instructive to our sociology of revolution. Earlier advantages in any nation – measured by the ability to keep pace with international developments – may lead to economic inertia. By contrast, the less fortunate, the relatively backward, must either innovate to gain advantages in the market or conquer other nations militarily, lest they be consigned to the world of also-rans. "Initial receptivity of a system to new forms does not lead to gradual continuous change but rather to the stifling of the change, whereas intial resistance often leads later on to a breakthrough" (Wallerstein, 1974: 59). Such a theoretical argument resonates with Gramsci's assertion that the higher the remnant of the feudal past in any particular society, the less likely will be the rise of a hegemonic bourgeois class. And Weber wrote, in *the General Economic History* that " the germs of modern capitalism must be sought in a region where officially a theory was dominant which was distinct from that of the East and classical antiquity, and in principle strongly hostile to capitalism" (Weber, 1961: 177).

There was therefore nothing inherent about England's internal organiza-tion that prompted that nation to its early capitalist development, despite the arguments of many English historians who adopt an evolutionary model. In fact, Wallerstein argues, it was England's earlier disadvantages that prompted such radical innovations, which included a political revolution that swept aside those social groups who constrained English development in the world economy. France's earlier advantages of a larger internal market and massive natural resources allowed the French to languish and the social forces opposed to capitalist development (the church, the king, and the aristocracy) to maintain enough resources to successfully defeat the same revolutionary efforts in the mid-seventeeth century Frondes (see Kimmel, 1988). Thus the second classical revolution, the English Civil War, and the century's most spectacular revolutionary failure, the Frondes in France, are both explained at the level of extending national participation in the capitalist world economy and becoming the center around which that economy revolved.

Many of these issues are discussed in the third volume of Wallerstein's projected four-volume work. Subtitled *The Second Era of Great Expansion of the Capitalist World-Economy, 1730–1840s*, this volume tackles the great historical revolutions of the late eighteenth century as well as the Industrial Revolution. But, he argues, the term is misleading; none were really revolu-tionary. "None of the great revolutions of the late eighteenth century . . . presented fundamental challenges to the world capitalist system," he writes (1989: 256). "They represented its further consolidation and entrenchment. The popular forces were suppressed, and their potential in fact constrained by the political transformations."

The notion of industrial "revolution" is, he asserts, "profoundly mis-leading" (Wallerstein, 1989: 33). Rather, we should think of the Industrial Revolution as "the reurbanization and reconcentration of the leading industries alongside an effort to increase scale" (Wallerstein, 1989: 78). The

French Revolution, in Wallerstein's view, was hardly a revolution at all, but rather an effort to domestically reorganize, and ideologically transform French society, to better compete with England in the struggle for hegemony in the capitalist world economy. In that sense, the French Revolution "was a relatively conscious attempt by a diverse group of the ruling capitalist strata to force through urgently needed reforms of the French state in light of the perceived British leap forward to hegemonic status in the world economy" (Wallerstein, 1989: 111).

But more than that, the revolution "created the circumstances of a breakdown of public order sufficient to give rise to the first antisystemic (that is, anti-capitalist) movement in the history of the modern world system, that of the French 'popular masses'," whose movement may have failed, but signalled the emergence of anti-capitalist possibilities (Wallerstein, 1989: 111). (Of course, by Wallerstein's own systemic logic, the first resistance to capitalism should not have had to wait almost two centuries to make its historical appearance, but should have been present at the moment of origins of the capitalist world economy. In fact, they were. In Wallerstein's own terms the first anti-capitalist movements showed up just as the bourgeoisie claimed their first political victory in England in the guise of the Levellers and the Diggers in England in the mid-seventeenth century.)

Finally, Wallerstein argues that the French Revolution "provided the needed shock to the modern world-system as a whole to bring the cultural-ideological sphere at last into line with the economic and political reality" (Wallerstein, 1989: 111). The economic reality had been established during the sixteenth century, and the political reality by the end of the seventeenth century with the consolidation of absolutism in France and the failure of absolutism and the emergence of the liberal state in England after the revolutions of 1640 and 1688. Thus,

> [t]he transition from feudalism to capitalism had long since occurred. That is the argument of these volumes. The transformation of the state structure was merely the continuation of a process that had been going on for two centuries . . . Thus the French Revolution marked neither basic economic nor basic political transformation. Rather, the French Revolution was, in terms of the capitalist world-economy, the moment when the ideological superstructure finally caught up with the economic base. It was the consequence of the transition, not its cause or the moment of its occurrence. (Wallerstein, 1989: 52)

Instead of revolutionary transformations, Wallerstein stresses the continuities between the various phases of the development of the capitalist world economy. The late eighteenth and early nineteenth centuries continued the processes of expansion into new geographic areas and the development of counter-cyclical movements of resistance and rebellion in some of those areas. Incorporation of new areas involved the "integration of the production sphere into the commodity chains of the capitalist world-economy" which, Wallerstein notes "tended to require, in the period of incorporation, both the establishment of larger units of economic decision making and the increased coercion of the labor force" (Wallerstein, 1989: 130). Thus incorporation has significant consequences for the domestic configuration of the newly incorporated areas: larger economic units of decision making and states that are "neither too strong nor too weak, but ones that are responsive to the 'rules of the game' of the interstate system" (Wallerstein, 1989: 187).

Again, all political movements in the periphery are to be understood within the context of incorporation into the capitalist world economy. This makes what non-structuralists had seen as blind irrational behavior suddenly appear very rational. "Far from being primitive resistance," Wallerstein writes of the Indian revolts, "the revolts were caused first of all by the involvement of the Indians in the capitalist world-economy, which had, only recently been made more efficacious by the various attempts to 'strengthen the arm of the central administration' " (1989: 220).

Wallerstein's Conceptual Model of Revolution

Wallerstein's world system theory offers some essential elements in the building of a sociological explanation of revolution. His insistence on a historical account offers a sharp contrast to modernization theory's ahistorical model-building. In a sense, Wallerstein is arguing that historically there was no theoretical inevitability to the rise of western Europe as the center of the capitalist world economy – nor, even, was capitalism the inevitable result of various cultural givens. Capitalism emerged in the vacuum created by the political standoff of the sixteenth century: no one country could create a world empire, though several, especially Spain, were interested in attempting it.

Further, Wallerstein challenges the evolutionist model that was shared by both imperialists and their critics (most notably Lenin) at the end of the nineteenth and beginning of the twentieth century. Imperialism is not, as Lenin suggested, a more highly advanced stage of capitalist development which results from the inability of industrial capital to further expand domestically its productive and consumption markets. Wallerstein argues that imperialism is a vital component of the very origins of capitalist development as a world economy – the unequal economic exchange between areas of the world is an integral part of the first historical manifestation of capitalist relations. Capitalism has always implied imperialism, Wallerstein argues; capitalism,

as a world economy, virtually requires imperialism. On the one hand capitalism "implies the inclusion of new nations into a single interconnected system
of dynamic growth. At the same time, it implies that the interests of the
peripheral countries are subordinated to those of the center" (Evans,
1975: 115). Wallerstein's strength is the focus on the mechanism by which
individual nations are tied into larger economic systems and the ways in
which this unitary economic institution transcends differing polities.

Three important consequences follow from this assertion. First, Wallerstein provides a compelling explanation to the contemporaneous historical
development of the nation-state and capitalist economy. In this sense, the
expansion of the world market is, as Marx saw in his analysis of imperialism, a
"progressive" force, which allows more "backward" peripheral nations to
integrate into the more "advanced," core-dominated market. Indeed, it
makes no sense to speak of societies as "isolated and self-maintaining
systems;" rather we must see how all individual nation-states articulate with,
and are themselves the products of, the development of the world system
(Wolf, 1982: 390).

Second, Wallerstein provides an analytic mechanism by which to view
those periphery countries not as "pre-capitalist," or "feudal" or anything of
the sort: they are capitalist and are oriented to the capitalist world economy,
althouh their position in the periphery prevents their maximizing their
possibilities in the market. "The character of the advanced core determines
that of the whole historical era. Once Western Europe has become capitalist it
no longer makes sense to describe the peripheral areas with which it is
involved as 'feudal' even if they are based on serfdom. Classes and groups
must always be analyzed according to their relationship to the world system as
a whole" (Thomas, 1975: 27). Following Wallerstein here, Wolf describes
how "the history of these supposedly history-less peoples [the indigenous
peoples of the colonies] is in fact a part of the history of European expansion
itself" (Wolf, 1982: 194). The history of the colonized is but one of "the
variable outcomes of a unitary historical process" so that in one population
after another around the world, "people's lives were thus reshaped to
correspond to the dictates of the capitalist mode" (Wolf, 1982: 231, 353).

Finally, Wallerstein's approach insists that we cannot understand the
revolutionary upheavals that have occurred in the Third World in the
twentieth century without reference to their position in the capitalist world
economy, since that economic location structures the possibilities for
domestic political activity, and the efforts by some elites to better that position become the pressures that can result in revolutionary explosion.
"Indeed, one of the most enduring legacies of the incorporation of the
periphery into the world system has been the splitting of their societies into
elites and masses, tying the elites to the universe of the center – its culture,

life style, and consumption patterns – and condemning the surrounding society to marginality'' (Hermassi, 1980: 91). Thus we can see that Wallerstein's model means that ''revolutionary movements develop in interaction with the trials of underdevelopment and the constraints of the colonial or postcolonial state'' (Walton, 1984: 27). In the contemporary periphery, ''the task of revolution is not simply to change the texture of values and privileges within a society, but also to put an end to external dependency and unequal exchange'' (Hermassi, 1980: 73).

Wallerstein locates the problem of revolution within both the temporal and the spatial development of the capitalist world economy. His concepts of core, semi-periphery, and periphery are suggestive of the location and the dynamics of revolutionary upheaval. For example, Wallerstein implies that revolutions are likely to occur in different zones for different reasons. In particular, a revolution in the semi-periphery will have a different character from a revolution in the periphery. In the former, we might see a movement of potential entrepreneurial elites attempt to move into the core by means of internal political realignments that would remove the barriers to successful participation in the capitalist world economy. In the periphery, by contrast, revolutionaries will be composed of nationalist peasants, who seek national withdrawal from the capitalist world economy because of the economic stagnation that incorporation as a periphery country implies. Instead, they seek economic self-sufficiency and internal industry development so as to rejoin the world economy as a semi-periphery nation. (Wallerstein interprets these periods of national isolationism as a kind of nationalist consolidation, a form of withdrawal from the world economy before reintegration in a better position, as in China's post-revolutionary isolationism, which was followed by its recent efforts to join the core.)

Temporally, revolutions are events that occur primarily in B-phase contraction periods of the capitalist world economy, as mobilized national actors seek to realign polities to maximize their position or to recapture lost advantages. During economic downturns, class conflict increases and warfare erupts as rivalry between core states intensifies for decreasingly available resources from the periphery. Increasingly, the periphery asserts nationalist revolution as well, since the intensification of pressure to extract resources by the core mobilizes nationalist sentiments among mobilized elements of the periphery. Thus Wallerstein offers an implied blueprint for the demise of the capitalist world economy, as we are in the midst of such a downturn in the history of the world system. Extended to the contemporary world, Wallerstein's argument is as follows:

> Once the reservers of unexploited land, labor and nonmechanized production have dried up, the core states will no longer be able to expand into a new periphery. The basic mechanisms of capitalist growth will have disappeared.

Class conflict at a high level of mobilization will become unavoidable throughout the world. The system will only be able to survive this final crisis by transforming itself into something entirely new – presumably a socialist world
government. (Collins, 1981: 53)

Geopolitical events – wars and revolutions – are linked to the expansion and
contraction of the capitalist world economy in both time and space.

Historically, Wallerstein's analysis of revolutions reflects this insistence on
placing the nation within the capitalist world economy, and therefore
locating the score of any explanation within the relationship of that nation to
the larger international economic sphere. Wallerstein maintains that the
classic bourgeois revolutions in England and France were made by those por-
tions of the nobility that felt the economic crunch of the feudal crises most
acutely. The English Revolution of 1640, for example, is characterized as a
"rebellion of the overtaxed 'mere' gentry againts a Renaissance court."
Consequently, it is not always a "rising" bourgeoisie that is the social class
that agitates for social change, but that fraction of the nobility as a class that is
most directly affected by precipitating economic causes. This fraction sweeps
aside those political obstacles to expanded participation in the world
economy, and in so doing transforms itself into a class of capitalist entrepreneurs – first as merchants, and later as industrialists. Theoretically,
Wallerstein suggests that revolutions "reflected particular historical circumstances that were the conjoint consequences of the conditions of the world-
economy and the interstate system as a whole at a given moment, the position
of the particular state in the whole system, and the existing distribution of
class and other social forces within the particular state. Each country has had
the revolution that was possible for it" (Wallerstein, 1984: 83).

Such apparent historicism, however, masks one of the most important
insights that Wallerstein's world system analysis holds for the student of
revolution, an insight that resonates well with those of several other theorists
we have discussed or will discuss in coming chapters. Wallerstein is arguing
that most revolutions occur neither in the most advanced nations, which are
already capable of manipulating the capitalist world economy to their advantage, nor in the most heavily exploited periphery nations, which have no
organizational or economic resources by which to sustain a challenge to the
division of world resources expressed by the capitalist world economy.
Revolution is a phenomenon of the semi-periphery at any given historical
moment, an effort at domestic realignment to allow participation in the
world economy in a way more advantageous to the owning class within any
particular nation. Revolutions are efforts on the part of slightly backward
countries to catch up quickly with those ahead of them (a notion that reminds
us of Trotsky's understanding of combined and uneven development, as well
as the salience of relative backwardness in the work of Gerschenkron). Thus

revolutions broke out in the mid-seventeenth century in those European states that lagged behind the true core country of the era, the Netherlands.

Problems with the World System Model

Despite this kernel of insight into the topography of revolutions, Wallerstein's world system model raises several problems. To argue, as I have quoted him above, that "[e]ach country has had the revolution that was possible for it" is to argue an overarching determinant cause of revolution within the world system, as well as to adopt the language of the functionalist in describing the properties of the social system. There are several problems with world systems theory, each of which has important ramifications in the sociology of revolution.

The incorporation and subsumption of all smaller units into the larger unit of the world system raises problems of reification. The capitalist world economy is a social system, the dynamics of which can only be understood in terms internal to it. Wallerstein's system theory has provoked a good deal of debate about the epistemological utility of a system approach. Wallerstein argues that his analysis "involves not the study of groups but of social systems" whose primary function it is to maintain themselves (Wallerstein, 1974: 11). What defines such a social system to Wallerstein "is the fact that life within it is largely self-contained, and that the dynamics of its development are largely internal . . . If the system, for any reason, were to be cut off from all external forces . . . the definition implies that the system would continue to function substantially in the same manner" (Wallerstein, 1974: 347). Capitalism is thus a self-contained, self-regulating system. "It is the world economy which develops over time and not subunits within it" (Wallerstein, 1989: 33).

Despite his earlier analogy with astronomy, Wallerstein relies more heavily on the analogy of the biological organism. Raw materials from the periphery flow to the core, where they are refined and returned as manufactured goods. Trade is the life-blood of the capitalist world economy. Above it all stands the inexorably rational market, the brain of the world system.

Systems theory, whether Marxist or Parsonian, lends itself to a certain historical teleology in which events occur because there is a systemic need for them to happen, and the dynamic internal engine of social change is replaced by a static, reactive capacity for adaptation and system maintenance. In part, this is a problem with any theoretical account of historical development that knows the outcome and seeks to generate its causes from what seems decisive at the end-point. But Wallerstein does not avoid this problem; at times he seems to revel in it. He begins his analysis well grounded in contemporary political economy – his goal, after all, is to explain the *modern* world system. He reaches backward into historical records to "discover" precisely those, and *only* those, elements in the historical origins of the world economy that will fit with the known outcome.

By explaining domestic political and social changes in relation to the overarching capitalist world system, Wallerstein tends to "downplay the impact of specifically political and military factors upon processes of social change in the modern world," as well as underplaying the central dynamic of social change that Marx observed in class conflict at the level of production (Giddens, 1985: 168). As a result, the specific national-level changes are minimized, since all nations relate to the capitalist world economy and their character is irrevocably branded by their interaction with that system. Just as there were no "feudal" countries after the origins of the capitalist world economy in the sixteenth century – just exploited periphery countries within the system – so too can there be no socialist countries within the contemporary capitalist world economy. As long as any nation-state relates to the capitalist world economy as a capitalist actor (exchanging for profit in the market) then its internal dynamics will be a reflection of that relation, *regardless* of its pronounced ideological allegiance.

This "uncomfortable amalgam of functionalism and economic reductionism" also leads to a curious anthropomorphism within the capitalist world economy as a whole (Giddens, 1985: 167). It is the system which has "needs" and "necessities" – a theoretical back-door made possible by Wallerstein's teleology. Thus he writes that the incorporation of new zones into the world economy "derived from the need of the world system to expand its boundaries, a need which was itself the outcome of pressures internal to the world economy" (Wallerstein, 1989: 129). In the 1790s, he notes, the American south "urgently needed a new crop." Cotton, of course, was that new crop, "and cotton needed Great Britain as a customer" (Wallerstein, 1989: 248).

Wallerstein's teleology and systems theory make it difficult, if not impossible, to gain a sense of the options open to any individual polity within the system. This assumes away one of the most pressing political questions currently on the agenda of every "socialist" nation: how to preserve the internal restructuring of the society through the seizure of state power and yet continue to operate in a world that is dominated and defined by a capitalist market. This is a question of revolutionary practice, and different socialist countries will opt for different approaches to it. And there is little analysis of the options open to the world system as a whole. By underplaying the idea of dynamic motion within the capitalist mode of production, Wallerstein leaves us with a steady-state system which seeks only self-perpetuation. This unbreakable interior logic assumes that system needs are somehow met, but does not provide a sociological analysis of how they are met, except in so far as they respond to previously asserted systemic "needs."

As with other systems theories, there is also an implicit voluntarism in Wallerstein's schema. Individual nations observe the system, and develop policies that will allow them to move up in the world system from one zone to another. This leads to political voluntarism, but only within the context of the world economy. Wallerstein does not incorporate political or military competition among states that is not strictly economic in character. What is more, economically mobilized social classes also observe the functioning of the world system, and attempt to maneuver themselves to a more advantageous market position. Thus they may take up arms against the state or against one another or press the state to take their position *vis-à-vis* other nations. Revolutions, in this model, are the responses of politically mobilized classes who see the state as a barrier to their fuller participation in the world market.

Wallerstein argues that state strength is, at base, a function of the strength of the ruling class in a particular society. In a capitalist world economy, he argues, the owner seeks a state that will perform two key functions: (1) help him gain or maintain advantage in the market, by limiting or expanding the "freedom" of this market at a cost less than the increased profit, and (2) help him extract a larger percentage of the surplus than he could otherwise extract, once again at a cost less than the resulting increased profit (Wallerstein, 1980: 113). Thus Wallerstein argues that state strength is an expression of the ruling class's capacity to mobilize political institutions for their own advantage *vis à vis* other owners in other nations and non-owners in their own nations. The state is nothing more than the political instrument of an owning class mobilizing for participation within the world economy. As Wallerstein puts it, [s]tate strength correlates with the economic role of the owner-producers of that state in the world-economy" (Wallerstein, 1980: 113).

Wallerstein constructs five measures of state strength from this simple systemic imperative: (1) mercantilism: the degree to which state policy can directly aid owner-producers to compete in the world market; (2) military: the degree to which states can affect the abilities of other states to do likewise; (3) public finance: the degree to which states can mobilize their resources to perform these tasks at costs that do not "eat up" the profits; (4) bureaucracy: the degree to which states can create adminstrations which will permit the swift carrying out of tactical decisions; and (5) class struggle: the degree to which the political rule reflects a balance of interests among owner-producers such that a working "hegemonic bloc" forms the stable underpinnings of such a state. Thus even the political institutions of the state are expressions of the position and trajectory of the nation within the world economy. Strictly political or cultural resources are interpreted as they contribute to the mobilization for the world economy.

Such a view of the state is inadequate to build a successful theory of revolution. Wallerstein does not fall into the trap of aggregate social psychological theories that cast the state as the disinterested passive distributor of resources, nor of social systems theory's almost Hegelian elevation of the state as the repository of political legitimacy within a fully integrated social system or as the coordinator of goal-directed political activities. But Wallerstein does seem to reduce the state to an epiphenomenon of international market forces. He argues that the strength of the state depends on the amount of surplus and the desire of the capitalist classes for state protection of industry and their role in international trade. This argument directly contrasts with Polanyi's analysis of the state's relationship to the development of the market. Where Polanyi saw the market as the creation of political actors, Wallerstein explains mercantilism as a consequence of the capitalist world economy; mercantilism is the effort on the part of economically mobilized classes to direct state policies towards the maximization of *their* (not the state's) interest. Wallerstein claims that the "economic development of particular states in modern times is and has been a function of their role in a world economy," and that "the political developments within such states have reflected the pressures that derive from the consequences for various groups of the condition of this world-economy at a given time" (Wallerstein, 1974: 101).

Such arguments lead him into deep waters, historically speaking. Wallerstein seems to argue that, as Skocpol asserts (1977):

> the core areas ended up with strong states primarily because there are more plentiful surpluses to tax and because the dominant capitalist classes want state protection for industry and their control of international trade; on the other hand, the periphery ends up with weak or non-existent states because it reaps less from world trade and because its dominant capitalist classes are interested in profiteering from direct dealings with merchants from core ares.

But such an argument leads Wallerstein to shaky historical conclusions as well as theoretical inadequacies. The reduction of state structures to market forces guides Wallerstein to an analysis that would predict the strongest states emerging in the core areas, which dominate economically, and inevitably serve the interests of the capitalist classes. Such a discussion is, therefore, instrumentalist, as when he writes that the Dutch state was "an essential instrument used by the Dutch bourgeoisie to consolidate an economic hegemony that they had won originally in the sphere of production and had then extended to commerce and finance" (Wallerstein, 1980: 65).

These problems are most evident in Wallerstein's treatment of absolutism.

Absolutism was a phenomenon of the semi-periphery, not the core; in Sweden, Spain, and France, political elites attempted to compensate for economic backwardness by creating powerful political institutions that could capture the market with military rather than economic muscle. The Dutch and English states were weak by comparison. Wallerstein argues that the character of the absolutist state was capitalist; these countries were after all, participating in the capitalist world economy. But this derives from his systemic symmetry that all institutions transform themselves, or, more accurately, are transformed, by the development of the capitalist world economy. Absolutism is more correctly observed as a political formation designed to redirect this capitalist world economy, to make it amenable to world empire, to stop capitalism in its tracks. Absolutism was the last gasp of feudalism in this sense, rather than the first political breath of capitalism. (I shall return to his question in chapter 6.) More importantly, the disjunction between an international economuc institution such as the capitalist world market and the feudal political institution of the absolutist state provides us with an analytic *disjuncture* between political and economic levels, between international and national arenas, in which the dialectical processes of social change and revolution can work themselves out.

Curiously, Wallerstein's theory of revolution would have been better borne out had he understood absolutist states as feudal reactions on the part of dying aristocracies rather than as political efforts to mobilize the nation towards more advantageous participation in the world economy. Revolutions in the mid-seventeenth century were revolts by coalitions of political opposition set in motion, in part, by the absolute monarchy's efforts to constrain trade and commerce and to abridge traditional liberties in the name of *raison d'état*. It was not the absolute monarchies that were capitalist; they were feudal. But the coalitions of political opposition to those monarchies were composed of disparate elements, among which were those groups who decidedly *were* capitalist and sought to lift royal restrictions on trade and better maximize the nations' participation in the capitalist world economy.

Finally, Wallerstein decisively undervalues the role of culture in general and ideology in particular. Culture is denied any causal significance, and is seen as functionally malleable, to be shaped by dominant forces at their will without a conception of how culture itself is shaped. "When the local dominant strata are threatened by any incipient class-consciousness of lower strata, emphasis on local culture serves well to deflect local internal conflict" (Wallerstein, 1974: 101). Culture, in this model, is a shallow reflection of deeper economic currents. Cultures are "the ways in which people clothe their politico-economic interests and drives, in order to express them, hide them, extend them in space and time, and preserve their memory" (Wallerstein, 1980: 65). Material interests don ideological clothing as wolves do sheepskins; moreover, the "ideological descriptions that systems convey about themselves are never true" (Wallerstein, 1980: 32).

But this misses what is essential about those ideological descriptions. Perhaps they are never true only at face value. They are crucially true below this surface level in that they are symbolic representations of a people to itself. This undervaluation of the role of culture leaves little room for ideology as a motivating force in revolutionary activity; culture itself has little role in the world economy, except in rounding off the rough edges.

Wallerstein's world system theory is critically important for our understanding of revolutions, even if Wallerstein's ambition overreaches the capacity of this theory to fully explain revolutions by itself. For Wallerstein has revitalized the study of world history as an integrated entity – a history not of discrete parts, distinct and separate from one another, each progressing through the different stages towards some identifiable future, but rather of a single, integrated whole, made up of separate parts that connect with one another. Wallerstein's theory makes it impossible to ignore the international context in which revolutions occur, even though revolutions cannot be wholly explained simply by their location within that international context.

In that sense, Wallerstein's world system theory makes a significant leap over the earlier non-structural theories of revolution. His work, as well as that of Polanyi and Trotsky, builds on the Marxian notion that capitalism is a world phenomenon, capable of transforming national and local units. The international economic context, the capitalist world economy, provides one of the three essentials levels of analysis of a sociological theory of revolution; it is essential to a structural analysis. Revolution within any one country must be understood by locating the country within the capitalist world economy, even though that revolution will also be explained by factors not directly traceable to the world economy alone.

5
Class Struggle and Revolution

A focus on the international arena may sensitize us to the crucial framing of revolutionary events by their global context. But revolutions are, after all, domestic wars, struggles within a society for political control, and any adequate structural explanation of revolution cannot stop with the context-ualization of the revolutionary event within the larger frame. Revolutions "are more responses to indigenous patterns of social conflict than manifesta-tions of a transnational wave" (Hagopian, 1974: 112). One needs to account for structural relationships within a society, as well as relationships between that society and others, and between domestic social groups and others from other societies acting on a global stage.

Following Marx's theory more closely than world systems theorists, at least in the sober economistic letter of his work if not in his ambitiously utopian spirit, some social scientists have insisted that adequate explanation of revolution rests on analysis of class relations at the level of production. The relations of production, the division of labor that defines the system of economic production in any society, determines the structure of power and wealth in a society, and is therefore a central component of a theory of revolution.

At first glance, this might seem to be obvious: revolutions, in the common-sense understanding, are revolts of the "have-nots" against the "haves" and the mechanism by which the haves have and the have-nots do not have is their relationship to the ownership of the means of production. Certainly, revolu-tionaries have endeavored to make their efforts sound this simple. Mao Zedong, for example, wrote that a revolution is simply "an insurrection, an act of violence by which one class overthrows another" (Mao Zedong, 1967: 7); and Engels wrote that every real revolution "brings a new class to power, and allows it to remodel society in its own image" (cited in Draper, 1978, Vol 2: 19). But the sociological realities are far more complex than such aphoristic devices, no matter how politically inspiring they may be.

Instead of examining the class origins of revolution, other simplistic formulae suggest that we look at the class composition of the revolution. Even Lyford Edwards, whose "natural history" of revolution was discussed earlier, was sympathetic to this class-based notion. To him, the English Revolution was "a struggle by British businessmen for power to pass laws like the Navigation Act;" the American Revolution was a "struggle of American businessmen to gain the like valuable privilege for themselves"; and the French bourgeoisie "gained this power in their Revolution, and, in addition, the peasants gained possession of the agricultural land of the nation" (Edwards, 1972: 198). (I will reserve criticism of this historical interpretation for later in this chapter.)

Still other analysts will insist that we can safely ignore the class origins or the class composition of the revolutionary events, and focus instead on the class outcomes, the ways in which subsequent political and economic configurations benefited some classes over and against others.

I believe, however, that class analysis will involve, to some extent all three, and more. Class analysis demands that we examine the overall organization of economic life within a society: the structure of production, the distribution of ownership, the division of labor, the access to political power that derives from economic control, as well as the relationship between domestic economic life and the world economy in which production takes place and towards which it is oriented. Revolution is caused by increasing antagonism between the two classes that compose the economic realm of production, those who own the means of production and those who do not and are therefore forced to alienate their labor power (sell to the owners their ability to work) in order to survive economically. The dynamic motor of revolution is the conflict between owners and producers.

Class struggle theorists often reverse the causal model of world systems theorists. To them, the international system is an emanation from domestic class struggle; it is class struggle writ large. Class struggle theorists also transform the attributions of causation to cultural and ideological variables of the non-structural theorists; in the class struggle model, culture and ideology merely veil the more central economic conflict that underlies all activity.

Such a model can best be understood by metaphor. In the class struggle model, a revolution is like a boxing match. Two fully mobilized classes get into the ring to slug it out. The winner is awarded, both literally and metaphorically, the "crown," political power, control over the state. (The state in this model is always the unitary prize captured and held by one class at a time, and the institutions of the state always act to promote the interests of that class.) Each combatant might call itself by a name, such as "Democracy," "Freedom," or "Liberté, Egalité, Fraternité," but these clever titles are simply ideological ruses that mask the narrowly conceived class interests that they might represent.

Granted, such a metaphor also caricatures the model it is intended to portray. But it also points out the danger of the class struggle model, a danger to which we will return later in this chapter. The model flirts with the reduction of other levels of analysis – the state, the international context, culture and ideology – to mere epiphenomena. Even Lenin noted the inadequacy of this exaggerated view. "Those who imagine," Lenin wrote (Lenin, 1929, vol. 6: 527) "that in one place an army will line up and say 'we are for socialism,' and in another place another army will say 'we are for imperialism,' and that this will be the social revolution will never live to see it."

Lenin's Class Theory

None the less, it is Lenin who presents one of the strongest arguments for the class struggle model, at least in theory. In 1917, as the Bolsheviks prepared to seize political power, Lenin defined revolution: "The passing of state power from one class to another is the first, the main, the basic principle of revolution, both in the strictly scientific and in the practical political meaning of that term" (Lenin, 1929, vol. 20: 119). To Lenin, a revolutionary situation is caused by the decay and collapse of the ruling class and the simultaneous anger of the oppressed class; it involves "a crisis in the policy of the ruling class which causes fissures through which the discontent and the indignation of the oppressed classes burst forth.' This crisis of the ruling class sharpens the discontent of the lower classes, and results in "a considerable increase in the activity of the masses" (Lenin, 1929, vol. 5: 174). When the working class revolts, they seize the state apparatus, transforming irrevocably the class character of the society. As Stalin explained in *Leninism*, his explication of Lenin's theory (cited in Colton, 1935: 6):

> The bourgeois revolution, being no more than the replacement of one group of exploiters by another in the seat of power, has no need to destroy the old State machine; but the proletarian revolution means that the groups of exploiters one and all have been excluded from power, and that the leaders of all the workers, the leaders of all the exploited, the leaders of the proletarian class, have come to occupy the seat of power, and they therefore have no option but to destroy the old State machine and to replace it by a new one.

Although it may appear consistent with Marx's insistence on the centrality of class struggle as the determinant cause of revolution, Lenin's understanding of the revolutionary process actually makes a significant departure. Marx argued that the increasing immiseration of the oppressed class was the crucial causal factor in precipitating revolution; revolution bubbled up from below as the working class became increasingly angry and restive. The ruling class, in this model, simply went about its business of being a ruling class – generating profits, squeezing the working class, controlling the state. Lenin, by contrast, suggests that revolution comes not when the ruling class is succeeding, but when it has failed, when its collapse has begun, when it is scrambling to reconstitute its rule and deploy the repressive apparatus of the state to maintain its domination of the society. In Lenin's view, revolution is precipitated by the collapse of the power of the ruling class, which is the mechanism that sets working-class discontent into action.

Lenin's theory also departs significantly from Marx's in the his emphasis on the centrality of political parties in the process of revolution.[1] Where Marx seems to have believed that the working classes would rise spontaneously after they had been increasingly dispossessed and oppressed by ruthless class exploitation, Lenin argues that trusting the working class to rise spontaneously is a tactical error; he believes that left to themselves the working classes will not progress to a revolutionary class-consciousness that will incite revolution. In what is perhaps his most important analytic legacy to the sociology of revolution, *What is to be Done?*, Lenin argues that the working class needs to be led to revolutionary class-consciousness by a vanguard political party, a group of dedicated revolutionaries who are able to discern the opportunity for revolutionary activity even in the absence of a concerted revolutionary movement among the workers themselves.

What is to be Done? contrasts Lenin's views with those of "economism". Economistic theorists believe that revolution grows out of the experiences of the working class, both within the factory and as they try to make their political aspiration tangible as policy. Trade unions, the organizations of workers at the level of factory production, are therefore revolutionary organizations, because they activate workers, bringing them into increased contact with the ruling class, which then heightens revolutionary consciousness. Therefore, the economistic position supports the development of trade unions among the workers as a way of meeting increasingly politicized challenges as the conflict between the two classes becomes increasingly sharp.

Lenin's work is a sustained critique of these positions. Lenin believes that left to themselves, the working class will develop only a "trade union consciousness," a consciousness that will promote their immediate economic well-being. But beyond this they will not move on their own. It is the vanguard party that will push the working class to articulate increasingly political claims, and that will transform the narrowly conceived, immediately economic concerns of the working class into the visionary activities of a revolutionary class. The vanguard party builds its organization from the vague discontent of the working class by attempting to demonstrate the larger social significance of specific dissatisfactions and by indicating the ways in which solutions to workers' problems lie not in incremental reforms within capitalism but in a sustained revolutionary effort to overthrow capitalism.

To Lenin, revolution is not a spontaneous uprising but a carefully planned political event, too important to be left to the diffuse anger of the oppressed class. Revolutions do not happen but are made, shaped by a small cadre of professional revolutionaries. The revolutionary vanguard party gives direction and shape to the revolution, which draws on popular discontent for its propulsion, but is not directed by it. Popular participation must be contained and shaped, for "the broader the popular mass drawn spontaneously into the struggle, which forms the basis of the movement and participates in it, the more urgent the need for such an organization, and the more solid this organization must be" (cited in Bell, 1973: 103).

The need for a small, highly organized, cadre of professional revolutionaries takes us far afield from Marx's earlier formulations about workers rising in spontaneous anger because they have nothing to lose but their chains. Lenin provides a distinct psychology of revolutionary motivation – revolutionary activity will not, of itself, happen from the material conditions of the society but must be willed into being. The professional revolutionary organization orchestrates revolutionary activity from above, and the masses follow in dumb anger as the revolution sweeps aside the pre-existing system.

What is interesting about Lenin's theory, then, is that although both dimensions of revolution we have discussed here – the origins of the revolutionary situation and the process of revolutionary organization – concern the seizure of state power by the oppressed class as the foundation of revolution, each dimension refuses to generate its causal mechanism from the bottom up. The working class does make revolution, but only after the ruling class has become so decadent and corrupt that it is incapable of ruling. Movement at the bottom depends on collapse at the top. Once the agitation from below is begun, it requires an elite to choreograph it, a vanguard party of dedicated professionals to shape it and give it direction and purpose. Even the working-class movement requires a ruling elite.

Barrington Moore and the Politics of Agricultural Production

Perhaps the most influential contemporary class struggle theorist of revolution is Barrington Moore, whose *The Social Origins of Dictatorship and Democracy* (1966) is a masterful account of the causes and consequences of industrialization and revolution in several different cases. Unlike Lenin, who stresses the urban organization of an industrial working class, Moore focuses on the countryside, examining the traditional agricultural organization of production, and tracing the relationships between owners and producers through the processes of capitalist industrialization and political transformation.

Moore is one of the first theorists within the Marxist tradition to understand the decisive role the commercialization of agriculture has in the shaping of politics and the dynamics of revolution. Marx assumes that agriculture equals feudalism, and that the interests of the feudal (rural) lords will eventually come into conflict with those of the urban bourgeoisie, who will sweep the landlords aside and institute a capitalist mode of production. Marx assumes that the locus of production in such a transition will shift from countryside to city, from manor to factory. But Moore stresses the role of *agrarian capitalism*, arguing that an intermediate stage in this process is the commercialization of agriculture by rural landlords. The different routes to political modernization – fascism, communism, democracy – are shaped decisively by the dynamics of the commercialization of agriculture; it is the intermediate step in the transition from feudalism to industrial capitalism that structures the possibilities and the outcomes of revolution.

Such an argument also diverges from Marx in another important way. Since Moore's theory focuses almost entirely on rural class relations, he develops a theory of the revolutionary potential of the peasantry.[2] For Marx, the peasantry is never a revolutionary class, but is instead either an incoherent mass or a potentially counter-revolutionary force with a frightening potential to be enlisted to serve the forces of restoration of the old regime. The structural ambivalence of the peasantry – at once isolated and separate and collective and communal – makes solidarity problematic. They are thus incapable of being a revolutionary class. To Marx, it is the transformation of the peasantry into the proletariat that constitutes the creation of a class for whom solidarity is assumed by the collective nature of production, and who are therefore capable of revolutionary organization.

Moore approaches this problem of rural class relations from several different positions. First, his work is a sustained analysis of the process by which peasants are transformed into proletarians; in this sense he extends Marx's original formulation. Second, he describes the mechanisms by which the peasantry becomes a revolutionary class itself, through the process of commercialization of agriculture. If the peasantry is transformed into proletarians, this often happens without them ever leaving the countryside. This allows Moore to explain peasant revolution in China, for example, as at the same time, a revolution against both feudalism and capitalism, both the old regime of the imperial state and rural landlords, and the transformation of the countryside into a capitalist production site.

Moore's overall goal is to explain why industrialization produces such different political forms; that is, to examine how democracy, fascism, and communism come into being through the process of industrialization. Moore argues that early developers, such as England and France, followed a route that was both capitalist and democratic. Later developers, such as Germany, Italy, and Japan, reproduced the economic form of capitalism, but required a totalitarian state (fascism) in order to institute capitalist industrialization. Finally, China and Russia reject capitalist economics, but at the cost of political democracy; this route is politically totalitarian and communist economically. Schematically, we can observe this relationship between economic and political outcomes of industrialization among early developers in figure 5.1.

What determines the political outcome of the modernization process is the line-up of class forces in the countryside. The critical change in society that is the essential long-run precondition for revolution is the way in which agriculture is commercialized. The immediate consequence of this transformation of the mode of production is the change in the relationships between agricultural classes, lords, and peasants. The relationship between agricultural classes and urban classes changes as a result, and thereby enters the revolutionary equation. The state is the political outcome of the line-up of class forces and their relative degree of strength and mobilization.

Much of Moore's analysis of specific cases is designed to demonstrate the comparability of historical cases by examining how mobilized particular classes were in the process, how they articulated their interests, and the dynamics of their conflict with other classes.[3] The outcome of a revolution, its trajectory, and the sequencing between revolution and industrialization, are all shaped by three variables: (1) the size and strength of the bourgeois impulse, that is, the ability of a bourgeoisie to pursue its interests in industrialization; (2) the intensity of repression of the peasantry by the agricultural landlords; and (3) the capacity of any of these classes to maintain control over the state.

Moore first examines the process of early industrialization and the commercialization of agriculture to determine the ways in which various classes will be set in motion. For example, if the aristocracy commercializes agriculture by evicting the peasantry and replacing them with hired labor, the

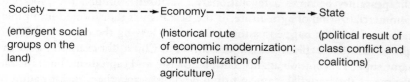

Society — — — — — — — — → Economy — — — — — — — — → State

| (emergent social groups on the land) | (historical route of economic modernization; commercialization of agriculture) | (political result of class conflict and coalitions) |

Figure 5.1   Moore's model of the path of early developers.

aristocracy becomes part of the bourgeoisie and therefore favors democracy. At the same time, the forced eviction of the peasantry removes a potentially revolutionary or reactionary force from the land (the peasantry). This was the case in England. If the aristocracy keeps the peasantry on the land and forces them to hand over their produce for the market by intensifying traditional labor discipline, the aristocracy will favor fascism, which is a way of transferring traditional agrarian authoritarianism to industrial society. At the same time, the peasantry is utterly immobilized and removed from potential resistance. This was the case in Prussia and Japan. Finally, if the aristocracy leaves the land (coming to court in urban centers, for example) and its members become absentee landlords, the peasants will be allowed to produce directly for the market. Thus the aristocracy demobilizes itself politically, while the peasants are radicalized by their participation in the market and are thus mobilized for revolutionary activity. This is what occurred in China and in France.

The complex interplay between these two agricultural classes also sets the conditions for the types of political institutions favored by each class. As Moore sees it, the bourgeoisie favors democracy, as the form of government they can most easily control as the most mobilized group. However, if there is a strong threat of socialism from an organized working class, they will fall back on their second choice: fascism. The landowning aristocracy favors democracy if it can remain the most mobilized class and can control the state, but if not, it will favor fascism to preserve its traditional privileges in the face of either a bourgeois or a working-class challenge. Within the state, bureaucrats are likely to favor fascism if they are linked to the landowning aristocracy. If other classes revolt against the bourgeoisie, however, state bureaucrats will opt for socialism as the form of government that will enlarge bureaucratic state power. The peasantry are largely unmobilized, and their revolt provides the "shock troops" for other groups. If mobilized directly for the market, they can become revolutionary because their market position is so vulnerable. If, however, the society has instituted a form of peasant land-ownership, the peasants throw in their lot with the bourgeoisie and join a fascist coalition in the face of a challenge by the working class. For their part, the working class supports either democracy or socialism, "depending on the extent to which their employers have made an alliance with the traditional state in order to enforce labor discipline" (Collins, 1973: 203).

Moore's Typology of Revolution

Moore's model of "the social origins of dictatorship and democracy" – the analysis of political outcomes of the relations between agricultural classes – also has important theoretical lessons for the study of revolution. Revolution itself can be the political outcome of a long economic struggle between agrarian classes, in which the state is transformed to realign political institutions with the changes that have already taken place on the land. Such is the case of the classic bourgeois revolutions – of England and France – where revolution expressed politically the changes that had already transformed economic life. On the other hand, revolution may be the political event which sets in the economic processes of industrialization in motion; revolution may precede industrialization because a strong state is necessary to provide the economic push to modernize. This is the case with later developers, such as Japan and Germany.

Moore's class analysis leads to a typology of revolution based on these structural relationships – those between agricultural classes at the level of production, between the ruling class and the state, and between the ruling class and bourgeois impulse. The sequence, dynamics, and even the level of violence in the revolution all depend on the ways in which these relationships sort themselves out. By providing a typology of political outcomes of industrialization, Moore has also constructed a typology of revolution.[4]

The "bourgeois revolutions" – those of England, France, and the United States – were characterized by a relatively strong bourgeois impulse. In England, an alliance of commercially minded gentry and urban merchants defeated the traditional landowning aristocracy; this alliance became the backbone for English industrialization. In the United States, the northern urban commercial interests triumphed over southern plantation-owners. This was not a triumph of capitalism over feudalism, but of one form of capitalism, industrial capitalism, over another form of capitalism, cash-crop agrarian capitalism. In France, a combination of a small number of agrarian capitalists (who extracted rents from the peasants to generate profit) and urban merchants and professionals overthrew the old regime to institute a capitalist society.

Though bourgeois revolutions share certain characteristics, the specific cases are vastly different. The English landlords had forcibly evicted the peasantry; the peasantry in France was large, exploited, and revolutionary; the peasantry in the United States non-existent. Agrarian labor relations in France were repressive; in England and the United States mobilization for the market led to little repression. The English state was relatively independent of the various classes, though the monarchy supported the rural aristocracy; conversely, the "independence of the landed gentry and nobility from the crown [and] their adoption of commercial agriculture partly in response to the growth of a trading and manufacturing class with its own strong economic base" marked the English case (Moore, 1966: 40). In France, the state was intimately linked to the aristocracy, who had "become a decorative appanage of the king" through venality of office and the routines of court life (Moore, 1966: 40). The English lower nobility had become capitalists and effected the transition to capitalist industrialization without much violence; in 1789, however the French aristocracy was destroyed. Moore does not hesitate to call the French Revolution a "bourgeois revolution" since it "mortally wounded the whole interlocking complex of aristocratic privilege: monarchy, landed aristocracy, and seigneurial rights, a complex that constituted the essence of the *ancien régime*. It did so in the name of private property and equality before the law. To deny that the predominant thrust and chief consequences of the Revolution were bourgeois and capitalist is to engage in a trivial quibble" (1966: 105).

Finally, in the United States, the central government was seen as the prize that would go to the victorious capitalist class, either southern agrarian capitalists or northern industrial capitalists. Southern planters "took over the defense of hereditary privilege", transforming themselves into the guardians of the old regime even as they were capitalist actors in the world economy (1966: 121). Southern chivalry did not grow organically from southern society; it was a defensive reaction against northern industrialism. (Here, Moore departs markedly from Wallerstein's world system theory, which holds that one's participation in the world economy determines the character of one's interests. Moore is suggesting that different forms of capitalism can coexist, and that some may be more amenable to positions ordinarily held by hereditary aristocracy.) But the consolidation of industrial capitalism after the war did not lead to full democracy in the United States either. "Under attack from radical agrarians in the West and radical labor in the East, the party of wealth, property and privilege in the North was ready to abandon the last pretense of upholding the rights of he propertyless and oppressed Negro laboring classes" (1966: 149).

Moore's treatment of fascism demonstrates the fallacy of modernization theory's equation between capitalism and democracy, the argument that capitalist economics necessarily and inevitably produce democratic political regimes. Towards the end of his treatment of the American Civil War, Moore prefigures his theoretical treatment of revolutions from above (1966: 152):

> The evidence indicates very clearly that plantation slavery was an obstacle to democracy, at least any conception of democracy that includes the goals of human equality, even the limited form of equality of opportunity, and human freedom. It does not establish at all clearly that plantation slavery was an obstacle to industrial capitalism as such. And comparative perspective show [*sic*] clearly that industrial capitalism can establish itself in societies that do not profess these democratic goals or, to be a little more cautious, where these goals are no more than a secondary current. Germany and Japan prior to 1945 are the main illustrations for this thesis.

There is nothing inevitably or necessarily democratic about capitalism; the two emerged and reinforced one another in the early bourgeois developing countries because of specific historical circumstances. In fact, it is possible that these circumstances reinforced both democracy and captalism for the last time in world history in those countries. Fascism opts for capitalism without democracy and communism rejects capitalist individualism and economic freedom to institute its version of radical democracy.

Moore's treatment of revolution from above and fascism in late developing nations amply illustrates this. Here, the bourgeoisie was socially and politically weak, though they had some economic power. The traditional landlords were comparatively strong politically, though economically weak, and eager to participate in the market themselves, which required that they transform existing agricultural class relations themselves. As Moore puts it, the central feature of the class positions that lead to fascism is "a coalition between sections of the old agrarian ruling classes that have considerable political power with a shaky economic position with an emerging commercial and industrial elite with some economic power but political and social disadvantages" (Moore, 1966: 305). (Such an explanation underscores the potential disjunction between economic power and political power; economic elites may be politically or socially impotent, while groups that are traditionally politically powerful may not also be economically powerful. This argument provides an important corrective to *both* Marxist theory and modernization theory, which both tend to equate economic power with political power.) The peasantry was relatively weak and unorganized, and therefore unable to mount an effective revolutionary challenge when the landlords intensified the degree of repression of labor as a method of generating increased profits from the land.

The key to revolution from above is the state which was deeply allied with the traditional aristocracy, and committed to preserving its power in the countryside and to accomplishing urban industrialization "from above," in the absence of a strong independent bourgeoisie. The state "served as an engine of primary capitalism accumulation, gathering resources and directing them toward the building of an industrial plant" (Moore, 1966: 440). A strong state plus traditionally politically strong aristocracy plus weak bourgeoisie and weak peasantry provides the alliance for fascist revolution, which destroys the traditional peasant economy to create the conditions favorable to capitalist industrialization and yet does not allow the development of socialism among a new and small industrial working class. Fascism provides a significant amount of political repression designed to rapidly create a disciplined and skilled labor force. "Essentially," Moore concludes, "fascism protected big agriculture and big industry at the expense of the agricultural laborer, small peasant, and consumer" (1966: 452).

Finally, Moore suggests that peasant revolutions, or communist revolutions, are produced by an entirely different configuration of these class alliances. In his empirical discussion of China, and in his later work on Russia (Moore, 1978), he describes the ways in which these forces came into play. In both cases the bourgeois impulse was quite weak; in China, Moore writes, the entrepreneurial push ways "puny" (1966: 177). Rural class relations were highly conflictual. The old regime state was long associated with the landed upper class, but the balance of power between them was different from the fascist combination. In Germany and Japan, the traditional landowning aristocracy was dependent upon the state to effect a modernization program and to maintain labor discipline; in Russia and China, the state was more dependent upon the power of the landlords to maintain traditional rural relations and prevent large-scale peasant uprisings which had marked the history of both countries. The inability of the state to institute an effective program for development, in part a consequence of imperialism and a response to the rapid industrialization of other countries in the late nineteenth century, weakened still further the authority of the state. In China, the peasantry was large and unorganized, but potentially radical because of the enormous amount of repression that characterized the traditional landlord-peasant relationship. Large-scale peasant rebellions had been common in Chinese history, and the Communist Party was able to tap this well of peasant resentment and turn it against the Manchu state as well as individual landlords. In Russia, the peasants were highly solidary in autonomous villages, and their conflict with traditional landlords had historically burnished this solidarity with class resentment. The traditional village of autonomous peasants was thus both potentially radical and extremely easy to organize.

Finally, Moore also includes an exemplary "non-revolutionary" case, India, the analysis of which can reveal some of the salient dimensions of the occurrence of revolution in the first place. India was characterized by a weak bourgeois impulse and a large conservative peasantry, both of which were shaped in part by imperialism (the outward expression of earlier successful bourgeois revolutions). If either of these variables had not been present, the political outcome could not have been a non-revolutionary transition to democracy. A radical peasantry would have produced peasant communist revolution; a stronger bourgeois impulse coupled with a push from the state would have produced fascism; a strong bourgeoisie that could control other classes would have produced a bourgeois revolution. Clearly from this example of the non-revolutionary situation, we can see how the combination of forces, their relative strengths, and their alliances and outlooks are the determining factors of the development process, as well as the determinant causes of revolution. This typology can be seen in table 5.1.

It is interesting to observe how this typologial construction contains an implicit challenge to modernization theory's ability to adequately explain

Table 5.1 *Moore's specific case studies*

Outcome	Cases	System of agriculture	State/class relationship	Peasant revolutionary potential	Strength of bourgeois impulse
Non-revolutionary	India	Labour-repressive	Dependent	Low	Weak
Peasant communist revolution	China, Russia	Labour-repressive	Dependent	High	Weak
Fascist revolution	Germany, Japan	Labour-repressive	Dependent	Low	Moderate
Bourgeois revolution	France, England, US	Labour-repressive Market	Dependent Independent	High Low	Strong Strong

Source: Taylor (1984: 31), *Social Science and Revolution*. New York: St. Matin's Press.

social development. Bourgeois revolutions took place between the mid-seventeenth century and the mid-nineteenth century; by the late nineteenth century the states that had already had successful bourgeois revolutions had so transformed the rest of the world that the relationships among the variables that produce the type of revolution had disappeared. A qualitatively new type of revolution – revolution from above (fascism) – characterizes the late nineteenth and early twentieth centuries. Finally, the twentieth century is the era of socialist revolution, in which the former peripheries of the bourgeois societies themselves undergo the process of industrialization. Bourgeois democracy, implies Moore, is no longer an option for countries seeking to industrialize; the success of the earlier developers has so transformed the structure of agricultural class relations in those former colonies that the bourgeois impuse is stymied and the relationship between the state and the ruling class distorted by imperialism.

State Autonomy and Cultural Variables in Moore's Class Analysis

We have examined Moore's work in detail because of the analytic power of his typology of revolutions and because it represents an unsurpassed effort to explain the relationship between revolution and industrialization from within a neo-Marxian perspective, focusing on the class relations at the level of agricultural production. There are, however, some problems with this analysis, which make the work less than complete in explaining revolution. Some critics have argued that the most serious of these is the systematic devaluation of the casual property of political variables, so that the state is treated as an epiphenomenon of class relations. Other critics have pointed to the systematic devaluation of non-structural variables such as culture and ideology as casual mechanisms, and the implication that motivation for political behavior is derived solely from the rational calculation of interests by collective actors (classes). While I agree with these latter claims, I do not share the critics' reservations about Moore's treatment of the state.

These critics unfold Moore's argument in a way that is instructive to our general effort to understand and explain revolutions. Moore argues that the presence and preferences of particular groups determines the political outcome of the revolutionary process. The intermediate variables are the strength of those groups and their political disposition, not the relative strength of the state and *its* disposition. The balances of class forces and the political coalitions of these mobilized classes determine the forms of the state. One type of coalition leads to one specific political outcome, another coalition leads to another political outcome. Thus, for example, in England, "relationships with commercial and industrial elements and with the king were *decisive* influences in *determining* the characteristics of the nobility" (Moore, 1966: 56; emphasis added). Schematically, Moore's argument appears as in figure 5.2. This "undervaluation" of the autonomous role of the state, however, is present only when Moore examines bourgeois revolution in England, France, and the United States, where the bourgeois impulse is strong and class forces are relatively independent of the state and can generate an entrepreneurial thrust on their own. In his discussion of revolution from above and fascism Moore assigns an explicitly causal role to the state, arguing that "the government has to carry out many of the same tasks performed elsewhere with the help of revolution from below" (Moore, 1966: 438). In later-developing nations, Moore argues that "the government has to become separate from society, something that can happen rather more easiliy than simplified versions of Marxism would have us believe" (Moore, 1966: 441).[5] Can it be that the autonomy of the state – seeing the state as a causal variable, relatively independent of class forces, pursuing *its own interests* – is only operative in some empirical cases had not in others? If the relative autonomy of the state operates in some countries, surely it must operate in others. Moore, himself, seems aware of this; in discussing Japan, he writes that "differences in internal social structure constitute only one major variable" and that one must also take into account "differences in timing and in the external circumstances under which premodern institutions broke down and adopted themselves to the modern era" (Moore, 1966: 250–1).

Political outcomes

		Democratic	Totalitarian
Economic outcomes	Capitalist	England France United States	Germany Japan
	Socialist		Russia China

Figure 5.2 Economic and political outcomes derived from Moore's work.

But this is precisely the point to Moore; he claims that the relative autonomy of the state is not an abstract principle that must be sought out in each empirical case, but a historical process created by the conjuncture of specific social forces that occur only among the early developing countries. When Moore turns his attention to revolution from above, the fascist route to modernization, suddenly the state emerges as a casual variable in its own right, directly and managing class relations in the interests of societal development. The purpose of the state is to "coordinate as far as possible the activities of a society in the pursuit of a single goal, such as conquest, defense against an enemy, the prevention or the promotion of social change" (Moore, 1962: 75). Here is Moore on the active role of the state (1966: 441):

> Certain conditions seem to have been necessary for the success of conservative modernization. First it takes very able leadership to drag along the less perceptive reactionary elements, concentrated among, though not necessarily confined to, the landed upper classes . . . Reactionaries can always advance the plausible argument that modernizing leaders are making changes and concessions that will merely arouse the appetites of the lower classes and bring on a revolution. Similarly, the leadership must have at hand, or be able to construct a sufficiently powerful bureaucratic apparatus, including the agencies of repression, the military and the police . . . in order to free itself from the influence of both extreme reactionary and popular radical pressures in society.

Here, it is not the state being produced by class forces, but the state that introduces revolution from above, the state that preserves the aristocracy and keeps the bourgeoisie weak and dependent, the state that plays the balance of class forces to effect its own ends. One might be tempted to retitle Moore's book "The Social Origins of Democracy and the Political Origins of Dictatorship".[6]

The emergence of the state as a determinant agent in the development process (rather than as a passive prize or an aristocratic bulwark against modernization) partially explains why the sequencing between revolution and industrialization differs between early developers and later developers. Among early developers revolution precedes development; by sweeping aside the old regime state and its social foundation, the aristocracy, the stronger entrepreneurial forces are able to transform the state and to propel the economic development of the society. Among later developers, if revolution comes at all, it follows state-sponsored industrialization efforts. Here, newly created and mobilized social groups (working classes, peasants) can effect socialist revolution, since the industrializing state has already pushed aside those old regime forces (aristocracy, monarchy) that retarded development. Fascism may be seen as a revolution from above that facilitates industrialization but suppresses the working-class revolution. Thus the sharp divergence in the historical trajectories of countries such as Germany and Japan on the one hand, and Russia on the other. The historical specification of the causal agency of the state is therefore not a glaring weakness of Moore's argument but one of his less-celebrated strengths. Different forms of development will reveal different line-ups of class forces and state autonomy, which will produce different political outcomes of the development process. Thus Moore provides a powerful corrective to modernization theory's earlier assumptions about universal patterns of development based on the experiences of the early developers.

Similarly, the role of ideas and culture are contextualized in a way that does not set them up as casual. Moore continually underplays the roles of ideas and culture as active agents. For example, he notes that certain ideas about feudalism contributed to democratic development (1966: 415):

> the most important aspect was the growth of the notion of the immunity of certain groups and persons from the power of the ruler, along with the conception of the right of resistance to unjust authority. Together with the conception of contract as a mutual engagement freely undertaken by free persons . . . this complex of ideas and practices constitutes a crucial legacy from European medieval society to modern Western conceptions of a free society.

But how do such ideas act? If we accept Moore's own internal logic, political institutions themselves result from material and social interests, not from political ideas. Thus to invoke political ideas as causal would demand a logical restructuring, which Moore explicitly rejects. "Why was this reactionary upsurge no more than a passing phase in England?" he asks (1966: 444). "Anglo-Saxon liberties, Magna Carta, Parliament and such rhetoric will not do for an answer." In discussing France, he asks if there were "some sort of legal and cultural barriers that prevented the *noblesse d'epée* from making a success of commerce? How important were such barriers in explaining the economic and political characteristics of the French nobility or the fact that a great revolution overwhelmed them?" Moore suggests that the "evidence leads me to offer a very firm negative to the question and to argue that it is the wrong question to ask" (1966: 49). Again, in France, when Moore inquires about the counter-revolutionary peasantry of the Vendée, he argues (1966: 98-9):

> To invoke the special religious sentiments of the peasants in the Vendée to explain the fact that they followed their *curés* into the counter revolution is to look at the situation the wrong way around. Very likely these sentiments were stronger here. But if they were, what could have kept them alive other than the fact that the *curé* played a special role in this distinctive rural society, that he did things a good many countrymen wanted done for rather obvious reasons? An attack on the *curé* was an attack on the linchpin of rural society.

In yet another discussion, Moore theorizes that "one may see the material interests that tied together the agrarians and the industrialists . . . In the light of current inclinations to take these ideas seriously, it is necessary to emphasize again that they were rationalizations and nothing more'' (1966: 296).

Moore's treatment of ideas can be easily observed in his chapter on India, since religious ideas have often been seen as the central determining agents of India's particular trajectory:

> The standard explanation runs about as follows. According to the theory of reincarnation, a person who obeyed the requirements of caste etiquette in this life would be born into a higher caste in the next. Submissiveness in this life was to be rewarded by a rise in the social scale in the next. This explanation requires us to believe that the ordinary Indian peasants accepted the rationalizations put forth by the urban priestly classes. Perhaps the Brahmans did succeed in this way to some extent. But it can only be a small part of the story. As far as it is possible to recover the attitudes of the peasants towards the Brahmans, it is fairly clear that the peasants did not passively and wholeheartedly accept the Brahman as a model of all that was good and desirable. Their attitude toward the monopolist of supernatural power seems to have been a mixture of admiration, fear, and hostility, much like that of many French peasants towards the Catholic priest. ''There are three blood suckers in the world,'' runs a North Indian proverb, ''the flea, the bug and the Brahman'' . . . Secular sanctions were obviously part of the caste system. And in a general way we know that human attitudes and beliefs fail to persist unless the situations and sanctions that reproduce them continue to persist or, more crassly, unless people get something out of them. (1966: 335)

In part, Moore's analysis is a sustained critique of the uses to which Weber's sociological theories had been put by modernization theorists. This leads Moore to undervalue the role of culture and ideas:

> Since transition to commercial agriculture is obviously a very important step, how is one to explain the ways in which it took place or failed to occur? A modern sociologist would be likely to seek an explanation in cultural terms. In countries where commercial agriculture failed to develop on a wide scale, he might stress the inhibiting character of aristocratic traditions, such as notions of honor and negative attitudes towards pecuniary gain and toward work. At the beginning stages of this research, my own inclination was to search for such explanations. As evidence accumulated, grounds appeared for taking a skeptical attitude toward this line of reasoning. (1966: 421)

Here, Moore's critique of a reading of Weber as a cultural determinist is strongest. Weber argued that a certain type of character, the historical product of religious ideas becoming secularized and activated in the economic sphere, played a significant role in the emergence of modern capitalism, giving modern capitalism its rational, ''sober, bourgeois'' form.

Moore considers such arguments to be psychologistic reductionism, a non-structural analysis that explains historical development by individual personality configurations.

In all these passages, Moore seems to suggest that ideas are epiphenomena to history, exerting a minimal effect on social change and political outcomes of development. But Moore also gives ideas some causal weight when he turns to revolution from above. Here, he argues that ideas do seem to have some agency; they are used to manipulate by groups that may not even believe them:

> As we look back on Fascism and its antecedents, we can see that the glorification of the peasantry appears as a reactionary symptom in both Western and Asiatic civilization at a time when the peasant economy is facing severe difficulties . . . To say that such ideas are merely foisted on the peasants by the upper classes is not true. Because the ideas find an echo in peasant experience, they may win wide acceptance, the wider, it seems, the more industrialized and modern the country is. (1966: 452)

Although these ideas may have been rationalizations from the point of view of political elites, they were taken seriously by the groups that such ideas addressed.

Though Moore rejects the causal role for culture that earlier non-structural theorists celebrated, he does place cultural variables in context as intervening, intermediate variables that give coherence and meaning to economic forces. And historically ideas and culture become increasingly important in later developing nations. Thus culture becomes one of the framers of social action, even if culture does not cause that action:

> [H]uman beings individually and collectively do not react to an ''objective'' situation. There is always an intervening variable . . . between people and an 'objective' situation made up from all sorts of wants, expectations and other ideas derived from the past. This intervening variable . . . culture, screens out certain parts of the objective situation and emphasizes other parts. There are limits to the amount of variations in perceptions and human behavior that can come from this source. Still the residue of truth in the cultural explanation is that what looks like an opportunity or a temptation to one group of people will not necessarily seem so to another group with a different historical experience and living in a different form of society. (1966: 485)

Moore's understanding of human motivation, however, is significantly limited. He assumes that motivations are exclusively rational, as groups calculate and pursue their economic interests as unanimous and collective wholes. In place of a Weberian actor motivated by cultural and material interests, Moore provides *Homo economicus*, the rational actor who pursues his or her rationally calculated material interests. Such a model is most clear when Moore deals with entrepreneurial activity. Instead of being hampered by a cultural overlay that impedes their capitalist economic activity, the nobility in Moore's scheme rationally pursues its economic interests:

> There was a repressive component in the adaptation of the rural upper classes to the rise of commerce and industry. That . . . is the key, rather than parasitism *tout court*. From this standpoint, the problem of the evidence concerning energy, ambition, economic drive, disappears. Talk about a psychological drive for achievement tells us nothing unless we know how the drive manifests itself. (1966: 286)

Moore provides us with an image of the landed nobility in each country responding on the basis of similar orientations to maximize their material interests, but doing so within different historical, political, and social contexts. In Japan, a rice-based agriculture and a strong state offer one set of possibilities, while in England, a wool-based agriculture and relatively weak state offers other. But the historical actors are everywhere essentially the same; the historical and cultural features of their situation are insignificant compared to the constant economic drive that propels them. In each case, the historical actors (and this includes the bourgeoisie and even, occasionally, the peasantry) are clear-eyed, hard-headed opportunists who rationally pursue their interests. Moore fails to contextualize motivation in the ways in which he subtly contextualizes the role of culture and ideas and the role of the state; his political psychology remains one of the theory's central weaknesses.

Despite this, however, Moore's work remains unsurpassed among contemporary social scientists in providing an overall explanation for revolutions that is sensitive to historical differences and yet explains general causes. His work makes it impossible to ignore the relations of classes at the level of agricultural production in determining the political outcomes of revolutions, and the role of revolutions within the larger framework of industrial development. And Moore's intellectual posture makes it difficult to remain objective. In recounting the revolutionary calculus, Moore does not equivocate about where he stands:

> Those of us who are skeptical of revolutionary changes at once point to the reign of Terror as part of the terrible price of revolution. But the mere continuation of the existing social order exacts its tragic price too. How many children die in India each year as part of the price of a ''reasonable'' rate of economic advance? How many adults died in two world wars as part of the price of a system of ''free and independent'' states? The calculus of suffering likely to result from revolutionary violence must include that which will come from prolonging the present state of affairs. (Moore, 1962: 206)

Although class relations are not the whole story, they are central analytic variables. Any adequate explanation of revolution must take into account the relations between owners and producers at the level of production (agricultural and industrial), the relations between ruling classes and the state, and the relations between entrepreneurial classes and the alliance of traditional landowners and the state that characterizes the old regime.

The Fusion of Class Analysis and the World System

Moore's work pulls the analysis of revolution back to the level of agricultural production, and away from the international world of trade and commerce. Some social scientists have sought to synthesize these two levels of analysis. Jeffrey Paige, for example, in his impressive *Agrarian Revolution* (1975), explains political change, from reform to revolution, by examining the ways in which political options are limited both "by the irreducible role of land in agriculture and by the compelling force of the international market in agricultural commodities" (1975: xi). Certainly, like Moore, Paige argues that revolutions are, first and foremost, "shaped by the relationship between upper and lower classes in rural areas" (1975: xi), but these relationships themselves, Paige argues, are transformed in the process of the commercialization of agriculture. Class relations shape the possibilities for commercialization, and the mobilization of agricultural production for a world market also feeds back on those traditional class relations. Paige is clear that the prime mover, the originator of these changes, is rural class relations; mobilization for the international market, however, can and does transform these relations.

Paige's theory is that political mobilization of both cultivators and noncultivators (landlords and peasants) can be predicted from the interaction of two variables: the source of income of each (land or capital for landlords, land or wages for peasants) and the ways in which the commercialization of agriculture transforms these sources of income. The source of income of each class shapes the economic form of agricultural production, and therefore determines the degree of tactical mobility in political behavior that either class may have in restructuring itself to handle new pressures from commercialization. The "relative dependence on land versus either capital or wages is the most important determinant of the political and economic behavior of cultivators and noncultivators" (Paige, 1972: 11). When landords' income is derived from the land, when they receive rent in kind or in labor, they are less tactically mobile than if their income derives from capital, which ties them to larger economic networks and allows them some strategic mobility in staving off working-class revolt. Similarly, when cultivators derive their income from land, they are less able to mount a significant rebellion against landlords; when they are tied to the market, however, and

Cultivators

		Land	Capital
Non-cultivators	Land	Commercial hacienda Agrarian revolt	Sharecropping Migratory labor Revolution (nationalist or socialist)
	Capital	Small-holding Commodity reform	Plantation Labor reform

Figure 5.3 Forms of agricultural organization and types of agrarian social movements described by sources of income for cultivators and non-cultivators. *Source*: Paige (1975: 11). Reprinted with permission of The Free Press, a Division of Macmillan, Inc. from *Agrarian Revolution: Social Movements and Export Agriculture in the Underdeveloped World*. © 1975 The Free Press

derive their income from wages, they are also more strategically mobile and capable of sustaining a revolt. Figure 5.3 shows the model that Paige constructed. In this figure, the direction of "modernization," that is, commercialization of agriculture, moves from top to bottom and from left to right. Thus the most highly developed agricultural form is the plantation system, in which landlords draw their income from capital and the cultivators draw their income from wages – that is, both are tied to the commodity market and have some tactical mobility. The plantation system is agrarian capitalism, since both classes are tied to the market and thus their relationships are between captial and wage labor. Political conflicts between landlords and peasants in these societies yield reform of labor conditions as their outcome, since working-class solidarity is high, but the capacity of the landlords to extend political rights, their ability and willingness to make concessions, is also high (1975: 358).

The least modern cell in the chart is that in which both landlords and peasants draw their income from the land, in which, therefore, commercialization of agriculture has proceeded least. This form of agricultural production Paige labels as "commercial hacienda"; here, peasant revolt will most likely be a "short, intense movement aimed at seizing land but lacking in long-run political objectives" (Paige, 1975: 43).

Commercialization of agriculture ties agrarian classes to the market and is, therefore, a potentially reactionary or revolutionary force. When landlords draw their income from the market and laborers still draw their income from land, the situation is the *least* revolutionary, as landlords maintain a degree of tactical mobility that is impossible for laborers to achieve; they are to embedded in traditional relationships on the land, which give them a secure and stable livelihood. This small-holding system leads to what Paige calls "commodity reform" movements, and landlords take the initiative to change the methods of production. "The greater flexibility, wealth, and negotiating ability of the upper class dependent on commercial income focus conflict on the market," Paige writes (1975: 48). The aim of a commodity reform movement will be "to force landlords to yield a greater share of profits through an inflated currency" (1975: 48).

By contrast, a system in which landlords retain their connection to the land as a source of income and peasants become connected to the market by drawing their income from wages – a sharecropping system of migratory labor system – is potentially the *most* revolutionary system, in which landlords remain desperately wedded to traditional methods of labor exploitation to stay afloat and the laborers are doubly squeezed by the landlords and their disadvantaged market position as non-owners. When landlords are less modern than either workers the possibility of a revolutionary outburst is increased. "Revolutionary movements are most likely to occur when cultivators can form strong, radical, and cohesive political organizations, but noncultivators are unable to grant political and economic concessions because they must rely on legal or extra legal force to maintain their position" (Paige, 1975: 57–8).

Paige thus defines a revolutionary situation in terms of the capacity for solidary organization among the working class and the ability or willingness to grant political concessions by the upper class. These postures are themselves the result of the respective classes' sources of income through the process of the commercialization of agriculture. Paige expands this model by exploring the political options open to both classes as a result of the source of their income. Non-cultivators who draw their income from the land tend to be economically weak, and therefore need to rely on political controls to keep order in the countryside. By contrast, when landlords draw their income from capital, they are economically stronger and therefore able to be independent of non-economic (political, military, police) controls of labor. Conflicts in this case "tend to be focused on the distribution of income between the upper and lower classes, not on the ownership of property" (1975: 20). Further, income from land politicizes the relationships between cultivators and non-cultivators, since the owners are inflexible about extending political rights to the workers in such a stagnant economic system.

When cultivators draw their income from the land, they develop a stake in the system and therefore are less likely to take political risks. Land as a source of income also makes peasants economically competitive with one another, thereby reducing the possibility of political solidarity. Again, we can see how Paige believes that landownership represents a conservative political force and the market generates a progressive impulse.

The best system of agrarian class relations from the point of view of the landlord is therefore one in which landlords are independent of the land and laborers are dependent upon the land: the small-holding system. The best system from the point of view of the peasant would be the opposite case, where workers are connected to the market and draw their income from capital while landlords remain tied to the land as a source of income. But, what is "best" for the worker is also the worst: the sharecropping or migratory system results in the most significant amount of political repression and economic exploitation of the laborers by the landlords, who exploit them economically and repress them politically, just as they are subject to the vagaries of the market unprotected by any political or economic shelters provided by landlords. Thus we begin to see how Paige's theory is an interesting elaboration of Marx's basic premise that immiseration leads to a revolutionary working class. Though Paige locates this immiserated working class among the most heavily exploited agricultural workers (where Marx focused on the most oppressed industrial workers) the principle is the same: the worse things get for the worker, the more likely s/he will become revolutionary. Thus we are likely to find revolutionary social movements emanating from the most oppressed agricultural workers. However, unlike Marx, Paige does not make a revolutionary upheaval solely dependent upon the experience and organizational efforts of the working classes. The experience and organizational capacities and proclivities of the landed classes must also be taken into account. Agrarian revolution "is a product not only of organizational resources on the part of cultivators but also of political inflexibility on the part of the non-cultivators" (Paige, 1975: 349).

The bulk of Paige's book is a systematic application of these principles to three cases in which three different sets of agrarian class relations resulted in three different political outcomes via different social movements. In each of these, the potential for revolution or revolt was present, that is, the landlords drew their income from the land. In Peru, *haciendados* drew their income from the land, but so did the laborers, and the outcome was agrarian revolt. In Angola, the peasants were tied to the market by migratory labor, while landlords were still tied to their income through landownership. There, however, the revolt was nationalist, not socialist. Only in Vietnam did the mix of a landowning class that derived its income from the land and a peasantry that derived its income from the market present a truly revolutionary situation. And within Vietnam, it was only in the south, in the Mekong Delta, that a truly revolutionary situation obtained. In the north and central parts of the country, a small peasants were far more tied to the land than in the south, where commercialization of agriculture made the greatest strides in the short period of Vietnam's colonial connection to France. In the north, greater community cohesion of peasant villages led to a greater adherence to traditional peasant life, greater economic individualism, and often peasant competition. The northern peasantry was characterized by "divisive individual plots, individual mobility, and a conservative oligarchy" (Paige, 1972: 299).

In the Mekong Delta, "economic and social organization of the villages . . . not only created political instability, but also led to new forms of class conflict and class-based political organization" (Paige, 1975: 302). Here, in the south, the commercialization of rice production was extensive, and the entire region depended entirely upon rice; there were, in a sense, no economic distractions from other crops or non-affected areas (see Paige, 1975: 310). The social organization of rice production resulted in a class of landlords who were "economically weak and dependent on outside military force and political power" and an "agricultural proletariat" of laborers who were paid in wages and heavily exploited economically, as well as being politically repressed by the landlords' reliance on the military. Decentralized sharecropping in southern Vietnam produced a genuinely revolutionary situation, in which potentialities for "class based cultivator organizations" and "bitter landlord resistance to cultivator rights" could spring up side by side. Here was a "landless agricultural proletariat with a strong incentive for political organization and an economically weak and politically rigid landed elite" (Paige, 1975: 318). This combination of a weak and intransigent upper class and a strong and oppressed working class is the recipe for revolution. Only in this system "is an inflexible upper class combined with a cultivator class strongly organized along class lines, and only in decentralized systems is the cultivator class able to overcome the political controls of the noncultivators" (Paige, 1975: 375). The National Liberation Front (NLF), the revolutionary social movement, focused its attention on the redistribution of land and on immediate economic reforms, rather than political reforms in the administrative center.

Like Moore, Paige has a sophisticated understanding of the complex relationship between capitalism and revolution. The relationship is not unidirectional nor deterministic. In some cases, to Moore industrial capitalism was the *outcome* of revolution (as in England, France, and the United States) while in later cases, Page and Moore agree that the penetration of capitalist relationships into the countryside in the form of the commercialization of agriculture has a galvanizing effect. In some specific cases, that effect may be revolutionary not because capitalism successfully penetrates the countryside but precisely because it is constrained from doing so by an intransigent and relatively weak upper class. In Vietnam, Paige writes (1975: 320), "it was not capitalism that led to revolution, but the constrained capitalism of a landed elite that used the political advantages of colonial rule to restrict the workings of the market and protect itself against both political and economic change."

The Limits of Paige's "Agronomic Determinism"

Like Moore, Paige's work has also been subjected to serious and telling criticism for its inability to treat political variables as casual, for casting the central state as simply the prize for which revolutionary struggles are fought. In Pagie's model, a revolutionary social movement "attempts to destroy both the rural upper class and the institutions of the state and establish a new society" (Paige, 1975: 358–9). It does not contend *with* the state, struggling with a political regime that is both allied with and relatively independent of the landed upper class, but against a state that is the instrument of class power.

In an interesting critique of the "agronomic determinism" of Paige's model, Somers and Goldfrank also suggest that Paige makes a serious conceptual error reminiscent of that of earlier non-structural theorists who saw revolution as a form of collective behavior. Like Smelser and others, Paige considers as social movements "collective behavior that occurs outside the established institutions of a society and involves participants who are united by some sense of intention or belief" (Paige, 1975: 87; see also Somers and Goldfrank, 1979: 448). These episodes – Paige calls them "events" – would be indicators of the dependent variable at the same time as they are part of the definition of the independent variable.

By maintaining that social movements, revolutionary or otherwise, are measured by extra-legal events from the lower classes alone, Paige loses sight of those revolutionary events which are initiated from above, by paramilitary vigilante groups composed of the police or the army, or citizens' groups inspired by the ruling forces, or even by the activities of the police or army themselves. By insuring that "the definition of social movements will be limited to the cultivators alone," Paige also decontextualizes their activities from the world of official and extra-legal violence that often precipitates it (Somers and Goldfrank, 1979: 449). Further, the "identification of a revolution with a revolutionary social movement" and the positing of "the activity of the cultivators alone as constitutive of the social movement" allows Paige to fall into a trap of many studies of social movements: "a revolution is like a revolutionary movement, only a little more so" (Somers and Goldfrank, 1979: 450).

Somers and Goldfrank push this conceptual critique of the definition of revolutions and social movements to its limits. "Had Paige stuck with his relational model," they write, "he would have been led to pursue the activities and repressive capabilities of the upper classes, and he would have had to bring the structure of the state – including most importantly its relation to those upper classes – to bear on the very characterization of the dependent variable" (Somers and Goldfrank, 1979: 450).

Further, Paige's understanding of motivation runs into the same problems as Moore's political psychology. Paige assumes a linear relationship between level of exploitation and likelihood of political mobilization. When all goes according to theoretical plan, the most heavily exploited laborers are the ones most disposed to revolt. Of course, occasionally, traditional society gets in the way, by providing an alternative source of political authority, economic rewards, or cultural meaning. In those cases, there must be "the introduction of political organization from outside the workers' community. The workers themselves are too divided to provide the coherent political organization necessary for armed insurrection" (Paige, 1975: 68). This implies the historical importance, occasionally, of the Leninist vanguard party, not as theoretically central to the analysis of revolution, but to be introduced on an ad hoc basis when historical circumstances warrant it.

In ordinary immiserationist circumstances, Paige searches for revolutionary actors among the most oppressed. And when he turns to Vietnam, this means searching for them in the rice paddies of the Mekong Delta in Vietnam. The source of change is the export sector of the agricultural economy, where the economy is most developed along capitalist lines but where class relations are least developed. But several scholars have questioned the empirical accuracy of locating the revolutionary impulse among the most heavily exploited workers in south Vietnam. Wolf (1969), Mitchell (1967), and Scott (1976) all locate the source of revolutionary opposition to the old regime among the middle peasants of the north and central regions of Vietnam. These peasants maintained high levels of traditional community solidarity in peasant villages and yet also maintained some tactical mobility to gain exposure to political ideas and ideologies of political reform and democracy. They were rural actors from tight-knit communities who were capable of developing some ties to urban centers of learning. Some were even educated.

Such a position requires that we see the traditional peasant village in different terms than Paige sees it. He believes that the traditional peasant village is universally and inevitably a bastion of reaction, constraining revolutionary behavior by adherence to tradition and peasant competitiveness, or by providing political and economic opportunities that change potentially revolutionary misery into a higher degree of satisfaction within the existing system. For example, in discussing Angolan migrant workers, Paige suggests

that tribal social structure "remained a viable source of economic oppor-
tunites and political authority for Africans cut off from white society"
(1975: 224). By contrast, Scott, Wolf, and the others cast the traditional
peasant village as a source of potential revolutionary sentiment, since their
traditional solidarity is threatened by the penetration of the capitalist market.
Peasants therefore become revolutionary to defend their traditional way of
life, not to overthrow capitalism; they react to major social dislocations set in
motion by overwhelming social changes brought about by the spread of the
market. Paige argues that the proletarianization of the peasantry is the *cause*
of their political mobilization and proclivity for revolution; Scott, Wolf, and
the others argue that the peasants become revolutionary to remain peasants,
to *prevent* proletarianization. All they really want is to be left alone – by the
state and by colonialists and capitalists.

From this perspective, northern and cental peasants in Vietnam were
defensive revolutionaries, reluctant to engage in political behavior, but
strategically placed so that they were capable of revolutionary activity.
Revolution does not happen when a society's most exploited groups revolt
because of increased exploitation in the most advanced sectors of the
economy, but when groups of middle-level, relatively autonomous peasants,
deeply anchored in their communities, draw upon the symbolic and material
resources of that traditional way of life to protect and defend it from invasion
from outside, either in the form of the state or the capitalist market. Peasants
revolt not when they have nothing left to lose, but when they feel they have
something precious to defend.

In part, the resolution of this debate depends on empirical support, on
which side of the debate can marshall enough convincing evidence to
demonstrate that its position is valid. While I agree with Paige's sensitivity to
the centrality of agrarian class relations, I am more convinced by the
theoretical perspective and the empirical evidence offered by those who argue
that the middle peasants, individualistic and tactically mobile, yet deeply
embedded in traditional communities, are the social group most likely to
develop revolutionary potential, precisely because their way of life is
threatened both by the processes of state centralization and capitalist
industrialization. This position can frame the analysis of revolution in terms
of the structural interplay among the international arena, class relations at the
level of production, and the state (cast as a partially autonomous, interested
actor), and still develop a political psychology of revolutionary motivations
that understands political behavior as stemming from more than the rational
calculation of individual interests. Revolutionary movements are composed
of those groups whose traditional ways of life – community solidarity, political autonomy from centralized political power, economic autonomy – are
most threatened by capitalist industrialization and state centralization. They

act rationally from what are sometimes non-rational sources of meaning. They draw on resources that are both material and symbolic and cultural.

Sadly – tragically – they always lose. Even when they win, they lose. For in winning a revolution, these groups must now face the arduous task of reconstituting political power and encouraging and sustaining economic development. And the processes that these victorious groups develop to successfully build a revolutionary political infrastructure and promote economic development are likely to bring about the very things that they struggled so heroically and successfully against: a centralized state apparatus and a form of industrialization that links the nation into the capitalist world economy.

Before we turn our attention to the tragic fate of these revolutionary actors, we must put one more structural element into the analytic equation. We must turn our attention to the role of the state, not as the object of contention between mobilized classes or as the arbiter of rewards, but as an interested party in its own right, a political actor seeking to maximize its interests in the national and international arena.

6

The State and Revolution

The state is more than the object of revolution, the prize to be won by the victorious party in revolutionary struggle. The state itself – its administrative bureaucracy, representative institutions, executive leader – is intimately involved in revolution, as cause and consequence, and as historical agent in its own right. Sometimes state initiatives, such as military expansion or economic development, set various groups in motion to oppose political efforts; these groups may become a revolutionary coalition of opposition which struggles with the state over the political and economic future of the nation. In other cases, state efforts to constrain military adventures or retard economic development spark the conflict with domestic political actors. In still other cases, segments of the state's bureaucratic administration may clash with one or more different segments, and provoke a political struggle that mobilizes mass political opposition or transforms the nature and direction of the political administration.

Many social scientists are today focusing on the state as a central variable in the revolutionary equation. As famed French historian Fernand Braudel put it slightly more than a decade ago (Braudel, 1986 [1979], vol. 3: 62):

> The state is back in fashion again, even among philosophers. Any analysis which does not grant it an important place is placing itself outside a developing trend, one which has its excesses and simplifications, of course, but which has at least the advantages of making some . . . think again and pay attention to something they were ready to dismiss, or at least any rate neglect, in the past.

Paying attention to the state as an active agent in revolutionary struggles means treating the state as an analytically distinct category from either the class structure upon which it is based or the social values that it may embody. The state must be seen as more than the "executive committee of the ruling class," the way that Marx had originally characterized it, and it must be seen as more complex than the simple repository of political legitimacy and the expression of generalized and consensually held political values, the way, for example, structural-functionalists such as Huntington, Parsons, or Gurr understood it. The state neither passively reflects the ideology of the ruling class nor simply expresses consensually held values. "Power and right are unfortunately not very tidily related in the world" (Dunn, 1972; 245). Further, the state is more than a mechanism by which a social group attempts to maximize its position in a capitalist world economy, as, say, Wallerstein might have it, and less than the sole guarantor of individual liberty and equality in a society organized by social privilege, as Locke or Hobbes believed. The state does not stand entirely above society, nor is it reducible to any other level of analysis.

At the same time that we treat the state as analytically distinct from class forces and transnational structures, our efforts to build a structural analysis of revolutions must also take care not to reify the state, to treat the state as if it were uniform and unified, cohesive and coherent, without internal divisions that represent more than momentary political factions. The state is not a thing that analytically transcends social organization, but it is an integral part of it. The state comprises an enormous collection of individuals and social groups. We might even speak of the state as a historical *process* by which these individuals and groups organize themselves around specific poles of interest for specific purposes, following diverse logics drawn from rational and non-rational sources. States are fluid assemblages of political actors, but states are also powerful sets of institutions that exert a significant influence over daily life, establishing parameters for social action, and maintaining (and even, sometimes, undermining) the capacity of the powerful to remain in power.

Often students are tempted to grant social structures a larger causal power than is warranted; I occasionally hear comments such as "Society made us this way" or "How can an individual challenge the State?" This type of reification grants too much autonomy and power to political institutions or to some abstraction called "society." The state is an active agent in revolutionary events – it is not only present but participates in its own destruction. But it does not live outside the realm of human life. We will speak of *states* as active agents, but not of the State, of an institution so powerful and free of constraints that it moves in a universe of its own. Sociological analysis of the state must recognize the divisions between its various institutions – military, judicial, administrative, legislative – as well as remain historically grounded, to understand the ways in which political power is aggregated and disaggregated at the level of the state.

The historical grounding of our analysis is critical, because the autonomy of the state from other levels of analysis is not a categorical given, but is, itself, a historical product. State autonomy was not always historically necessary or possible. "States provide *territorially centralized organization* and *geopolitical diplomacy*," writes Mann (1986: 514). "The usefulness of such power organizations was marginal in the early Middle Ages. But its functionality for dominant groupings began to grow, especially on the battlefield and in the organization of trade." For this reason, Mann cautions students to remain historical, since "the power autonomy of states is not a constant" (Mann, 1986: 514).

Already, I have suggested some of the ways in which the state is a crucial actor in revolutions: as cause, as interested party pursuing its own interests, and as consequence. Of course, each of these three dimensions cannot be fully separated from the other two, but we will be concerned with those social scientists who have examined these particular roles of the state.

The Classical Legacy

Two distinct theoretical trajectories about the relationship between the state and revolution emerge from the works of the classical theorists of revolution. On the one hand, Marx and Lenin believe that the state is critical the understanding of the phenomenon, but both believe that the state can be largely understood by reference to class struggle. On the other hand, Weber and Hintze see in the state, and especially its bureaucratic administration, processes that can not be reduced to class analysis and that are directly relevant to the study of revolution.

As we have seen earlier, Lenin believed that the state was the object of revolutionary struggle, since the state was the instrument by which one class oppressed another. In fact, Lenin defines the state in class terms; in his treatise *State and Revolution* he writes that the state is "an organ of the rule of a definite class which *cannot* be reconciled with its antipode" and even further specifies its use of violence when he writes that the state is "a special organization of force; it is an organization of violence for the suppression of some class" (Lenin, 1970: 8, 28). If the state is so intimately tied up with class rule, then it can hardly be the guarantor of individual liberty against encroachment. Elections are farcical charades; "the oppressed are allowed once every few years to decide which particular representatives of the oppressing class shall represent and repress them in parliament" (Lenin, 1970: 105).

So intimate is the connection between the state and class oppression that the state becomes antithetical to individual freedom. "So long as the state exists there is no freedom. When there will be freedom, there will be no

state'' (Lenin, 1970: 114). Thus, the goal of revolution is the destruction of
the state:

> if the state is the product of the irreconcilability of class antagonisms, if it is a
> power standing *above* society and *"increasingly alienating"* itself from it'' then
> it is obvious that the liberation of the oppressed class is impossible not only
> without a violent revolution, *but also without the destruction* of the apparatus
> of state power which was created by the ruling class and which is the embodi-
> ment of this ''alienation''.[1]

Here, Lenin agrees with the traditional Marxian idea that the destruction of
the state is the proletariat's historical mission. What will be particularly the
object of their dismantling is the political quality of administration, the use
to which administrative institutions were put – namely the suppression of
the proletariat. Thus Lenin claims that ''the state will disappear as a result of
the coming social revolution, that is, that public functions will lose their political character and be transformed into the simple administrative functions of
watching over the true interests of society'' (1970: 73).

Lenin believes that such a process is historically situated; it is only the
proletariat that can destroy the state. Prior to 1917, Lenin argues, the
historical outcome of revolution has been to strengthen the state instead of
smashing it, making the state an even more effective instrument of class
domination (1970: 32). Bourgeois revolutions ''perfected'' the repressive
apparatus of the state, creating illusory democracy while enforcing class rule.
Working-class revolution will eliminate it.

Lenin also argues that the destruction of the state and political authority
does not occur all at once, at the moment that the working class asserts itself
politically. During the process of revolution, the power of the state remains
salient.

> A revolution is certainly the most authoritarian thing there is; it is the act
> whereby one part of the population imposes its will upon the other by means of
> rifles, bayonets, and cannon – authoritarian means, if such there be at all; and
> if the victorious party does not want to have fought in vain, it must maintain
> this rule by means of the terror which its arms inspire in the reactionaries.
> (Lenin, 1970: 74)

Unfortunately, such a statement raises difficult analytic – not to mention
strategic – problems. When does the terror end and political reconstruction
of a neutral administrative state begin? When has the process ended sufficiently to allow for the dismantling of this apparatus that served the
proletariat in its seizure of power? And how does this process begin? What
about those groups and individuals whose interests appear to be served by
maintaining *their* control over the means of repression? Are not the institutions of the state sufficiently adaptable that they can serve the interests of a

class fraction – say, the leaders of the revolution – against would-be leaders from the *same* class? The inability of Lenin's theory to answer these questions theoretically also suggests some of the strategic limitations of his ideas – for example, the strengthening of the state after the Bolshevik victory in 1917, and the reconstitution of one of the world's most powerful political apparatuses in a society in which it was to have disappeared.

This signal weakness of Lenin's derives also from Marx's insistence that both the form and the content of the state is an expression of and the instrument by which the ruling class maintains its power. It is the achievement of Weber and his followers, most notably Otto Hintze, that they divorce the form of the state from its content, and are thereby able to better comprehend one of the dynamics of state – society relations in the process of revolution.

On the one hand, Weber insisted that the administrative capacity of the state was ethically neutral, in the sense that it could serve either good or evil ends. On the other hand, he also believed that the increasingly pervasive power of state institutions reduced human capacity for individual freedom. These two claims are not contradictory, but carefully linked: the state can serve any end, but all polities circumscribe human volition and remove meaning from life.

Weber defined the state entirely in terms on its ability to achieve certain ends. "A compulsory political organization with continuous operations will be called a state insofar as it successfully upholds the claim to the *monopoly* of the *legitimate* use of physical force in the enforcement of its order" (Weber, 1978, vol. 1: 54). In *The Protestant Ethic and the Spirit of Capitalism* he specified some of the means by which the state is to be defined when he wrote that the state is "a political association with a rational, written constitution, rationally ordained law, and an administration bound to rational rules or laws administered by trained officials" (Weber, 1962 [1904]: 16–17). The definition of the state rests entirely on its means, never on its ends:

> It is not possible to define a political organization, including the state, in terms of the end to which its action is devoted. All the way from the provision for subsistence to the patronage of art, there is no conceivable end which *some* political association has not at some time pursued. And from the protection of personal security to the administration of justice, there is none which *all* have recognized. Thus it is possible to define the "political" character of an organization only in terms of the *means* peculiar to it, the use of force. (Weber, 1978, vol. 1: 55)

Although I do not share Weber's insistence that the means and end of the state be analytically separate[2], his claims about the autonomy of the state from any *specific* end, and the centrality of the means of violence as defining features of the state remain critical for our understanding of revolution. The problem of revolution for Weber is that it inevitably strengthened the state's capacity to constrain individual action, particularly in the realm of the economy. Without exception, revolutions strengthen the bureaucracy's hold over the market. What is more, revolutions are brought on by breakdowns in capacity to administer the means of violence, both internally (police repression of domestic opposition) and externally (military capacity to defeat foreign enemies).

This Weberian emphasis on bureaucracy and military capacity informs much of the work of structural social scientists since Weber's time, among them analysts such as Perry Anderson, Randall Collins, and Theda Skocpol, whose work we will consider later in this chapter. Before turning to them, though, we will briefly sketch some of the implications of Weber's theory as they found their way into the influential historical essays of German historian Otto Hintze.

Hintze was a devoted follower of Weber, who observed in transmutations of political forms the specification of political content. Hintze argued that revolutions were entirely political phenomena, both causally and consequentially. Like Weber, Hintze claimed that the process of state formation is the chief cause of the content of the state, its character and its intention. Determined to show a "causal connection between certain types of political bodies and certain constitutional forms of government," Hintze examined the historical emergence, and the roles and functions of various political institutions, such as local administrative bureaucrats (commisaries), regional legislative bodies (estates), and most especially the military (Hintze, 1975: 177). Revolutions became, for Hintze, important moments in a general process of state-building or state formation, itself the most significant process of social change.

Hintze stressed the significance of the military in both the history of the state and the process of state-building. The state has its origins in military organization, far more than class struggle. A state's organization "will not be determined solely by economic and social relations and clashes of interests, but primarily by the necessities of defense and offense, that is, by the organization of the army and of warfare" (Hintze, 1975: 215; see also p. 181). To adequately understand the state, Hintze argued that we must look outside of national borders as well as to the structure of social classes within the nation itself. Social classes will suggest the type of military organization that is most likely; for example, land-based armies are more likely when propertied classes dominate over commercial classes, while naval power is associated with commercial classes' ascendancy and the retiring of land-based propertied classes to their provincial estates. For this reason, "[s]ea power is allied with progressive forces, whereas land forces are tied to conservative tendencies" (Hintze, 1975: 214).

More significantly, though, the geopolitical relationship between nations is the single key determinant of the form and content of the state. The relations between states, the position of one relative to others and its overall position in the political line-up of nations are critical. "It is one-sided, exaggerated, and therefore false to consider class conflict the only driving force in history," Hintze writes (1975: 183). "Conflict between nations has been far more important; and thoughout the ages, pressure from without has been a determining influence on internal structure."

It is important to distinguish Hintze's emphasis on the global context of state building and Wallerstein's model of the capitalist world economy. In Wallerstein's schema, mobilized classes and states coalesce to pursue economic interests in the world market; the underlying cause of military competition is the driving force of the capitalist world economy: economic competition. To Hintze, the causal relationship is reversed. The underlying cause of economic competition in the world market is political and military competition between states, each of which seeks to augment its power at the expense of the others. "The rise and development of capitalism remains unintelligible without insight into how they were conditioned by the course of national formation" (Hintze, 1975: 183). The process of state-building is the effort to gain administrative control over larger and larger units of territory so as to more effectively pursue international agendas against foreign competition. To Hintze, "the development of military and political power and constant military preparedness were possible only on the basis of a larger, centrally ruled and administrative territory" (1975: 174) and the development of that territory was only possible by increasing centralized political power.

Historically, Hintze focuses on the development of the absolute monarchy or the absolutist state, which is the first state to both create and to need a modern standing army and a pervasive nationally centralized and administratively decentralized political bureaucracy.[3] The absolutist state was a military state, designed to make war on foreign enemies and to pacify domestic discontents, even while mobilizing the country for war. Here lies the important implication of Hintze's work for the study of revolution. Political centralization of administration and the development of a larger standing army siphoned resources from the countryside and abridged traditional liberties in order to generate revenues for state programs:

> Maintenance of the army became the chief task of the state's financial administration. This in turn led to unprecedented extension of the tax burden and consequently to a peculiar economic system that aimed at increasing the stock of ready money and at the same time fostering and stimulating production artificially, especially in industry. (Hintze, 1975: 201)

In this sense, states which centralize and expand political power to pursue their own ends against global geopolitical competition may generate domestic opposition from a variety of sources. This is the kernel of Hintze's theory of revolution, which describes how political opposition is first set in motion by autonomous states pursuing distinctly political interests in the global arena.

This is not to say that revolutions, in Hintze's view, do not have class consequences, but that their origins appear to be distinctly political. The strengthening of the state takes place with or without a revolution: a non-revolutionary society permits the state to grow stronger, while the aftermath of a revolution inevitably produces a state more pervasive and powerful than the pre-revolutionary state it overthrew. Contrary to liberal political theorists who claimed that capitalism was an economic form of a minimalist state, Hintze insists that capitalism requires a strong state; "the self-contained national state possess the guarantees for the survival of capitalism" (1975: 426).

Though Hintze agrees with the Marxian notion that "the affairs of state and of capitalism are inextricably interrelated, that they are only two sides, or aspects, of one and the same historical development," Hintze reverses Marx and Lenin's understanding of the causal sequencing between state and capital (1975: 452). "The development of capitalism was furthered in the interests of the state as an indispensible means to political power" (1975: 426). Hintze demurs from a political determinism that would be comparable to Marx's economic determinism, but his historical analysis of specific revolutions indicates the economic consequences of political transformation. In England, for example, "agrarian capitalism developed . . . as a consequence of the capitalistic class's acquisition of political power;" capitalism was not the cause. Similarly, in France, the revolution "did not create that class (the peasants) but it did preserve it and free it from feudal burdens. The Revolution thwarted agrarian capitalism at the outset" (Hintze, 1975: 444, 445). In short, as Hintze summarizes his position, "we are not dealing with the creation of a capitalistic form of economy by the state, but with the laying a foundation upon which it could develop, and with its explicit encouragement by the state" (1975: 446).

Of course, if Marx and Lenin erred by assigning too little autonomy to the state, Hintze appears to err in the other direction, assigning too much autonomy to the state – so much, in fact, that the state appears to conduct its foreign and domestic policies according to its own devices and informed by its own ideological justifications. Legitimacy seems hardly problematic as states pursue their interests against those of other states, and the most powerful state of all is able to effect its economic and political agenda on other states as well as on its own population. The dialectical interplay between states and classes is elusive and essential for adequate understanding of revolution.

Several contemporary social scientists, such as Ellen Kay Trimberger, have attempted to integrate political variables into a class-based theory of revolution; others, such as Randall Collins and Anthony Giddens, have worked to integrate economic variables into a state-centered theory of revolution. A few have attempted synthetic amalgams of class and state. In this chapter we will examine two of these synthetic efforts in the work of Perry Anderson and Theda Skocpol. (The next chapter will examine the work of Charles Tilly, who goes further by attempting to also integrate social psychological variables and political motivation.)

State-builders as Revolutionaries

By establishing the state as relatively autonomous from the structure of social classes or the world system, some theorists have explored the ways in which political actors within the state sector have become revolutionaries, and the types of revolutions that they accomplish. Ellen Kay Trimberger, for example, examines the ways in which state bureaucrats become revolutionary, seizing control of the state apparatus, and then rebuild the nation along nationalistic reformist lines by exercising bureaucratic efficiency. Such an event Trimberger calls a "revolution from above;" a revolution in which "military and civil bureaucrats, dissatisfied with the ineffective and vascillating policy of dynastic leaders in dealing with the West, launched unauthorized nationalist movements" (Trimberger, 1978: 13). In her empirical comparison of the revolutionary upheavals in Meiji Japan and Turkey in 1920, and later including Egypt and Peru in the 1950s as additional cases, Trimberger specifies both the structural and historical conditions under which revolution from above can occur.

What defines a revolution from above, in Trimberger's view, is the extra-legal takeover of political power led by some of the highest-ranking civilian bureaucrats in the old regime. There is little or no mass participation, as the revolutionaries attempt to achieve their ends by manipulation of elites rather than by mass demonstrations and protests. There is, in fact, little violence. There is also little appeal to radical ideology; the takeover is pragmatic, efficient, and accomplished in a step-by-step manner. And it accomplishes the destruction of the economic and political base of the aristocracy (Trimberger, 1978: 3). In sum, revolution from above is "an attempt by bureaucrats solely dependent on the state for their power, to eliminate the potential political opposition of those with economic power" (Trimberger, 1978: 29). They moved quickly to consolidate political power within the state because they both lacked mass support and they feared continued political opposition from economic notables and landlords (Trimberger, 1978: 36).

In order to accomplish revolution from above, certain structural features must be present in the society. Perhaps most important, the military class of officers must be independent of those classes that control the means of production. Military bureaucrats must be drawn from a different social class than the economic elites or even former political elites, not recruited from dominant landed, commercial, or industrial classes. And they must not form close personal and economic ties with those dominant classes, even after their ascencion to high office; instead they must remain dependent upon the state for their claims to power (Trimberger, 1978: 41–3; see also Skocpol, in Evans et al., 1985: 10). The autonomy of the military is itself produced, Trimberger suggests, by the "decay of feudal institutions, urbanization of standing troops, and infiltration of urban artisans and merchants into the military," all of which "hastened the decline of military skills and segregated those who held military positions from the political elite" (Trimberger, 1978: 64). The military bureaucrats are not recruited from dominant landed, commercial, or industrial classes. The autonomy of military bureaucrats is enhanced if they maintain regional bases of power that are geographically distant from the site of the central government (Trimberger, 1978: 43).

Not only must military bureaucrats be autonomous from the ruling class, but they must be cohesive and solidary as well. The solidarity of bureaucrats is generated, Trimberger argues, by the dependence of the nation on western powers. Military bureaucrats' nationalistic reaction to western dependence fosters a solidarity in the face of external threats to national autonomy (Trimberger, 1978: 42, 154). Thus, the military bureaucrats demand an end to national degradation by foreign powers; their ideology is nationalist, not socialist or authoritarian.

But military bureaucrats do not become revolutionary only within an international context of dependence and foreign domination. The existing ruling class must be unable to reform the nation sufficiently to oppose continued domination *and* there must be threats of revolution from within the country – that is, there must be the possibility of revolution from below. Revolution from above is a revolution without mass support; in fact, it may be a revolution in spite of the early rumbling of mass mobilization for a revolution from below. Into the breach caused by an impotent ruling class and the possibility of revolution from below, the military bureaucrats are able to effect a revolution from above: nationalist but not socialist.

Historically, Trimberger argues that revolution from above is a possibility only in those countries that are relatively backward in comparison to the dominant (core) powers, and whose traditional political elites or ruling economic class have been unable to improve the position of the country in the world at large or better the lives of its own citizens because of the continued domination of the western powers. In part, then, revolution from above is a revolution of what Wallerstein calls the "semi-periphery," those nations who have some national bureaucracy that is independent of the domination of the west but who are still held in the grip of unequal exchange and domestic poverty as a result of their dependence on the west. Revolutions from above are revolutions that seek to modernize the nation under a more nationalistic program, and seek to remove from power those traditional elites who are seen as complicitous with continued foreign domination and therefore retarding economic and political modernization (see Trimberger, 1978: 25).

As Trimberger sums up the historical circumstances in Japan and Turkey, the growth of a patrimonial government

> created a group of autonomous officials whose wealth and status were based on office and not on land. These officials were not modern bureaucrats for their positions depended on personal status and personal connections and not on merit, skill or specialized knowledge. But the growth of a social group with aristocratic status and power based on patrimonial office prevented the creation of an estate of landlords in Japan and Turkey with autonomous political and legal rights. (Trimberger, 1978: 54–5)

If nothing else, revolution from above can allow autonomous military bureaucrats to sweep aside the ruling class of the old regime, and to begin to implement a new program of capitalist industrialization.

But revolution from above is limited by the same structural and historical circumstances that make it possible in the first place. Within the context of a capitalist world economy, the bureaucrats' efforts to "achieve a stable and powerful nation state based on autonomous capitalist development" are constrained by the larger international political economy. In both Japan and Turkey, Trimberger reminds us, "the uneven, unequal, and distorted economic development created by dependent capitalism resulted in political instability which threatened the authoritarian political system consolidated by revolution from above" (Trimberger, 1978: 105, 127). The likely outcome of revolution from above, then, is dependent capitalist development, in which industrialization is geared towards the needs of an external market, and is oriented towards military needs and the subimperialist control over other countries in the region; industrialization takes place within a relatively narrow sector; technological dependence on more advanced countries is maintained; workers experience the superexploitation that comes from the interaction of class and world economy; and the country remains dependent on foreign capital. In short, national autonomy is sacrificed for modest industrial development that maintains the nation's dependence on foreign powers (see Trimberger, 1978: 124–6).

The failure of revolution from above to generate a genuinely autonomous form of national development is ultimately based on who is included and who is excluded from the revolutionary coalition. The only group, Trimberger suggests, that could prevent the slide into dependent capitalist development is, of course, the working class. Yet mass mobilization is precluded by the organization of the bureaucratic effort, and prevented by the initial success in sweeping aside the older traditional elites. But the lack of mass mobilization is decisive in constraining the scope of the revolution from above, and limiting the possibilities of effecting truly autonomous national development, a process that would require mass democratic institutions possible only, Trimberger believes, within a socialist context.

Despite the limits imposed on revolution from above by the lack of mass mobilization, the autonomy of military bureaucrats can pose a revolutionary threat to traditional elites. In a sense, creating a distinctly political bureaucracy may be dangerous for the continuation of the old regime, because such a development may create a potential base for political opposition among the servants of the state. If bureaucratic office becomes property, then the office-holders may become capable of mounting a successful challenge against the old regime. Such an understanding suggests one of the contradictions located within the old regime state, a contradiction that does have important implications for our study of revolution. In the effort to enlarge and sustain the power of traditional elites within the old regime, the political power-holders may develop an administrative bureaucracy that will centralize political and military administration. However, the relative autonomy of this administrative bureaucracy may result in it becoming the source of potential opposition against the old regime, if the traditional elites are incapable of generating a program of nationalistic development and reducing dependence on foreign nations. Such a pattern emerged not only in Turkey and Japan in the nineteenth and early twentieth centuries, but also in France and England in the mid-seventeenth century, and in France in the late eighteenth century and Russia in the early twentieth century. A fractious bureaucracy is capable of joining a coalition of political opposition that unites several discontented groups in a rebellious alliance against the old regime. It is coalitions such as these that make revolutions.

Revolution as Geopolitical Failure

Trimberger specifies the conditions under which state-builders, in this case military bureaucrats, may become revolutionaries and overthrow the traditional elites of the old regime, only to be limited in the scale of reform by their failure to mobilize the working classes. Randall Collins looks at the relationship between state-building and revolution from a different perspective.

For him, revolution is the domestic result of failed foreign policy, the inability of the state to pursue its political interests in an international arena of military and political competition. Note here that for Collins the global arena in which individual nations undergo revolutions is a political arena, a field of political competition and military conquest. Like Hintze and Weber, Collins stresses the strictly political dimension of revolution. This perspective is in sharp contrast to that of Trimberger, who, like Wallerstein and Marx, emphasizes the economic context of revolution; military bureaucrats become revolutionary when the old regime cannot successfully oppose the economic pressure of foreign domination. To Collins, state-builders who fail may become unwitting and reluctant victims of revolution.

Collins's geopolitical theory rests on certain assumptions about the relationship of state to society as well as of state to the geographic boundaries that constitute a nation. The state, he argues, is ultimately reducible to its historical origins: mobilization for war. The state had its origins in warfare, and its organization base remains the military. The military structure and the types of weapons available all compose the state's infrastructure. The economy is subsumed under military imperatives, and administrative resources become anything that the state can manipulate to more effectively mobilize the nation. Such variables as ethnicity, religion, or ideology are all cultural resources to be deployed by the regime to generate solidarity.

States are also spatially located, and here Collins offers a more geographic explanation for revolution than do other theorists. States, he argues, depend on the defensibility of heartlands and defensible barriers between states. Political relationships are composed of relations among states situated in heartlands. Conflict within this geopolitical world takes two general forms (see Collins, 1981: 71–2 *et passim*). First, there is the political competition between states over the boundaries between their heartlands – marshlands, waterways (oceans, seas, rivers), mountains, and the like. This competition can erupt into war, which will require mobilization of the domestic population – through taxation, conscription, billeting of troops, etc. As Collins sees it, this global geopolitical competition may have important domestic repercussions. He argues that "the major political changes have occurred because of international military dynamics; states which are strong enough to fight back against strong enemies have had to mobilize their populations, both for increasingly larger armed forces and to pay for increasingly expensive wars" (Collins, 1981: 60).

Second, there is the imprecision of the fit between the purview of the state and its domestic territory, which may also become a source of political tension and instability. Outlying areas traditionally maintain a troublesome relationship to the central state, and the regime must constantly patrol its borders not only against foreign aggression but also against the autonomy of its own borderlands. Stated axiomatically, the further a province is from the centralized political regime, the less strong its allegiance to that regime. Now, such an axiom does not hold all the time, but it does indicate the domestic sources of strain within any political nation. The purview of the state does not evenly cover the geographic boundaries of the nation.

Why, then, do revolutions happen? According to Collins, revolutions are the consequence of failed foreign policies. Global military competition leads regimes to mobilize domestic support for aggressive foreign policies – policies designed to expand geographic territory and grab other nations' economic resources. When such policies are successful, they pay handsomely and successful aggressive foreign policies can assure dominance in the inter-national arena and a consequent high standard of living (legitimacy, stability, luxury, absence of revolutionary opposition) for the successful nation. But failure can be disastrous, not so much because of the potential conquest by a foreign nation, but because the domestic population may become restive in the face of failure. Thus, "revolutions have been made possible by defeat in war which destroyed the coercive apparatus of the state, but happened to leave the defeated territory unoccupied by the conquerer" (Collins, 1981: 99). Military defeat in foreign wars ushers in a revolutionary situation.

It is not only military defeat that can bring about revolution however. Unsuccessful efforts to expand militarily can lead to military breakdown of the defensive capabilities of the state (against foreign aggression) as well as its coercive capacities (against potential domestic opposition and to maintain a high level of extraction of resources for war). Military "disintegration" is a crucial precondition for revolution, and the long-term cause of this military breakdown is "an unsuccessful effort to expand capacity, and hence internal structures of domination and surplus extraction." In this way, Collins argues that military strains can "produce" revolutions (Collins, 1981: 66, 67; see also Collins, 1986: 169).

Often, ironically, initial military successes may have dramatically different consequences than expected. In this sense, military *overextension* may be the ultimate cause of military breakdown, which can produce a revolutionary situation. "Geopolitical overextension is a key antecedent condition of revolution" (Collins, 1986: 169). This overextension may result from initial successes in geopolitical and military competition with other states. State expansion is potentially infinite, limited only by the farthest reaches of the globe. And Collins assumes that the need for expansion by states is quenched only momentarily; states are as rapacious and expansionist as their capacities allow. Thus states will continue to expand until they have crossed over a threshold point beyond which they should *not* have expanded. Having now done so they have gone too far, and the dire consequences of military disintegration and revolution may follow. Thus, the "military overextension of states typically leads to rapid disintegration of territorial power" (Collins, 1986: 164).

Collins's geopolitical theory also can be used to explain the relative rarity of revolutions. "Things stay the way they are because people are physically dispersed across the landscape in certain ways," Collins writes, emphasizing spatial distance as a barrier to political action. The "cognitive complexities of changing the physical organization of things tends to require more energy and more coordinative activities than simply leaving things as they are" (Collins, 1986: 160). This helps explain the inherent "conservatism" of the peasantry, for example, whose political wish is often to be left alone. "Much of the time the state can survive by routine, or by a relatively low degree of 'legitimacy arousal'," the mobilization of only a small amount of support keeps fragmented and disunified opposition from coalescing (Collins, 1986: 160).

Obviously, Collins gives a much greater emphasis to strictly political variables in his explanation of revolution. But in his discussion of non-revolutionary events, as we can see, he also allows room for political ideas, and even for emotions and experience as part of the revolutionary equation. "The revolutionary downfall of a state is due not simply to economic difficulties," he writes, or even "the disintegration of its military apparatus in defeat." One also must consider the "loss of legitimacy," the withdrawal of political consent from the domestic population (Collins, 1986: 164). And when the revolution breaks out, there is an experience of hope, of elation, of the possibility of personal transformation, which Collins interprets by using the metaphor of boundaries that he has earlier employed in describing the relationships between states. "The rare elation that accompanies a revolutionary uprising is probably due to there being on apparent boundary between one's own micro situation and that prevailing anywhere else" (Collins, 1986: 261). Revolution is the obliteration of boundaries, both personal and political.

Despite the many useful insights that Collins's strictly geopolitical interpretation of revolution may afford us, there are still some lingering problems with the model. In large part, these problems are a result of overinterpretation, making larger claims for his model than are warranted. Collins is correct, for example, that military defeat can been used to partially explain the outbreak of revolution. For example, as the Russian troops returned home defeated in 1904–5 from the Russo-Japanese war, or later from the First World War in 1917, Russia experienced its two great revolutionary upheavals, the first unsuccessful and the second quite successful. But such a model cannot explain all the underlying causes of those revolutionary outbreaks, since there are many examples of defeated armies returning home without a revolution being the eventual outcome. Collins's model can specify the timing of the outbreak in some cases, but the domestic structural causes – the tensions between social classes, between various classes and political power-holders, and among competing visions and ideologies of legitimacy – are not completely brought forward in this model.

Similarly, the notion of geopolitical overextension is a useful construct to explain revolutionary events after the fact, but as a predictive variable it is virtually impossible to measure. In fact, the concept of overextension implies a type of *post hoc ergo propter hoc* fallacy in which causality is assumed from the results, not by the historical antecedents. (Collins is not alone in raising this problem; it plagues all comparative historical sociology, but it is especially telling for those models which promote one level of analysis as pivotal.) We can only know that overexpansion occurred by the revolutionary outcomes, and assume that a nation without revolutionary events did not overextend itself. But how can we know when military expansion has reached its limits?

In addition, Collins falls victim to what we might label "the Goldilocks problem" in this model of overextension. Military expansion is necessary for states; without expanding they risk clientage to another state. But expansion can neither be "too much" (or else revolution) or "too little" (or else loss of legitimacy and/or vulnerability to attack). Military expansion must be "just right." Yet the analyst has no way of knowing beforehand how much is just right and how much is too much or too little. Further, Collins asks us to assume that the aggressive capacity of states knows no limits, that, like sharks, states must grow or die. Such assumptions may be warranted from a cynical, or at least coldhearted observation of contemporary geopolitical relations, but it ignores the theoretical possibility as well as the historical attempts to create a "just state," a state based on administering to its own domestic population without military adventurism and cutthroat competition with other states. Certainly, most such efforts have been relatively short-lived, but not all. If one were to write the history of geopolitical competition from the point of view of Switzerland or Norway or Denmark, global military competition would hardly be the prime mover of political or social life, as it might be from the point of view of England, France, Germany, Russia, or the United States.

Despite this, Collins has placed strictly political and military variables on the comparative sociological agenda if we are to understand revolutions. He insists that these variables cannot be reduced to other levels of analysis, either at the global level of international economic competition (which only serves to camouflage geopolitical competition) or at the level of class struggle (which only indicates the extent to which a state is tactically mobile to pursue its own objectives in the military arena). The dynamics of state-building – military expansion, diplomacy, maintenance of geographic boundaries – are all crucially linked to the occurrence of revolution.

Revolution and Modernity

Like Collins, Anthony Giddens stresses the centrality of the state in a theory of revolution, but takes a different historical slant on how to interpret both the causes and the prospects of revolutionary change. Though Giddens nowhere explicates his theory of revolution in significant detail[4], there are enough references to it throughout his works to allow us to tease out some of the theoretical threads. In particular, Giddens develops two partially over-lapping projects, each of which bears on a theory of revolution. First, he seeks to reconceptualize the fundamental characteristics of modernity; this is by definition a historical project concerned with social processes and change. The second project is a more ahistorical, nomethetic effort to develop ontological categories that define the structural parameters of social action at any one time. This is the project concerned with "structuration theory." Like Weber, then, Giddens seeks to specify what is unique about the contem-porary or modern configuration, understand its origins, and develop abstract concepts that can be applied across historical moments and social spaces.

A key to the modernity project is Giddens's insistence that the indepen-dent qualities of capitalism, the nation-state, and industrial production, as well as their historical conjunction in western Europe, makes modernity radically different from all previous moments in western history as well as from any non-western society. In this sense, then, Giddens argues that revolutions are a modern form of praxis, possible only within the historical epoch known as modernity. In pre-modern society, Giddens proposes a "secretional" form of social change, while in colonized societies, Giddens stresses the loose integration and articulation of colonial outposts of non-modern empires. These would imply that sweeping and abrupt revolutionary change would be impossible in such situations (see Giddens, 1985: 201).

Revolutions are also modern in so far as they are enacted by social move-ments whose focus, and in certain respects very existence, is shaped by the state. The nation-state is, to Giddens, the apotheosis of modernity, a distinc-tively modern system (see Giddens, 1985: 17–31); and what is more, the social movements which challenge the revolutionary formation of nation-states in most instances are also thoroughly modern social processes (see Giddens, 1985: 313–25).

Giddens also suggests that revolutions are modern because they presume as preconditions the play of a multidimensional and poorly integrated world system, composed of military, economic, and political contradictions. Thus the geopolitical context for national development is more than the context of revolution; it is, in part, the cause. "The European state system was not simply the 'political environment' in which the absolutist state and nation-state developed," he writes (1985: 112). "It was the condition and in substantial degree the very source, of that development. It was war, and preparations for war, that provided the most potent energizing stimulus for the concentration of administrative resources and fiscal reorganization that characterized the rise of absolutism."

Giddens's characterization of absolutism provides an instructive illustration of this. In contrast to Marx's (and Wallerstein's) argument that "the absolutist state was founded upon an alliance between the crown and the commercial capitalist bourgeoisie" – a position he terms "discredited" – Giddens stresses the distinctive conjuncture of political and military changes that made absolutism possible (Giddens, 1985: 96, 97). First, "a series of linked technological changes in armaments" made traditional land-based warfare methods obsolete. Second, "the emergence of greatly accentuated administrative power within the armed forces" changed the military capacity to engage in warfare. Particularly, the development of military discipline and formal ranking allowed for a larger and more bureaucratically organized administration. Finally, "the development of European naval strength" allowed Europe to expand beyond the capacity of earlier states. Europe provides, Giddens notes, "the only instances of far-flung empires based first and foremost on control of the oceans. However much traditional empires might have depended upon sea-borne communications, their expansion usually resulted from the control of large land-masses" (Giddens, 1985: 105–6).

As we can see, Giddens gives primary causal weight to the development of political and military institutions to create the transitional form of the absolutist state, which precedes the modern nation-state. The development of absolutism, and later of the nation-state, is both the cause of modern revolutionary movements – movements that contend with the state over scarce resources – and the object of the struggle. Revolutions are modern phenomena not only because they only take place historically within modern society, but because they are only able to take place within modern society.

Giddens's second project, the theory of structuration, also carries with it some implications for revolution (see Cohen, 1989: 254–73). Giddens insists that the underlying purpose of his development of these abstract concepts is to demolish the evolutionary notions embedded within earlier efforts to develop these abstract conceptualizations. (He is here referring to both Marxism and functionalism.) Revolutions are never inevitable, Giddens argues, either for reasons of increasing sharpness of structural contradiction or because of system breakdown and the failure of value consensus.

Instead, Giddens proposes a set of ahistorical structural contingencies. Modern class society is distinctively organized, in part, by both capitalism and the nation-state. Note here that class relations do not compose the state, but the state constitutes, in part, class society. And modern class society gives rise to specific sets of contradictions which may give rise to conflict, although contradictions need not do so. There is nothing inevitable about conflict or change being generated from contradiction.

In structuration theory as well, then, the state is a central actor in the conceptual possibility of revolution. But to argue that the state is conceptually and historically a crucial actor in generating the contradictions that may give rise to challenges says nothing about the social composition, origins, and ideology of that opposition. That there is no secure, empirically relevant conception of interests that are unacknowledged by actors in part stems from Giddens's understanding of the term "exploitation" (see Cohen, 1989: 188–93). To Giddens, "exploitation exists only to the extent that the interests of dominant groups of superordinate agents diverge from generalisable interests which superordinates share in common with subordinate agents" (Cohen, 1989: 190). But surely exploitation "cannot be defined in terms of the interests of superordinates alone. For exploitation to occur the interests of superordinates and subordinates must diverge" (Cohen, 1989: 190). Specifying the interests of actors that are unacknowledged by those actors themselves has always proven a theoretically nettlesome task for social theory – Marx's efforts to imbue the proletariat with an interest in the classless society without their quite knowing it is an obvious case in point. However it is a necessary one, for it allows us to specify the ways in which exploited, subordinate groups can become conscious actors in history. While Giddens offers one of the most sophisticated accounts of the structures of social life, there is a less developed theory of motivation and mobilization of social forces from below. This is the task of theorists of mobilization, to which we shall turn in the next chapter. For now, however, we acknowledge our debt to Giddens for the theoretical specificity of social structures and his insistence on the historical specificity of modernity, the context of revolutionary potentials. Here Giddens is articulate in his argument that the modern nation-state, emergent from the absolutist state in western Europe, is the key player in any historical account of revolution.

Anderson and Absolutism

One of the more intriguing efforts to understand the role of the state in revolution has been the work of Perry Anderson (1974). Anderson's historical discussion of the absolutist state specifies a distinctly political dimension of the transition from feudalism to capitalism – a dimension that had earlier either been assumed or ignored in Marxist theory. But of interest to us here are the implications of this historical model for building an adequate sociology of revolution. Anderson's model has some fruitful suggestions about the timing and trajectory of revolutionary events. These are deeply embedded in his work, so in order to understand them we must first place his analysis of a specific form of the state – the absolute monarchy – in its sociological context.

What was the absolutist state?[5] Was it an element of feudal reaction designed to repress rebellious lower classes and contain capitalist development, or an engine of precisely that capitalist development, clearing out residual vestiges of feudalism from economic control? Or was it a neutral arbiter in the class struggle, without a class character itself? These questions may appear to take us far from the theoretical analysis of revolution, but since many of the great historical revolutions were mounted against monarchies that struggled to become of and maintain an absolutist charac- ter – autonomous from class control, and capable of pursuing their interests against foreign opposition and repressive domestic discontent – the specifi- cation of absolutism will bear directly on how we understand the dynamics of revolution.[6]

Many of the theorists who confront these issues look to Marx and Engels for explications of the character of absolutism. But Marx and Engels provide ambiguous and shifting portraits of absolutism; at times they appear to characterize it in each of the three ways I have mentioned. For example, in *Anti-Duhring*, Engels seems to argue that the absolutist state is a feudal state when he writes that the "mighty [sixteenth-century] revolution in the economic conditions of society . . . *was not followed* by any immediate corresponding change in its political structure. The state order *remained feudal* while society became more and more bourgeois" (Engels, 1971 [1878]: 115; emphasis added). But in *The Origins of the Family, Private Property and the State*, Engels suggests that there are periods when "the warring classes are so nearly equal in forces that the state power, as apparent mediator, acquires for the moment, a certain independence in relation to both. This applies to the absolute monarchy . . . which balances the nobility and the bourgeoisie against one another" (Engels, 1970 [1884]: 157). And Marx seems to suggest a third position in the first volume of *Capital*, when he writes that capitalists "all employ the power of the state, the concentrated and organized force of society, to hasten, hothouse fashion, the interests of the nobility by securing feudal relations of production in an era of commuta- tion of labor services and the appearance of commodity relations. The simultaneous revival of Roman law gave juridical expression to this political power, and secured the right to private property, which buttressed feudal landownership in a transitional era. The absolutist state thus preserved feudal relations by incorporating the bourgeoisie through the sale of offices, and protected the aristocracy from challenge by an emergent bourgeoisie. In short, absolutism was "a redeployed and recharged apparatus of feudal domination designed to clamp the peasant masses back into their traditional social position . . . It was never an arbiter between the aristocracy and the bourgeoisie, still less an instrument of the nascent bourgeoisie against the aristocracy: it was the political carapace of a threatened nobility" (Anderson, 1974: 18; see also pp. 212, 260).[7] Even though the character of these states was feudal, Anderson does acknowledge that they also "represented a decisive rupture with the pyramidal, parcellized sovereignty of the medieval social formations" (Anderson, 1974: 15).

Anderson's discussion of specific absolutist states in both western and eastern Europe links together these historically diverse events by reference to international *political* pressure as opposed to reference to mobilization for increased participation in the capitalist world economy. He argues that one must "reinsert the whole process . . . into the international state system" since only the world economy of industrial (not commercial) capitalism was capable of the international integration that Wallerstein ascribes to it. While it is true that western and eastern versions of absolutism were alike in that both preserved noble class rule in societies in which feudal social relations still dominated, their origins and historical trajectories are somewhat different, partly because they influenced one another. In the East, then, "it was the international pressure of Western Absolutism, the political apparatus of a more powerful feudal aristocracy, ruling more advanced societies, which obliged the Eastern nobility to adopt an equivalently centralized state machine, to survive" (Anderson, 1974: 197). Political innovation in one arena, designed to cope with domestic restiveness, may be experienced as political pressure in another country, which has then to adopt the innovation or risk political domination. Thus Anderson explains the long-term decline of the Ottoman Empire, for example, by the "military and economic superiority of Absolutist Europe" (Anderson, 1974: 379).

The disjuncture between the political apparatus of the absolutist state and the economic mode of production provides, for Anderson, the dynamic source of motion in those societies. This disjuncture is historically decisive:

> In nature and structure, the Absolute monarchies of Europe were still feudal states: the machinery of rule of the same aristocratic class that had dominated the Middle Ages. But in Western Europe, where they were born, the *social formations* which they governed were a complex combination of *feudal and capitalist modes of production*, with a gradually rising urban bourgeoisis and a growing primitive accumulation of capital on an international scale. (Anderson, 1974: 428–9)

In effect, absolutism was the last gasp of a politically dominant class, the nobility, to maintain its power in the face of development of capitalist economic activity from below:

> Thus while capital was slowly accumulated beneath the glittering super-structures of Absolutism, exerting an ever greater gravitational pull on them, the noble landowners of early modern Europe retained their historical predominance, in and through the monarchies which now commanded them. Economically guarded, socially privileged and culturally matured, the aristocracy still ruled: The Absolutist State adjusted its paramountcy to the steady burgeoning of capital within the composite social formations of Western Europe. (Anderson, 1974: 430)

The disjuncture between the political and the economic is also theoretically significant to Anderson's theory of revolution, because it is in the seam between the political and the economic that revolutionary activity takes place. The revolutionary moment is precisely the moment when large and powerful states are constructed to retard capitalist development in the interests of a threatened landed aristocracy. These moments occur at different times in different countries, but always for the same reason: capitalist economic relations threaten to transform the pre-existing mode of production, over which the nobility has long held political and economic power. In their efforts to hold on to their economic power, they fortify their political power, creating absolutist states to clamp down on domestic opposition, and pursue geopolitical interests abroad. Ironically, of course, the very effort to repress domestic opposition in the form of the absolutist state provides precisely the opportunity for revolution.

Anderson observes this process most clearly in Russia. In the early twentieth century, he argues, "there was a dislocation between the social formation and State in the last years of Tsarism. The Russian social formation was a complex ensemble dominated by the capitalist mode of production, but the Russian State remained a feudal Absolutism" (Anderson, 1974: 355, see also pp. 353, 358). Contrary to Trotsky and Lenin, who argued that the Russian Revolution was a proletarian revolution against a capitalist state, Anderson argues (1974: 359; italics in original) that:

> *The Russian Revolution was not made against a capitalist State at all*. The tsarism which fell in 1917 was a feudal apparatus: The Provisional Government never had time to replace it with a new or stable bourgeois apparatus. The Bolsheviks made a *socialist revolution*, but from beginning to end they never confronted the *central enemy* [the capitalist state] of the workers' movement in the West.

The moment of revolution is the opportunity provided by a declining class in crisis which mobilizes to extend political power against the rising commercial or industrial classes.

From such an analysis, Anderson's theoretical claims begin to emerge. Revolutions are cataclysmic events that complete the work of the rising class in wresting political power away from the dominant class of the old regime which has used the state to advance and promote, and later to protect and defend, its interests. Revolution is made possible by the disjuncture between state and society, and made necessary by the increased political repression that the ruling class will use to protect its privilege. Thus Anderson rescues a traditional Marxian explanation of the class character of revolution, by organizing the character of revolution by the character of the rising class that successfully challenges the absolutist state. "In the West, the Spanish, English, and French monarchies were defeated or overthrown by bourgeois revolutions from below; while the Italian and German principalities were eliminated by bourgeois revolutions from above." At the same time, in the East, "the Russian empire was finally destroyed by a proletarian revolution" (Anderson, 1974: 431).

Why, then do we place Anderson here, together with theorists who put the state at the center of analysis, when he explains political changes by reference to class struggle? Why is Anderson's not approach regarded as similar to that of Moore, a contemporary effort to rescue the generally Marxian notion of the class character of revolutions, bourgeois revolution in France and England, proletarian revolution in Russia? Could Anderson not be thought of as a class theorist?

Actually, Anderson grants a tremendous amount of theoretical autonomy to the state, but he does so in *pre-capitalist* social formations only. The relative autonomy of the state is a historical, not a theoretical, issue; he is interested in specifying under what historical conditions the state is the autonomous agent. In fact, he makes the political level *the* level of definition of pre-capitalist modes of production, which has important implications for his theory of revolution. Here is Anderson's argument in brief. What makes capitalism unique?

> *All* modes of production in class societies prior to capitalism extract surplus labour from the immediate producer by means of extra-economic coercion. Capitalism is the first mode of production in history in which the means whereby the surplus is pumped out of the direct producer is "purely" economic in form – the wage contract: the equal exchange between free agents which reproduces, hourly and daily, inequality and oppression. (Anderson, 1974: 403)

Prior to capitalism, Anderson suggests that "the superstructures of kinship, religion, law or the state necessarily enter into the constitutive structure of the mode of production;" that is, these non-economic relationships and institutions are the defining features of the pre-capitalist modes of production (Anderson, 1974: 403). "They intervene *directly* in the internal nexus of surplus extraction," he argues, not simply at the level of reproduction of social relations. In capitalist societies, by contrast, these non-economic levels of analysis shape only indirectly the relations of production. In this way, Anderson sums up, the "pre-capitalist mode of production cannot be defined *except* via their political, legal, and ideological superstructures, since these are what determine the type of extra-economic coercion that specifies them" (Anderson, 1974: 404). In other words, in capitalist society, the economic relations between capital and wage labor determine the non-economic levels of social life; in pre-capitalist society, these non-economic levels structure and determine the ways in which economic extraction of surplus labor occurs in the first place. The political realm determines the structure of the economic oppression.

Such an argument immediately separates Anderson from classical Marxism, which argues that the political is reducible to the economic for all modes of production. Anderson argues that Marx's error was not with his specification of the capitalist mode of production, where he was correct, but in reading the dynamics of capitalism backwards into history. Anderson insists on a historical understanding of the shifting analytic causal weights given to the economic and the political. In pre-capitalist society, the political dominates over the economic.

The implications for a theory of revolution are significant. First, the analysis of revolution must be historically grounded in these shifting valences of the political or the economic. Anderson's analysis implies a definition of revolution that is historically flexible: revolutions that *produce* a capitalist mode of production – the so-called bourgeois revolutions – are understood as political revolutions, while those revolutions that occur *within* a functioning capitalist mode of production transform economic relationships. Even there, the state is a central variable in the analysis of revolution. "Secular struggle between classes is ultimately resolved at the political – not at the economic or the cultural – level of society. In other words, it is the construction and destruction of States which seal the basic shifts in the relations of production so long as classes subsist" (Anderson, 1974: 11).

Anderson's analysis of the crises of absolutism and its implications for a theory of revolution has also been strongly criticized. Some argue that he has gone too far in characterizing the absolutist state as feudal when capitalist social relations are bubbling up underneath and spinning all around the state in the world economy (see, for example, Hechter, 1977, who resurrects Wallerstein's notion that Anderson has specified the "lineages of the capitalist state"). Others suggest that he has not gone far enough, and is still undervaluing the autonomy of the distinctly political. For example, Miliband argues that Anderson underestimates the independent initiatives of monarchs and their administrative staffs and therefore makes it hard to understand why so many nobles resisted the monarchs as long as they did (see Miliband, 1977). After all, the high nobility were among the chief opponents of absolutism in France, where they sought to limit the efforts of Richelieu, Mazarin, and Colbert to "domesticate" the aristocracy and championed provincial autonomy against the political interests of the state. Any structural analysis of the role of the state in revolutions must also embrace this type of autonomous political sphere of activity. The state generates its own ideological justifications for its actions; the term *raison d'état* expresses the ways in which political justification of political activity is disconnected from class interests. States pursue their own interests in the international economic and political arena, promoting some types of trade and constraining others, and seeking diplomatic or military confrontations with some states and avoiding those confrontations with other states. What the state's interests are in such a global sphere is based on the calculations of the policy-makers.

But Anderson pays less attention to the international level of analysis, either geopolitical / military or economic. For him, each state undergoes its experience with absolutism when the internal, domestic class forces are amenable to it. Such an explanation is ultimately historicist, deriving absolutism directly from the dynamics of the feudal mode of production and the interests of its dominant class within any specific country at a particular time. Instead, "Anderson could have systematically explained the rise of the full range of European absolutist states partly in terms of the interstate military competition and partly by exploring the varying initiatives of monarchs as autonomous actors in relation to the dominant and subordinate classes" (Fulbrook and Skocpol, 1984: 205). In particular, Anderson could have paid more attention to the distinctly political relationships between states in the European state system, to discern the ways in which land warfare on the continent shaped the political options open to specific states at any one moment. "In both East and West there were possibilities and exigencies for monarchs to create and deploy standing armies within the multicentered state system that arose out of the medieval European political parcellization" (Fulbrook and Skocpol, 1984: 205).

Absolutism was a transitional social formation, the political form of the transition from feudalism to capitalism. This economic transition from one mode of production to another did not, and could not, happen entirely at the level of production, despite the assertions of orthodox Marxist theory, but required a political vehicle, both to sweep aside many of the intransigent feudal obstacles to capitalist development and to facilitate the more rapid development of nascent capitalist forces. Absolutism accepted its political charge to protect the traditional feudal order, but its mission was contradicted by its effect: the pressing to opposition of many of the constitutive elements of that system.

Absolute monarchies were innovative monarchies, reformist monarchies, developing institutional mechanisms by which to concentrate political power, ensure domestic order, and pursue their ambitious foreign policy objectives in the name of reason of state. All had inherited medieval political institutions that were inadequate to meet the increased political and financial needs engendered by the drive to participate more actively in the international arena. The possibilities offered by the expanding international market and the omnipresent possibility of war (even when there was no overt war), fueled this drive for increased revenues. War, or the threat of war, was perhaps the single most important pressure on the monarchy, forcing kings to innovate so as to raise enough revenues to support armies that could sustain increasingly costly war efforts. Absolutist monarchies expanded the army and the administrative bureaucracy, and greatly extended both the scope and the amount of taxation, as well as developing more efficient administrative instruments to extract taxes from an increasingly recalcitrant population.

These innovations were institutional responses to the persistent fiscal crisis that characterized the history of the absolutist state. The state's resources were stretched by the economic possibilities of a burgeoning capitalist market and the demands of war; any state that did not keep pace was faced with the uncertain and unhappy future of clientage to a more powerful state. The fiscal crisis of the absolutist state was located in its insufficient fiscal resources to pursue the economic and political objectives that seemed integral to its economic growth. Any solution to the fiscal crisis engendered a crisis of legitimacy as traditional social arrangements were abridged to garner greater shares of the nation's wealth. Resolution of the fiscal crisis, then, generated political opposition – an opposition that could, and often did, gel into a revolutionary coalition that would challenge the state for political power.

Such a perspective, which I develop and apply elsewhere,[8] indicates the merits as well as some of the drawbacks of Anderson's model. Historically, many revolutions were mounted precisely against absolutist states as they attempted to resolve fiscal crises by abridging traditional privileges. But the disjuncture between the state's calculation of its interests in the name of reason of state on the one hand, and the interests of the traditional landowning aristocracy as the ruling class, on the other, suggests the mechanisms by which the ruling class often was divided in its allegiance in revolutionary upheaval, and why some elements of the hereditary nobility supported the revolutionaries against the absolutist state. Understanding revolution requires an analysis of the disjunction between the state and the ruling class *as well as* the disjunction between the state and the rising class. It also requires that the entire set of these domestic structural disjunctions be placed in a context of international geopolitical and military competition as well as international economic development.

Revolutionaries as State-builders: Skocpol's Structural Model

Perhaps the most ambitious recent theoretical attempt to integrate the state as a primary independent causal variable in the outbreak of revolution has been the work of Theda Skocpol (see Skocpol, 1976a, 1976b, 1979a; Goodwin and Skocpol 1988).[9] Skocpol's major work, *States and Social Revolutions* (1979a) develops a distinctly structural theory of revolutions in which the state occupies center stage, and its relations with the international political economy and domestic social classes structure the possibilities for state action. On the basis of an examination of three empirical cases of social revolution – France, Russia, and China – Skocpol develops a general model of revolution and offers a strong challenge to existing perspectives on revolution.

Skocpol's argument has three essential components: (1) a definition of social revolution; (2) a theory of the causes of revolution; and (3) a theory of the outcomes of revolution. Social revolutions, Skocpol writes, are defined, in part, by their outcomes as well as by their causes; they are "rapid, basic transformations of a society's state and class structures; and they are accompanied and in part carried through by class-based revolts from below" (Skocpol, 1979a: 4). There are two critical elements to this definition. First, the transformation must be both social and political; social revolutions are distinct from rebellions, revolts, and political revolutions in that social revolutions require a successful transformation not only of the polity but also of the social bases of political power. "It is this combination of thorough-going structural transformation and massive class upheaval that sets social revolutions apart from coups, rebellions, and even political revolutions and national independence movements" (Skocpol, 1976a: 175). Second, this transformation must include a popular uprising; social revolution involves more than a change engineered from above by an elite.

Skocpol argues that social revolutions are best understood from what she calls a "structural perspective," one that stresses "objective relationships and conflicts among variously situated groups and nations, rather than the interests, outlooks, or ideologies of particular actorsin revolutions" (Skocpol, 1979a: 291). The essential elements in her analysis thus involve relationships (among classes, among states, and between classes and states) and exist independently of the consciousness of the individuals who enter into these relationships. By comparing three social revolutions with each other, as well as with selected cases of non-revolutionary change or failed revolutions – England in the seventeenth century (a political revolution), Prussia in the early nineteenth century and Japan in the late 1860s (revolutions from above), and Germany in 1848 and Russia in 1905 (failed revolutions) – she identifies three stages of revolution: (1) the collapse of the old regime state; (2) the mass mobilization of the peasantry into class-based uprisings; and (3) the reconsolidation of state power by a new elite. At each stage specific structural factors directly determine social outcomes.

Revolutions begin, Skocpol argues, with the weakening or outright collapse of the existing state structure. The state collapses not because of revolutionary action from within (this *follows*, rather than precedes, state collapse) but because of several structural pressures:

> Imperial states become caught in cross pressures between intensified military competition or intrusions from abroad and constraints imposed on monarchical responses by the existing agrarian class structures and political institutions . . .
> Their existing structures made it impossible for them to meet the particular military exigencies that each had to face. (Skocpol, 1979a: 285)

In other words, revolutions occur in relatively backward states faced with a crisis engendered by military or economic competition with stronger states in the context of unevenly developed international economic and political systems. Skocpol emphasizes military defeat and territorial overextension as the geopolitical forces that exert pressure on old regime states, while economic competition within an unevenly developing capitalist world economy exerts economic pressure. These international forces set the political processes in motion.

One of the important implications here is the centrality of political variables over economic variables in the causes of revolution. The conditions that give rise to revolutions are

> *political* contradictions centered in the structure and situation of states caught in cross-pressures between, on the one hand, military competitors on the international scene and, on the other hand, the constraints of the existing domestic economy and (in some cases) resistance by internal politically powerful class forces to efforts by the state to mobilize resources to meet international competition. (Skocpol and Trimberger, 1977: 104)

Note here that even domestic class forces are set in motion by political activity geared to the global arena.

Skocpol further specifies the structural origins of social revolutions by pointing to her three empirical cases and generalizing from them. All three, she argues, were ''agrarian bureaucracies'' situated in international fields dominated by more economically advanced nations. Agrarian bureaucracy denotes ''an agricultural society in which social control rests on a division of labor and a coordination of effort between a semi-bureaucratic state and a landed upper class'' (Skocpol, 1976a: 177). Even more specifically, these were large, agrarian capitalist societies dominated by top-heavy state machines which were losing out in the international sphere to more tactically mobile and more advanced *capitalist* nations. The pressure on the old regime state is enormous; it must either industrialize and commercialize or go under, becoming a client state to the more advanced nations.

Confronted with military collapse and/or fiscal crisis, one option allows the state to seek to strengthen itself through relevant reforms, such as ending the tax privileges of the upper classes or acquiring direct control over the agricultural surplus. How successful these reform efforts are depends in turn on two other structural relationships. The first is the role played by the landed upper class in national government. If the upper class maintains a powerful collective, autonomous presence (for example through bodies such as the Parlement of Paris), it can block reforms successfully, and the resulting conflict between the upper class and the state can immobilize the repressive and administrative capacity of the state. If the upper class is either uninvolved in national politics or integrated into it in a way that makes it wholly dependent on the state, the upper class can therefore not block reforms. The second structural relationship has to do with whether or not agricultural class relations allow for high productivity. The higher the potential productivity, the better the state's chances of weathering its crisis.

If international tensions are modest, if the landed upper class is politically weak, and if agricultural relations are suitable for high productivity, the state can enact reforms from above and overcome the crisis (for example Prussia in the early 1800s and Japan in the 1860s). If the crisis is severe (Russia in 1917), if the landed class is strong on the national level (France and China), and/or if agricultural class relations are resistant to increases in productivity (France, Russia, and China), the state cannot resolve its crisis. A combination of state crisis and upper-class insurrection immobilizes the state and opens the way for mass uprisings. These conditions for political crisis are summarized in table 6.1.

Political crisis is necessary for revolution, but it is not sufficient on its own. Social revolutions arise from a conjuncture of political crisis and widespread peasant revolt aimed at the landed upper class. The potential for peasant revolt in turn is determined by another set of structural factors: the degree of peasant autonomy and solidarity and the local strength of the upper class. "Historically, mass-based social revolutions from below have successfully occurred only if the breakdown of old regime state organizations has happened in an agrarian sociopolitical context where peasants, as the majority, producing class, possess (or obtain) sufficient local economic and political autonomy to revolt against landlords" (Skocpol and Trimberger, 1977: 109). (Note here the divergence from Paige's claim that an immiserated peasantry is most easily mobilized for revolutionary behavior). Peasant uprisings are likely (a) when the peasant community is strong and the

Table 6.1   *Conditions for political crisis*

	Monarchy / dominant class	Agrarian-economy	International pressures
France	Landed-commercial dominant class has leverage within semi-bureaucratic absolute monarchy	Growing, but no breakthrough to capitalist agriculture	Moderate. Repeated defeats in wars, especially due to competition from England
Russia	Highly bureaucratic absolutist state; landed nobility has little political power	Extensive growth; little development in core regions	Extreme. Defeats in 1850s and 1905. Prolonged participation and defeat in First World War
China	Landed-commercial dominant class has leverage within semi-bureaucratic absolutist state	No developmental breakthrough; near limits of growth, given population and available land	Strong. Defeats in wars and imperialist
Contrasts			
Prussia / Germany	Highly bureaucratic absolutist state; landed nobility has little extra-local political leverage	Transition to capitalist agriculture	1806 – Strong 1848 – Mild
Japan	Highly bureaucratic (though not fully centralized) state. No true landed upper class	Productivity increasing within traditional structures	Strong. Imperialist intrusions
England	No bureaucratic state. Landed class dominates politics	Transition to capitalist agriculture	Mild

Source: Skocpol (1979a: 155), *States and Social Revolutions*. New York: Cambridge University Press.

peasants have some economic and political autonomy, and (b) when landlords lack direct economic and political control at the local level.

In both France and Russia peasants owned a substantial proportion of the land and lived in cohesive, self-governing communities, while the landed upper class did not directly control either production or the local administrative or coercive apparatus. The collapse of the state thus left a peasantry capable of organized insurrection against a landed upper class incapable of stopping them. In China, where the peasant community was weak and the

Table 6.2 *Conditions for peasant insurrection*

	Agrarian class structures	Local politics
France	Peasant smallholders own 30–40% of land; work 80% + in small plots. Individual property established, but peasant community opposes seigneurs, who collect dues	Villages relatively autonomous under supervision of royal officials
Russia	Peasants own 60% + and rent more; control process of production on small plots; pay rents and redemption payments. Strong community based upon collective ownership	Villages sovereign under control of tsarist bureaucracy
China	Peasants own 50% + and work virtually all land in small plots. Pay rents to gentry. No peasant community	Gentry landlords, usurers, and literati dominant local organizational life; cooperate with imperial officials
Contrasts Prussia/ Germany	West of Elbe: resembles France. East of Elbe: large estates worked by laborers and peasants with tiny holdings, and no strong communities	Junker landlords are local agents of bureaucratic state; dominate local administration and policing
Japan	Communities dominated by rich peasants	Strong bureaucratic controls over local communities
England	Landed class owns 70% + . Peasantry polarizing between yeomen farmers and agricultural laborers. No strong peasant community	Landlords are local agents of monarchy; dominate administration and policing

Source: Skocpol (1979a: 156), *States and Social Revolutions*. New York: Cambridge University Press.

local landlord power strong, the collapse of the Manchu state did not lead directly to a successful peasant uprising; this occurred decades later when the peasants had been organized and local landlord power broken by the Chinese Communist Party (CCP). The conditions for peasant insurrection are summarized in table 6.2.

These two sets of structural antecedents – political crisis and agrarian class struggle resulting in peasant uprising – produce the revolutionary situation in which formerly marginal elites reconstitute state power along new lines.

Preconditions of revolution

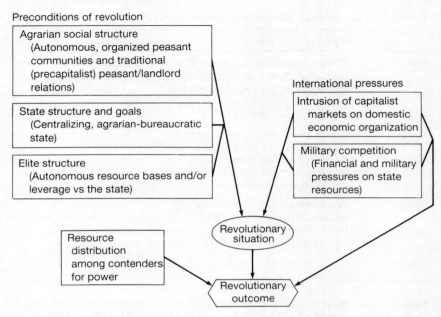

Figure 6.1   Schematic model of Skocpol's analysis of revolution.   *Source*: Goldstone (1980).

This can be seen in figure 6.1, which summarizes the causes of revolution according to Skocpol.

Once the state has been weakened and peasant uprisings have occurred, the main activity of revolution is the reconsolidation of state power by a previously marginal political elite. The general outcome of revolution is the creation of a stronger, more bureaucratic, more highly centralized state. Revolutions are caused by the collapse of the state, and they are completed by the construction of larger, more power states. State cause revolutions, Skocpol seems to argue, and revolutions ''cause'' states.

The way that state power is reconsolidated, as well as the fate of the would-be political leaders, depends on the structural opportunities available in each case. In this sense, the old regime leaves ''legacies'' to the post-revolutionary state-builders (see Skocpol, 1976b). The relatively developed industry of Russia, for example, provided an urban base for the reconsolidation of power not available in either France or China. Because power had previously been so centralized, everything crumbled when the tsarist regime did, and the Bolsheviks needed no mass base to seize power. The autonomy of the peasantry, in fact, made them an unlikely mass power base, and also insured that post-revolutionary developments depended more on the city than the countryside. In China, the lack of an indigenous peasant organization provided a rural base not available in either France or Russia. Without as strongly centralized a political power, and without an industrial base as developed as Russia's, the Chinese case offered no such urban possibilities, either for the Kuomintang or the CCP. Thus the Bolsheviks rooted themselves successfully in the cities, the CCP in the countryside and the Jacobins in neither. The dynamics of reconsolidation of state power can be seen in table 6.3.

In recent work, Skocpol has turned her attention to the dynamics of revolutions in the contemporary Third World (see Goodwin and Skocpol, 1988). Here, Goodwin and Skocpol argue that the occurrence of revolution can be predicted by the type of state that exists and its relationship to social classes. Specifically, they argue that "revolutionary movements . . . typically coalesce in opposition to 'closed' or 'exclusionary' as well as organizationally weak (or weakened) authoritarian regimes" (Goodwin and Skocpol, 1988: 13). In such situations, economic grievances of excluded groups can quickly become politicized. As Seymour Martin Lipset writes (quoted by Goodwin and Skocpol, 1988: 15):

> The exclusion of workers from the fundamental political rights of citizenship effectively fuse[s] the struggle for political and economic equality and cast[s] that struggle in a radical mold. Where the right to combine in the labor market

Table 6.3   *Outcomes of revolutions*

France	1787–9: Breakdown of absolutist state; and widespread peasant revolts against seigneurial claims
Russia	1860s–1890s: Bureucratic reforms from above 1905: Unsuccessful revolutionary outbreak 1917: Dissolution of state; widespread peasant revolts against all private landed property
China	1911: Breakdown of imperial state; spreading agrarian disorder, but no autonomous revolts by peasants against landlords
Contrasts	
Prussia/ Germany	1807–14: Bureaucratic reforms from above 1848: Failed social revolution; bureaucratic monarchy stays in power
Japan	Political revolution centralizes state; followed by bureaucratic reforms from above
England	Political revolution establishes parliamentary predominance within non-bureaucratic monarchy

Source: Skocpol (1979a: 157), *States and Social Revolutions*. New York: Cambridge University Press.

[is] severely restricted . . . the decision to act in politics is forced on trade unions. Whether they [like] it or not, unions [must become] political institutions; they [have] first to change the distribution of political power within the state before they [can] effectively exert power in the market.

In addition, closed authoritarian regimes provide a common enemy and a highly visible focus of opposition, and have a tendency to radicalize or at least neutralize moderate reform-minded groups who might have competed with revolutionary leaders. Thus, Goodwin and Skocpol conclude, the "*ideal* formula for the growth of a broad revolutionary coalition is a repressive authoritarian regime which does not thoroughly penetrate and control its entire territory or its borders; or else what was once an effectively repressive state that suddenly weakens in these respects" (Goodwin and Skocpol, 1988: 17).

This is not to say that Goodwin and Skocpol completely reduce revolutionary outcome to the type of state, and give no weight to the strength of the opposition. Such a position would be akin to Huntington's non-structuralist political theory, which held that revolutions take place in either "highly centralized monarchies," in "narrowly based military dictatorships," or in "colonial regimes" (Huntington, 1968: 275). Goodwin and Skocpol suggest that it is the type of state *and the class base of its rule* (for example its relationship with the ruling class) that determines the revolutionary event and outcome:

revolutionaries are most likely to succeed where and when civil society *as a whole* may be mobilized against an autonomous and narrowly based colonial or "Bonapartist" regime . . . By contrast, when civil society is polarized and revolutionaries confront a state with a significant social base – even if that base is principally the upper and middle classes – then success is much more difficult. Furthermore, if a state traditionally dominated by economic elites can incorporate at least some popular sectors or organizations, then success becomes more difficult still. (Goodwin and Skocpol, 1988: 29)

Thus they argue that "the structures of states and armies, as well as the political relations between states and various sectors of society, provide the analytic keys to explaining revolutions in the Third World" (Goodwin and Skocpol, 1988: 31).

These three dimensions of state-society relations – level of inclusion, bureaucratization, and penetration into civil society, can be seen clearly in figure 6.2.

This summary of Skocpol's argument, and its contemporary extension, suggests its resolute structuralism, and its systematic effort to avoid recourse to voluntarist factors, as well as its location of the state squarely in the center of analysis. The main fruit of Skocpol's work is a new perspective on revolu-

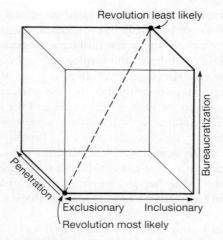

Figure 6.2 Likelihood of revolution as a function of type of state structure: a graphic representation of states according to degrees of (1) penetration (of national territory), (2) incorporation (of socially mobilized groups), and (3) bureaucratization (of the state administration and the armed forces). *Source*: Goodwin and Skocpol (1988: 38).

tion. This perspective has three components: (1) a distinctive set of general principles for studying revolution, which logically imply (2) a critique of Marx's (and, by extension, any class-based) theory of revolution, which in turn provides the basis for (3) a drastic rethinking of the nature of revolution in the contemporary advanced capitalist world. I shall examine each of these in turn.

As Skocpol notes, "three major principles of analysis" underlie her work: first, a "non-voluntarist, structural perspective" on the causes and processes of revolution; second, a "systematic reference to international structures and world-historical developments" and third, a conception of states "as administrative and coercive organizations . . . that are potentially auto-nomous from (though conditioned by) socioeconomic interests and structures (Skocpol, 1979a: 14). These principles are formulated in self-conscious opposition to four prevailing models of revolution: Marx's theory of self-conscious movements rooted in class conflict; the "political conflict" approach of Charles Tilly,[10] the aggregate social psychological models of Ted Gurr, and the value-system consensus models of Parsons and Chalmers Johnson. All of these models, according to Skocpol, overemphasize the voluntarist elements in revolution, ignore the international context, and undervalue the autonomy of the state. These pointed critiques are especially aimed at Marxism.

Skocpol's resolute anti-voluntarism is based on several observations. She claims that revolutions are not made by conscious actors; they happen. They are not caused or even begun by revolutionary vanguards, with (or even without) an organized, mobilized, and ideologically imbued mass following. They arise from certain structural conditions: a political-military crisis in conjunction with certain relationships between the peasantry and the landed upper class, and between the landed upper class and the state. Second, she argues that actors in revolutionary situation are not always clear about what they want; their motives are often complex and ill-formulated. Third, even when some revolutionary actors have clear aims, the outcomes of revolution are often at variance with those aims: although revolutionary groups in all three revolutions studied by Skocpol sought to reduce or limit the extent of state power, each in fact created a new, more centralized and more powerful state.

We can more easily understand this argument if we think metaphorically. Skocpol uses the metaphor of a structurally unsound bridge to represent the old regime state structure. The bridge forms a link between domestic institutions and transnational economic or geopolitical institutions, but cracked, weak and overextended as it is, a heavier truck than usual (that is, more advanced social forces) puts increasing pressure on it. Eventually the bridge collapses under this new weight. In the resulting power vacuum, a new group of engineers builds a structurally sound bridge that will be more resistant to environmental erosion and can accommodate additional weight.

All three of Skocpol's central arguments make a great deal of sense, and they clearly point to a conclusion we reached in our discussion of earlier non-structural theories of revolution: an analysis of ideology and organized, self-conscious social action is not alone sufficient for understanding revolution. Skocpol, however, goes even further in her actual analysis. In effect, she argues that these voluntarist elements are not even necessary for understanding revolution. Consciousness and conscious social action play an ambiguous role in her analysis: they are there, but she does her best to ignore them.

Skocpol's insistence on transnational relations and world historical developments is also a significant departure from Marxism, and here she finds herself in the company of analysts such as Wallerstein, Collins, and Weber. Revolution, she argues, does not arise simply from the contradictions and conflicts internal to a society. The path of revolution is shaped partly by the opportunities and requirements of the historical moment, and partly by reference to transnational structures and institutions and world historical events. For example, the Chinese revolutionaries already had the historical example of the Bolshevik revolution from which to draw inspiration and information, while the Bolsheviks obviously did not. Revolutions are also shaped by relations between states. Skocpol argues that underlying all social revolutions is the 'internationally uneven spread of capitalist economic development and nation-state formation'' (Skocpol, 1979a: 19). Revolutions occur ''only in countries situated in disadvantaged positions within international arenas'' (Skocpol, 1979a: 23).

Though Skocpol's analysis bears a surface resemblance to Wallerstein's world system model, Skocpol is also departing from Wallerstein's model in significant ways. Skocpol is not saying that revolutions occur in countries on the periphery or semi-periphery of the world capitalist system. Her position is more complex. Following Hintze, she holds that there are two international systems, a capitalist economic system and a nation-state system, neither of which is wholly reducible to the other. Indeed, she argues that although ''uneven economic development always lies in the background, developments within the international state system as such . . . have directly contributed to virtually all outbreaks of revolutionary crises'' (Skocpol, 1979a: 23). So the French revolutionary crisis was precipitated by decades of political-military competition with England, the Chinese by western imperialist intrusion and defeat by Japan, and the Russian by the First World War.

Skocpol's emphasis on the independent role of the international state system leads naturally to her third general principle. She objects to the view that political structures and struggles can be reduced to socioeconomic forces or conflicts, or that the state is simply an arena in which social conflicts are fought. Instead, she argues, the state must be seen as an autonomous structure with its own logic and interests – a set of administrative, policing, and military organizations headed, and more or less coordinated by, an executive authority'' (Skocpol, 1979: 29). While she notes that it is true that ''states are greatly constrained by economic conditions and partly shaped and influenced by class forces, nevertheless, state structures and activities also have an underlying integrity and a logic of their own, and these are keyed to the dynamics of international military rivalries and to the geo-political as well as world economic circumstances in which given states find themselves'' (Skocpol and Trimberger, 1977: 107). In addition, she argues that the power of the state must be treated as a crucial independent factor in revolution.

This notion of state autonomy is very different from arguments made by either world system theorists or class theorists, and it has important implications for the study of revolution. Both world system and class models eventually explain state action by reference to another level of analysis. Even neo-Marxists, who follow Marx's analysis of the state in *The Eighteenth Brumaire*, argue that the autonomy of the state from direct class control by the dominant class makes the state more able to preserve the existing mode of production and thus protect the interests of the dominant class in the longer run. The state is seen still in terms of the class interests it serves. Skocpol, by contrast, sees the state primarily as a separate set of institutions, though she, of course, acknowledges their connections with socioeconomic forces.

The state appears as the main actor in Skocpol's account of revolution; the origins, processes, and results of revolution are portrayed largely in political terms. Revolutions begin with a breakdown of the state apparatus, which is shaped not by class struggle, but by relations between the state and both the dominant class and other states; the revolutionary process involves the building of new state forms, an effort in which class struggles are important but not central; revolutions end with the consolidation of new state power. This last point is particularly important; for Skocpol, the central result of revolution is not a more advanced mode of production but a more centralized, mass-incorporating bureaucratic state.

As Skocpol notes, her emphasis on the autonomy of the state goes well beyond virtually all Marxist theory. Her focus on the relations between the state and the various social classes, moreover, separates her from Weber, whose main concern was the relations within the state between rulers and their staffs. Finally, her stress on the uniformity of both the cause and the outcome of all three revolutions goes against the neo-Marxist tendency of Moore's class theory, dependency and world system theory, and others who pointed to several different trajectories towards modernity. The categories "early," "late," and "dependent" development thus have no place in Skocpol's analysis, as France ("early"), Russia ("late"), and China ("dependent" in a sense) manifest to her eyes similarities rather than differences.

Her approach is not without its theoretical antecedents, though they are scarcely acknowledged. Hovering just out of sight at every point in her argument is the spirit of Tocqueville. Indeed, one might say that Skocpol reintroduces Tocqueville to a contemporary theory of revolution by incorporating his ideas into a framework generally sympathetic to Marxism. Like Tocqueville, Skocpol is concerned with the relations between the state as an autonomous institution and society. Like Tocqueville, she sees growing political centralization and autonomy as *the* consequences of revolution. (Her general assessment of the French Revolution follows that of Tocqueville's *The Old Regime and the French Revolution*.) Also like Tocqueville, she presents the irony of revolutions made in the name of freedom but culminating in a much strengthened state.

In bringing Tocqueville in, Skocpol has not ushered Marx out. The two are hardly incompatible, and Skocpol does a good job of combining a Tocquevillian approach to the state with a Marxian conception of "class relations as rooted in the control of productive property and the appropriation of economic surpluses from direct producers and nonproducers" (Skocpol,

1979a: 13). At the same time, however, Skocpol does challenge the specific Marxian theory of revolution, and her own account is at odds with it at every major point. There is, she argues, a "lack of fit between Marx's theory of revolutions and the actual historical pattern of social revolutions" (Skocpol, 1979a: 292).

Skocpol's very selection of cases crosscuts Marxian categories: the French case, a bourgeois revolution in Marxist terms, is lumped together with socialist revolutions in Russia and China. Her intellectual journey goes in a direction counter to the conventional, in effect interpreting the Russian revolution in terms of the Chinese, and the French in terms of the Russian, rather than the more common opposite approach. She thus begins – and stays – with a very different image of revolution: the marker revolution is China not France, not "western bourgeois revolution," but "agrarian bureaucratic revolution." Thus it is not surprising that most of the categories central to conventional Marxian analysis are absent from Skocpol's book. Revolutions, according to her analysis, do not arise from a contradiction between the forces of production and the relations of production in a society. They arise from a state crisis conditioned by the state's position in international political and economic systems and by its relation to the dominant social class.

From Marx's position, revolutions are made by more or less self-conscious rising social classes, and these rising classes give their name and character to the revolutionary events themselves – the bourgeoisie in the case of bourgeois revolutions, and the proletariat in the case of proletarian or socialist revolutions. These classes combat the dominant social classes and the pre-existing mode of production. And what they portend is a new mode of production. In Skocpol's analysis, nothing of the sort happens. Not only are rising classes not the major agents of revolution, but sometimes they are not even present as distinct social classes at all (for example the bourgeoisie in France in 1789). Instead of rising social classes, we find peasant uprisings, conflict between the landed upper class and the state, and marginal elite movements.

The Marxian perspective on revolution generally gives some role to a "vanguard party" in the making of socialist revolution – whether the relatively ambiguous role of the *Communist Manifesto* or the quite clear role given the party in Lenin's analysis. In contrast, "vanguard parties" do not appear in Skocpol's analysis at all; instead we find "marginal elites" struggling for state power. This difference is important: To call a political group a "vanguard party" implies that it has a natural or unproblematic relation to a revolutionary social class. To call it a "marginal elite" suggests that this relation is less immediate, more problematic. Marginal elites may mobilize particular social classes in their efforts to consolidate state power, but they are not, by definition, the representatives or partisans of those classes. Vanguard parties are understood in terms of the class interests and the wider social goals they pursue; marginal elites in terms of their immediate activity, consolidating state power. In short, although, "vanguard party" and "marginal elite" may be used to refer to the same political group, the latter term implies a more critical approach to that group's goals and social base.

Finally, the "withering away of the state" is central to the Marxian conception of revolution. Since the state is the "organized power of one class for oppressing another" in Marx's view, the abolition of classes necessarily means the gradual disappearance of the state. In Skocpol's analysis, far from withering away, the state flourishes after a revolution, whether capitalist or socialist.

If we accept Skocpol's model, then we must rethink entirely the approach to revolution that has dominated western social science since the mid-nineteenth century. Marx's model allowed us to draw analogies between the bourgeois revolutions of the past and the socialist revolution of the future. Just as capitalism emerged from a contradiction between productive forces and feudal social relations, so socialism would emerge from a contradiction between productive forces and capitalist social relations. Just as capitalism was built by a rising bourgeoisie, so socialism would be built by a rising proletariat. As Marx remarked in the *Communist Manifesto*, the two processes involved a "similar movement." The past is necessary prologue to the future, as well as the future's central metaphor.

Skocpol's model of revolution destroys any possibility of such analogies: the revolutions of the past simply do not provide relevant models for revolution in advanced capitalist societies, although they may yield some insights into contemporary Third World societies' potential for revolution, as we have seen. Unlike the old regime states studied by Skocpol, the advanced capitalist state is hardly in a disadvantaged position in international economic and political arenas. Previous revolutions, therefore, do not provide any direct model for the ways in which an initial political crisis could develop. At the same time, if the advanced capitalist state is relatively autonomous, as current theories of the state claim, the upper class should be unable to block the state from enacting the reforms necessary for weathering its crisis. Thus previous revolutions do not provide a model for exacerbation of the initial state crisis by successful internal resistance. Advanced capitalist societies also lack any producing class with the economic and political autonomy of the French and Russian peasantries. Hence previous revolutions do not provide a model for the structural conditions that might generate a mass uprising and turn an exacerbated state crisis into a social revolution. Most important, the revolutions of the past resulted in the rise of strong, bureaucratic, centralized states – their outcomes in this respect directly contradicting the ideals of the revolutionaries. Thus they do not provide a model for transformation of the strong, bureaucratic, centralized states already existing in the advanced capitalist societies. Instead, they provide a cautionary tale, an admonition.

None of this implies that major progressive social change is impossible in the advanced capitalist societies. It merely suggests that such change must be of a quite different nature from the revolutions of the past and, thus, that the past cannot provide much of a positive model. Skocpol in effect urges us to stop aping the past and get on with transforming the present. Marx once said that "the social revolution of the nineteenth century cannot draw its poetry from the past but only from the future." Skocpol's work reveals that Marx drew his revolutionary prescriptions precisely from where he cautioned one from looking. What is more, by reading her analysis chronologically backwards from China to Russia to France, she argues and demonstrates how the same admonition ought be true for the twentieth century.

The Limits of Skocpol's Structural Perspective

Skocpol has much to tell us about revolution, and the implications of her work are both stimulating and unsettling. There is a curious problem of historical causation at times, however, in which successful revolutions and unsuccessful revolutions seem to come from utterly different sources. She writes that "successful social revolutions probably emerge from different macro-structural and historical contexts than do either failed social revolutions or political transformations that are not accompanied by transformations of class relations" (Skocpol, 1979a: 5). Not only is the outcome incorporated into the definition of revolution, then, but it becomes the *post-hoc* vehicle to explain the success of the revolution itself. (See Walton, 1984, for an elaboration of this point.)

Most centrally, there is one striking gap in her approach, which is rooted in the general analytic principles and which in turn underlies several of the substantive problems in her work: although she has a great deal to say about the causes and consequences of revolution (and the correlations between them), she devotes scant space to the *process* of revolution, to how human beings actually make a revolution.

This omission arises directly from her insistence on a structural perspective with no admixture of voluntarism. Because of her uncompromising stand against voluntarism, Skocpol forgets that human beings, thinking and acting, (however haphazardly), are the mediating link between structural conditions and social outcomes. Structural conditions moreover, do not dictate absolutely what humans do; they merely place certain limits on

human action or define a certain range of possibilities. Within the revolutionary moment, there is more than one potential outcome, the one that
actually occurs. That outcome x did result from structural conditions, a, b,
and c does not logically mean that outcomes y or z were not possible.
"Structure and situation interact, and determine the limits of decision and
action; but what determines the possibilities of action is primarily situation"
according to Hobsbawm (1975: 12). Structural conditions may define the
possibilities for mass uprisings or the options available for consolidating state
power in a revolutionary situation, but they do not fully explain how particular groups act, what options they pursue, or what possibilities they realize.
Here is the nineteenth-century French historian, Michelet, writing about the
moment of revolution in France in 1789: "On that day everything was
possible . . . the future was present . . . that is to say time was no more, all a
lightning flash of eternity." Talk about outcomes not being inevitably
contained in structural antecedents!

In short, even if Skocpol is correct about the relationships between
structural conditions and revolutionary outcomes, her analysis is incomplete.
She ignores the mediating factors – human consciousness and action – that
are always part of the story and sometimes crucial to it. Or, more precisely,
she simply assumes that the appropriate actors are always there, waiting to
perform the role required by the structural conditions: peasants ever ready to
make massive uprisings and marginal elites ever able to reconsolidate political
power. She rarely regards their response to structural conditions as
problematic, and thus systematically undervalues the role of ideology, political organization, and self-conscious social action.

This gap in her analysis manifests itself at different points in her argument,[11] but it is especially crucial in two instances: the peasant uprising in
China and the role of the Bolsheviks in Russia. Skocpol argues that the degree
of peasant autonomy/community and the extent of local landlord power
determine the potential for peasant uprisings, but she leaves little room in
her analysis for the ideological and organizational factors that actualize this
potential. The omission undoubtedly mars her analysis of all three revolutions, but it is particularly glaring in the case of China. Structural conditions
there were *not* wholly ripe for a peasant uprising, which did not occur until
peasants had been organized by the CCP. In other words, the self-conscious
activity of an organized revolutionary group was crucial – a fact which
Skocpol discusses but the implications of which for her structural perspective
she ignores. if the CCP played a central role in the peasant uprisings,
however, we must ask how they turned the historical trick. Through what
combination of ideology and organization did they create a mass rising in
unpromising structural conditions? The very "voluntarist" factors that
Skocpol seeks to play down become quite important.

Skocpol also argues that structural opportunities determine how state power is reconsolidated after the revolution. She seems to assume, however, that given a set of structural conditions, the reconsolidation is more or less automatic. The case of Russia in particular is problematic in this regard and raises questions that force us beyond a structural perspective. Granted that the developed urban industrial world of tsarist Russia created a potential base for reconsolidation of political power that was available to neither the French Jacobins nor the CCP in China, how did the Bolsheviks manage to take advantage of the opportunity? We cannot simply assume that a group capable of doing so just happened to exist. What ideological and organizational resources allowed the Bolsheviks to survive through all those lean years prior to 1917 and to capitalize on the possibilities created by the conditions in Russia? Successful realization of these possibilities required a distinctive ideology, one that justified the importance of immediate revolutionary action from an urban base. A group whose ideology stressed waiting for the fuller development of capitalism, or placed an emphasis on the peasantry as the revolutionary class simply would not have had the proper orientation for reconsolidating power successfully. In other words, in the Russia Revolution, the specific ideology of the Bolsheviks was an important factor in its own right in determining the future.

Skocpol's analysis takes us a long way from non-structuralist, voluntarist theories of revolution, and she holds the autonomy of the state to be a central construct, so that the state is not reduced to another level of analysis – either international or domestic class struggle. While she at times overemphasizes the autonomy of the state, and underemphasizes the independent causal role of ideology and culture, she has established the structural foundations of a theory of revolution. What is still missing, of course, stems from her anti-voluntarism: an analysis of people's motivations to participate in revolution, a social psychology of revolution. The specification of a social psychology of revolution from *within* a structural analysis of revolution (as opposed to *instead of* a structural analysis, as in the work of Gurr or other social psychologists) is the chief contribution of the work of Charles Tilly, to whom we shall turn in the next chapter.

7

Motivation and Mobilization: A Structural Social Psychology of Revolution

---

> I hate those absolute systems which make all the events of history depend on great first causes linked to each other by a chain of fate and which thus, so to speak, omit men from the history of mankind. To my mind, they seem narrow under their pretense of broadness, and false beneath their air of mathematical exactness.
>
> Alexis de Tocqueville

From Motivation to Mobilization: A Contextual Social Psychology of Revolution

Structural theories of revolution, whether they stress the causal role of the international system, class relations at the level of production, or the state, are important and necessary correctives to the analytic poverty of non-structural theories that stress social disorganization, system breakdown, or eruption of discontent. Structural theories make clear that social conflict is the analytic center of gravity for social theory, and that this conflict – between different classes, between classes and the state, between different states, and between different classes within a transnational economic arena – forms the starting-point for theories of social order as well as of revolution. But though structural theories can take our inquiry far, they stop short of completely explaining revolutions because they leave out several crucial elements.

In a resolute effort to avoid psychologizing revolution, many structural theorists leave out human beings altogether. States collapse, classes struggle, states are rebuilt, with nary an analytic thought for the people who actually carry out this work. As one historian put it:

It is not that men's motives are unimportant; they indeed make events, including revolutions. But the purposes of men, especially in revolution, are so numerous, so varied, and so contradictory that their complex interaction produces results that no one intended or could even foresee. It is this interaction and these results that recent historians are referring to when they speak so disparagingly of these "underlying determinants" and "impersonal and inexorable forces" bringing on the Revolution. Historical explanation which does not account for these "forces," which, in other words, relies simply on understanding the conscious intentions of the actors, will thus be limited. (Wood, 1973: 129)

Perhaps, however, the effort to take these forces into account has propelled the theoretical pendulum too far in the other direction, too far away from motives and emotions. Surely, the remarkable variety, number, and incoherence of these motives would make them an even more important subject for sociological scrutiny. Human agency is essential to the phenomenon of revolution, and sociological analysis that fails to take into account the experiences and motives of the actors themselves, however complex, varied, or contradictory, will also be limited. "Even in its most sociological moments, history cannot neglect the drama of personality and chance," Crane Brinton wrote (cited in Bell, 1973: 129–30). People may not make history exactly as they please, but people do make history. We need to recognize and build our theories around, an understanding that "social phenomena are, on the one hand, man-made and man-changeable, and on the other, occur within tremendously powerful and pervasive social structures" (Urry, 1973: 181). The effort to place structural relationships and institutions at the center of analysis has left people out in the cold. What is needed is an understanding of *mobilization* not motivation, a contextually situated social psychology that relies on the interplay of social structural contexts for collective action.

Perhaps the undervaluation of a revolutionary psychology in structural models stems from the de-emphasis that structural theories place on the *process* of revolution. Structural theories tell us much about the causes of revolution or the consequences of revolution, but rarely do they investigate the revolutionary process itself. Granted, most structural theories seek to avoid the serious drawbacks that "natural history" models tend to display, and thereby downplay the events themselves, except in so far as one can observe during the revolutions the seeds of the consolidation of the post-revolutionary social order. But "nothing is inevitable in the birth or the course of revolution" and the failure to examine the process itself blinds the analyst to the trajectories not taken, the possibilities contained in the revolutionary moment rather than the inevitable outcomes (Leiden and Schmitt, 1968: 73).

It could be argued that natural history theories of revolution also downplay the sponteneity of the revolutionary process, that seeking for indicators that the revolution has passed from one stage to another also blinds those theorists to the possibilities contained within any particular moment in the revolution. These possibilities, such as the revolutionary sections in Paris during the first years of the revolution, or the factory councils in revolutionary Petrograd, or the Leveller organizations in mid-seventeenth-century London, are "spontaneous organs of the people," always emerging "during the revolution itself," springing "from the people as spontaneous organs of action and of order" (Arendt, 1965: 253, 275). These social movements, or even small groups, articulate radically new visions of social reconstruction, and contain "an entirely new form of government, with a new public space for freedom which was constituted and organized during the course of the revolution itself" (Arendt, 1965: 253). Though these movements may not succeed, they leave lasting legacies for future dissidents who seek models for the future from the failures of the past. They cannot be left out of the analysis of revolutions, any more than we can leave out the study of revolutions that fail if we want to understand why some revolutions succeed.

What is central, then, is that the process of revolution creates structural possibilities for transformation that were not present prior to the outbreak of the revolution. "What the revolutions brought to the fore was the experience of being free," writes Hannah Arendt (1965: 26–7). Revolution "transforms a concrete situation of oppression by establishing the process of liberation," adds Paulo Freire (1972: 31). Revolutionary outcomes cannot be calculated solely from structural antecedents; even if these processes of liberation are foiled, they must be taken into account.

The undervaluation of human agency is also fed by structural theorists' minimization of culture and ideology as motivating forces. But culture is essential because it provides an ideational foundation for the structures and institutions that interact to form revolutionary crises in structural theories. Revolution "does not follow spontaneously from the system of under-development or the machination of the state. It is only as these interact with the cultural practice that political consciousness finds its theme and expressive vehicle. Revolutionary movements are successfully organized in proportion to the strength and relative unity of their cultural bases" (Walton, 1984: 156). Collins recognizes this problem when he notes that the "revolutionary downfall of a state is due not simply to economic difficulties or disintegration of its military apparatus in defeat, but also to its loss of legitimacy" (Collins, 1986: 164). *Things* (states, class power, world economic or military position) do not simply fall apart, as Yeats had it; people must cease believing in the legitimacy of the things of the old regime.

Cultural questions inevitably involve values, a socially derived morality that people apply to the institutions and structures which exert such inexorable power over their lives. These values involve a culture's traditional way of life, a way of life that is threatened by the substantive social changes augured by the development of institutions such as the state, classes, or the world economy. Far from being necessarily a retardant of social change, tradition, culture, and values may propel a people towards revolutionary challenge, as I will argue below. Cultural morality is applied to matters both temporal and spiritual; that domination that inheres in structural arrangements must appear to be legitimate by reference to some system of values (or that system must be so powerful and repressive that it need not seek legitimacy, although such systems may be as vulnerable to revolutionary upheaval as they are seemingly omnipotent). Political theorist John Dunn makes this moral capacity central to his understanding of revolutionary timing:

> A revolution happens, then, when a set of revolutionaries with quite complex ideas succeed in arousing in vast masses of men already deeply discontented with the prevailing order a sufficient sense of their own superior political and moral capacity to justify the masses in struggling to destroy the prevailing political (and to some degree social) order and to replace it with the political control of the revolutionaries. (Dunn, 1972: 15)

At least some people must want the state to collapse or hope that class conflict will erupt into full-scale violence.

Downplaying human agency also downplays the role of the individual as historical actor. This unfortunate research strategy may make some sense when one is examining social institutions, but the capacity of individuals to act, to make strategic choices, and to influence one another are all especially salient during revolutionary upheavals. Particularly, how could we understand the important role that charismatic leaders have played in revolutionary events without an understanding of culture and ideology, on the one hand, and of individual agency on the other. Charisma is a capacity to revolutionize people "from within," offering a "revolutionary will" as an alternative to legal or traditional orders (Robertson, 1985: 253–4). Charisma involves the rejection of convention, of established political order, and creates the possibilities of new and different forms of rule. Thus the withdrawal of adherence to a particular social order so that people may follow a charismatic leader may open the possibility for the withdrawal of legitimacy that structural theorists admit is a precondition for revolutionary upheaval. This is not, of course, to imply that charismatic authority is a necessary condition for revolution. Revolutions may (and do) occur without charisma, but this does not mean that we ought to theoretically ignore the human possibilities that charisma may mobilize.

According to Weber's original formulation, charisma is a non-rational form of authority, in which obedience inheres in the charismatic leader's capacity to mobilize sentiments and emotions and give a coherence and meaning to life that the established order cannot provide. Often revolutionaries may be graced with a certain amount of charisma in the eyes of their fellow citizens, which might allow us to enlarge the definition of revolutionary charisma to a collective sense as well. "What revolutionaries offer themselves and their own societies is above all else an image of power, control, certainty, and purpose in a world in which impotence, incomprehension, and the terror of sheer meaninglessness are permanent threats" (Dunn, 1972: 256).

So constituted, either at the individual or at the collective level, charismatic authority is inherently unstable, since the individuals in which authority inheres are threatening enough to the establishing order that they are often exiled or executed. Even if they are not, authority is invested in a person, and people are mortal, so the authority must be transformed following the removal of the leader. A discussion of this process would take us far from our discussion of human agency in revolutionary events, but it reveals a central component of revolutions: charisma is about emotions – mobilized, activated, politicized – and an adequate analysis of revolutions must account for the emotions that give rise to revolutionary upheavals themselves and those that are aroused by the revolution and, in its course, sustain the revolution and give it some of its direction.

As is evident from my earlier arguments, I believe that revolutions are, at their center, about two emotions – hope and despair – which can set people in motion against a constituted order and can sustain that rebellion and propel it into a revolutionary upheaval. Pre-revolutionary despair is evident; revolutions are the "outcome of a long process of dissatisfaction, dissent and organization," writes one sociologist (Urry, 1973: 128). Such dissatisfaction must be "sufficiently general to create not merely a certain slough of subjective despair but an epidemic desire for action" (Gottschalk, 1944: 5–6). In short, the despair that precedes political action must also contain the capacity for hope.

And here some theorists are positively eloquent. Revolution reinvents history; "the course of history suddenly begins anew, than an entirely new story, a story never known or told before, is about to unfold" (Arendt, 1965: 21). John Berger writes that "[e]very revolutionary protest is also a protest against people being the objects of history. And, as soon as people feel, as a result of their desperate protest that they are no longer such objects, history ceases to have the monopoly of time" (Berger, 1972). "The rare elation that accompanies a revolutionary uprising," writes Collins (1986: 261), "is probably due to there being no apparent boundary between one's own micro-situation and that prevailing anywhere else."

Let me be clear that to call into question social psychological levels of analysis, to incorporate human agency into the theory of revolution, is not to imply the direction that social actors will take in their efforts to reconstitute the world. As Aya perceptively notes, the aims of many revolutionaries "have been largely conservative, even reactionary, in the literal sense of trying to preserve older economic and political arrangements under attack by the state or upper classes." Thus

> their radicalism has been tactical, their collective violence the cutting edge of defensive conservatism, and their "revolutionary" intervention an attempt to turn political crises to their own sectional advantage, grabbing the opportunity afforded by breakdowns of state power to reclaim property and prerogatives lately usurped by dominant groups. (Aya, 1979: 72–3)

People become revolutionary when they become desperate enough to mobilize themselves politically to attempt to overthrow or to preserve the existing system, and when they become hopeful enough to believe that by mobilizing themselves to take political action they stand some chance of success. When people make revolutions, they are acting on their dreams. The foundation for those dreams is often a reminiscence, a recollection of the world as it once was, a desire for restoration.

Rational Actors and Moral Economy

Two groups of social scientists have attempted to understand motivation for revolutionary behavior from within a structural perspective, embedding their revolutionary psychology in a discussion of class, state, and international relations. One group assumes that people act rationally, calculating their interests and joining the side that promises to deliver the most to them as individuals. Another group assumes that people act emotionally, attempting to hold on to the ethical and material world they have created, to maintain existing relationships that permit them to survive and give their lives coherence.

These theories are part of a literature on social movements and collective behavior, which seeks to explain revolutionary events by the psychological conditions under which people are motivated to join social movements. But neither the *rational actor* nor the *moral economy* model of motivation falls into the trap of psychological reductionism that I described earlier. Both clearly link their understandings of human action to the structural shifts that give rise to revolutionary movements in the first place. Both models draw their empirical examples from the literature on recent or contemporary peasant movements, both because peasant revolutions have been the most common form of contemporary revolution and because peasants may represent a ''purer'' form of mobilization to rebellion, a mobilization based entirely on their experiences as peasants.

The rational actor model assumes that people act as if they are rationally maximizing expected utility. Drawing from Olson (see chapter 3), analysts such as Samuel Popkin describe the peasant as a rational problem-solver who becomes a revolutionary because the expected return is greater than if he or she does not become a revolutionary. Popkin's peasants are rational individuals who ''evaluate the possible outcomes associated with their choices in accordance to their preference and values'' (Popkin, 1979: 31). In his study of peasant mobilization during the Vietnamese revolution, Popkin applied his model of the rational peasant.

Peasants behave rationally, Popkin argues, in both market and non-market situations, seeking to maximize the potential benefits for themselves and their families. His image of the peasant village is that of a corporation, a collection of rational actors each of whom is seeking the same ends as everyone else. He notes that individual peasants have always been competitive with each other, quite willing to thwart another villager's success if it will bring profit. Peasants do not live in a primordial village of harmony and meaning, he argues, but are competitive and conniving individuals, who often see other villagers as competitors. Here, Popkin follows Mintz's caution that an ''accurate comparative sociology of rural life will have to escape from preconceptions about the countryside: to minimize its emphasis on isolation to suspend its judgements about the coherence, homogeneity, and solidarity of preconceived groups, tribes and communities'' (Mintz, 1982: 185).

However, this makes collective action problematic, since collective action ''depends on the ability of a group or class to organize and make demands,'' that is, on individuals setting aside their individual rationality and agreeing to group activity. It also opens the way to the ''free rider'' problem, in which the likelihood of participation in an activity that is in the interests of the individual is actually reduced by the probability of others acting, since any individual can have his or her interests promoted without actually doing anything. Thus they become ''free riders'' on others' actions.

Popkin's solution to the problem of collective action and the free rider problem is to locate peasant behavior not in psychology but in political economy. Popkin maintains that commercialization of agriculture and colonial state-building are not necessarily harmful to peasants, that these ''cannot be directly equated with a decline in peasant welfare due to the destruction of traditional villages and/or elite bonds'' (Popkin, 1979: 81; see also p. 79). Traditional institutions within the peasant village are harsh, and allow little mobility for the individual peasant. The commercialization of agriculture – the penetration of market forces into that traditional peasant village – and the development of strong central political authorities, which push aside traditional constraints on economic profit maximization, may instead provide *opportunities* for the individual peasant. Thus, Popkin argues, peasants rebel not to preserve their traditional village life, and not because of increased immiseration as a result of being transformed into proletarians. Rather, peasants rebel because they seek upward mobility. "Throughout the world, peasants have fought for access to markets, not as a last gasp when all else has failed them, but when they were secure enough to want to raise their economic level and 'redefine' cultural standards!" (Popkin, 1979: 80).

Individual peasants, therefore, join revolutionary movements when they each determine that the revolutionary movement offers them a higher likelihood of upward mobility than the old regime. Popkin insists that Vietnamese peasants did not support the Communist Party until they each became convinced that it could deliver the material goods, enabling them to better their material position. Their support would also last as long as they continued to believe this. In that sense, peasant communism is less about ideology and still less about nostalgia for a lost world of peasant harmony and "primitive communism", which is evoked by the Communist Party. It is about the capacity of one political party to deliver the goods to the peasants and their allegiance to any group that can deliver those goods.

In Vietnam, Popkin argues, the peasants supported the Communist Party because the communists provided what Olson called "selective incentives," that is immediate rewards in the form of lower rents and taxes, and provided political entrepreneurs who appeared responsive to the needs of the peasants on a daily basis. What is more, the communists were honest, and they could be trusted with the taxes they collected. In a sense, then, the communists did not offer a return to a mythic bucolic past, but a concrete alternative to the past, in which the communists stressed communal structure of the village and the notions of collective goods. These arose not from the primordial structure of the village, but through the process of mobilization by the Communist Party itself. Peasant communalism is thus a *product* of political mobilization for rational ends, not a cause of it.

Popkin's model is useful in its insistence that we not romanticize the peasant village as a world of material abundance or ethical harmony. But like Olson, Popkin's model is more persuasive when applied to elite behavior than to mass participation in a revolutionary movement:

> It is doubtful that the people engaging in these actions had any hopes of winning a high political office or securing other material benefits. Nor is there evidence that these people were coerced into risking their lives. And, it is hardly

reasonable to suppose that one demonstrator, more or less, would have significantly affected the course of events. (Salert, 1976: 45)

Like Olson's, Popkin's model attempts to generate collective behavior
from individual calculation of interests, as if collective action were simply the
sum total of all individual actions. Even if collective action *were* the simple
aggregation of individual rationalities, there is no logical ground for
assuming that a set of individual rationalities adds up to collective rationality.
Each actor individually seeking to rationally maximize his or her interests in
the market yields not collective rationality but the classical "anarchy of the
market," in which collective rationality – planning – requires the active
intervention of the political administration to coerce individuals to set aside
their momentary rational interests for the longer-term interests of
maintaining the system as a whole. In short, the unit of analysis for a
comparative historical sociology of revolution must always be on the collectivity, embedding individual behaviors within the larger structural frames in
which those individuals experience their social location.

Rather than accepting Popkin's model of individual rational actors, others
have returned to Durkheimian concerns about the non-rational bases of
solidarity. But unlike Durkheim, *moral economists* do not condemn
collective behavior as irrational, nor do they place much faith in the
inevitable stabiliation of a morally coherent social world in which the state is
the expression of the collective conscience. Moral economists argue that
people experience themselves as rooted in the social world, anchored to time
and space through a sense of place, a social center from which point the world
is viewed as meaningful and coherent. It is the disruption of this world that
transforms peasants (or any other group) into potential revolutionaries.

The moral economy perspective has often been dismissed by Marxists
because the revolutionaries look backward to an age of community rooted in
immediate face-to-face contact of political intimates rather than forward to a
proletarian utopia. Thus Marx himself dismissed the reactionary nature of the
lower middle classes, as did Lukacs, who wrote that

> The outlook of other classes [petty bourgeois or peasants] is ambiguous or
> sterile because their existence is not based exclusively on their role in the
> capitalist system of production but is indissolubly linked with the vestiges of
> feudal society. Their aim, therefore, is not to advance capitalism or to transcend
> it, but to reverse its action or at least prevent it from developing fully. Their
> class interest concentrates on symptoms of development and not on develop-
> ment itself. (Lukacs, 1971: 59)

However, we will be concerned here to specify the conditions under which
these potentially backward-looking classes may become visionary.

The moral economy school stresses the two disruptive forces that I have

referred to at various places throughout this book: the economic incorporation into the capitalist world economy (capitalist industrialization) and the
political incorporation into a national political entity (state centralization).
Peasants, independent artisans, villagers – in short, any people who experience economic autonomy in their work and political community in their daily
interactions among neighbors – are likely to become politically mobilized for
participation in revolutionary social movements when these two experiences
are threatened. When they are threatened, peasants (or artisans) draw on any
resource they can to preserve their threatened way of life, including appeals to
rational self-interest, cultural tradition, religious ideology, or self-defense.
Thus "revolutionary and other radical mobilizations take place when people
who do have something to defend, and do have some social strength,
confront social transformations which *threaten* to take all that from them and
thus leave them nothing to lose" (Calhoun, 1983: 911). In ordinary times
such daily experiences as cultural tradition, ideology, religion, and community may not be radical at all; in fact they are most often conservative in the
proper sense of the term, seeking to conserve, or preserve, the meaningful
texture of everyday life (see Calhoun, 1980 and 1983). But large-scale
changes in which they become enmeshed transform these conservative forces
into revolutionary forces. "During times when the existing order seems
deeply threatened," writes Calhoun (1983: 911), "such communities may
find that they can be traditional only by being radical." Their radicalism is,
as Calhoun argues, "reactionary," as well as reactive to macro-level social
transformations that disrupt daily life.

The moral economy school stresses the analytic importance of the impact of
these larger-scale forces on autonomous social groups who come to participate
in revolutionary social movements. In particular, scholars have examined the
"moral economy of the peasant," in the term of James Scott, one of the
school's principal advocates, which consists of a general communal sensibility
in which all are entitled to survive (the right to subsistence) and each is
obligated, through an elaborate ideological chain, to help others out in times
of crisis and to share in relatively prosperous times (the norm of reciprocity).
The individual is not the center of the peasant universe, but the kin group, or
the village, or, at the very least, the domus – the peasant household which
most often consists of the extended family. The peasant is "less than an
unimpeded actor" who acts independently; the community impedes,
structures, constrains, and defines his or her individual actions (Migdal,
1974: 133). The goal of the peasant is not to maximize his or her economic
interests in a market, but to be left alone, to eke out his or her existence
within the social world into which each was born and in which each finds
meaning and both moral and material sustenance. "Woven into the tissue of
peasant behavior, then, whether in normal local routines or in the violence of

an uprising, is the structure of a shared moral universe, a common notion of what is just" (Scott, 1976: 167). The autonomy of the peasant village was captured by Sir Charles Metcalfe, writing of India in 1832 (cited in Migdal, 1974: 50): "The village communities are little republics, having nearly everything they want within themselves, and almost independent of any foreign relations. They seem to last where nothing else lasts. Dynasty after dynasty tumbles down; revolution succeeds revolution . . . but the village community remains the same." If "the power of the state stops at the bamboo gates of the village" as one Vietnamese proverb put it, then the social world of the peasant also stops there; the village is relatively disinterested in the world beyond its borders.

But the tragedy of the nineteenth and twentieth centuries, the tragedy, perhaps, of the history of capitalism, is that the peasant is not left alone, cannot be left alone; he or she is brought into contact with the world economy, with political elites, and with economic elites, all of whom increase the pressure on the peasant and threaten the peasant's day-to-day experience of community. "The commercialization of agriculture and the growth of bureaucratic states produced systems of tenancy and taxation that increasingly undermined the stability of peasant income and provoked fierce resistance" (Scott, 1976: vii). And the history of the threatened peasantry is also the history of any social group that experiences economic autonomy from the criteria of capitalist production (exchange value in a market) or political community that is decentralized and stateless – "to steadily reduce the reliability of subsistence guarantees to a point where peasants had hardly any other alternative but resistance" (Scott, 1976: 40). As we have argued earlier, it is the intrusion of capitalist industrialization and political centralization – markets and states – that erodes the foundations of traditional life and mobilizes those groups. As Wolf puts it:

> it is precisely when the peasant can no longer rely on his accustomed institutional context to reduce his risks, but when alternative institutions are either too chaotic or too restrictive to guarantee a viable commitment to new ways, that the psychological, economic, social and political tensions all mount toward peasant rebellion and involvement in revolution. (Wolf, 1969: xv)

What this means is that neither immiseration nor upward mobility are the concerns of potential revolutionaries. "The great majority of peasant movements historically, far from being affairs of rising expectations, have rather been defensive efforts to preserve customary rights or to restore them once they have been lost" (Scott, 1977b: 237). Peasants rebel not when they have nothing left to lose and not when they seize an economic opportunity. Immiseration is a poor basis for revolution, since "people who face starvation are too busy just surviving to plot the overthrow of governments or to formulate blueprints for alternative social orders" (Adas, 1979: 75–6). The powerless are "easy victims;" rebellion requires a sense of strength and possibility (Wolf, 1969: 290). "To rebel is not only to seek food when hungry, for animals do that as well, but it is to recover one's culture, one's self-esteem, one's rights – in short, to assert one's humanity" (Scott, 1977b: 248).

Seizing the opportunity for upward mobility could hardly account for the conditions that give rise to peasant mobilization. "[L]egitimacy rather than economic survival was the major issue employed by those who sought to recruit peasant supporters for rebellion" (Adas, 1982: 105).

Several long-run preconditions for peasant revolution may be inferred from our earlier structural analysis combined with our current interest in the sources of peasant mobilizations (see Wolf, 1969: 135). A worsening geopolitical situation is experienced as continued foreign encroachment on the old regime state. These increased pressures are experienced both directly and indirectly by the peasantry, and they establish the conditions for state collapse. The spread of industry and trade to the countryside transforms rural class relations, as well as the peasants' relationships to their networks of family and meaning. Intra-elite dissent may be indicated by the infighting of warlord armies; the dissolution of elite unanimity indicates a vulnerability among landlords, which suggests that a peasant movement might succeed. And finally, the impinging of all these three factors on traditional peasant autonomy will deepen agricultural discontent and perhaps propel it into mobilization for rebellion.

Wolf identifies three sets of social conditions that endow a peasant populations with the tactical leverage necessary to make possible political rebellion. These three sets of conditions also indicate why revolutionary peasants are more likely to be "middle peasants" – small landowners and secure tenants farming chiefly with family labor – as opposed to poor and landless peasants. First, middle peasants exercise some control over their own means of production, a margin of economic independence that, in a struggle, may become an important political asset. Second, the location of the peasantry is important; those peasants who live in marginal, outlying areas – "poor but free" – are often beyond the effective control of the landlord and official agents of political repression. Again, middle peasants have the tactical mobility to survive without complete dependence on local landlords. Finally, Wolf argues that some external agent must set the process in motion, especially the intervention of some foreign power or state collapse which erodes the established lines of repressive power. Another way to describe these there variables is to see peasant mobilization as contingent on (1) peasant solidarity; (2) peasant capacity for collective action; and (3) landlord vulnerability (Goldstone, 1982: 198). Peasant participation in revolutionary social movements depends on their experience of the erosion of their traditional way of life and their belief that participation my restore the world they appear to be losing.

Moral economists are careful to distinguish their theories from earlier models of collective behavior, which often saw peasant behavior in terms of its irrational adherence to traditional, pre-modern, forms of cognitive organization. Peasant mobilization may be reactionary or restorative, but it is also *collectively rational*. Even millenarian movements or charismatic movements, according to one historian, must be seen as rational; their magical or millenarian content "was not only consistent with the basic premises of their broader belief systems but it formed a vital part of the process by which the grievances of the colonized were transformed into what may be perceived to be a viable mode of collective protest" (Adas, 1979: 162). Remember Marx's famous description of the function of religion in his *Contribution to the Critique of Hegel's Philosophy of Right* – noting particularly his sensitivity to the material basis of religious searching, which occurs just before his most famous sentence: "Religious distress is at the same time the expression of real distress and the protest against real distress. Religion is the sigh of the oppressed culture, the heart of a heartless world, the spirit of a spiritless situation. It is the opium of the people" (Marx, 1978: 54).

Charismatic leadership also has a material foundation; often it is made possible by the erosion of the state and intra-elite discontent in the first place:

> the ineptitude of colonial regimes actually gave impetus to rebellion by either provoking prophetic leaders or providing opportunities for them to mobilize supporters. Government inaction or initial bungling also obscured its potential military might in the eyes of the colonized peoples. In many instances disgruntled groups saw government failures as signs of the great power of prophetic leaders and as a promise of their inevitable victory. (Adas, 1979: 128)

It is in this context of structural transformations creating the possibilities of peasant mobilization that earlier efforts to understand the social psychology of revolution come into sharper focus. Peasant mobilization occurs within the space opened up by the collapse of the old order and before the constitution of the new order, between what Skocpol identifies as the causes and the consequences of revolution. "It is precisely when the peasant can no longer rely on his accustomed institutional context to reduce his risks, but when alternative institutions are either too chaotic or too restrictive to guarantee a viable commitment to new ways, that the psychological, economic, social, and political tensions all mount toward peasant rebellion and involvement in revolution" (Wolf, 1969: xv). In this context, we can resurrect the notion of, for example, relative deprivation, as Adas does, suggesting a structural context for a form of relative deprivation that goes beyond Gurr's formulation, and allows us the possibility of understanding how deprivation, experienced here as the loss of autonomy and community, may, under some circumstances lead to rebellion:

> As a result of European colonialism, new groups, ideas, objects, and organiza-
> tional patterns were introduced into non-Western societies, where they altered
> and threatened the positions of previously established indigenous groups. In
> these circumstances, significant numbers of individuals and whole groups
> among the colonized came to feel that a gap existed between what they felt they
> deserved in terms of status and material rewards and what they possessed or had
> the capacity to obtain. This perception of a discrepancy between expectations
> and capacities led to a sense of deprivation, which was both relative and collec-
> tively experienced . . . Because the stress and frustrations that accompanied
> these feelings of relative deprivation were sufficiently intense and shared, they
> produced collective protest movements designed to ameliorate strain by closing
> the gap between the participants' expectations and their capacities. (Adas,
> 1979: 44)

While the moral economy perspective has been most usefully applied to peasant movements – in part, because peasant revolution is the dominant form of revolution in the twentieth century – it is also useful in explaining the participation in revolutionary social movements of other groups. In dealing with lower-middle-class movements among urban artisans, crafts-people, skilled tradespeople and small shopkeepers – who have composed the backbone of the urban popular support for revolutions from the English Revolution until the present day – the moral economy perspective is excep-tionally useful (see, for example, Arendt, 1965; Kimmel, 1984; Bonnell, 1985). These works stress the ways in which these urban groups experience their daily lives as expressing economic autonomy – control over their labor, control over the products of their labor – and political community in a decentralized world of neighbors and friends. The disruption of that world by state centralization or economic industrialization threatens to transform these groups into both citizens and proletarians, and for them these two positions would represent significant downward mobility. In these conditions, as they lose one world of meaning, they invoke it as a past utopia to which they want to return. They invoke tradition, "grounded less in the historical past than in everyday social practice" (Calhoun, 1983: 888). It is not really that such a world existed in the past; rather it is the world in which they currently live, and which the believe is threatened.

Artisans and peasants share several characteristics which might lead either group to become "reactionary radicals", characteristics that distinguish their revolts from the revolts of the organized working class in capitalist society. It is "precisely the fact that peasants and artisans have one foot on the pre-capitalist economy that explains why they have provided the mass impetus for many 'forward-looking' movements. Their opposition to capitalism, based as it is on a utopian image of an earlier age, is as tenacious, if not more so, as the opposition of a proletariat which has both feet in the new society" (Scott, 1977c: 231). Thus, Calhoun argues, "we need to see revolutions against capitalism as based not in the new class which capitalism forms, but in the traditional communities and crafts which capitalism threatens" (Calhoun, 1988: 49).

It is the spontaneous outbursts of these groups that often ignite the revolutionary event itself; the outbursts are against the erosion of a world in which people have found meaning and coherence (see Arendt, 1965: 246–7, 263, 266, 268 *et passim*). They articulate an ideology of both freedom *and* democracy, of both liberty *and* equality, fused through an active, transcendent political community. The history of revolution is replete with social movements of urban lower-middle-class artisans and petty producers who articulated these claims of economic autonomy and political community: Levellers, Diggers, *sans-culottes*, Chartists, Luddites, soviets, anarchists, populists, and many others. Here is how some radicals put it in England in 1859 (cited in Thompson, 1963, chapter 10):

> Those relics of the feudal yoke
> Still in the north remain unbroke.
> That social yoke, with one accord
> That binds the peasant to his Lord.
> And Liberty, that idle vaunt,
> Is not the comfort that we want.
> It only serves to turn the head
> But gives to none their daily bread.
> We want community of feeling
> And landlords kindly in their dealing.

Like their peasant counterparts, these lower middle classes fight neither for a return to the world they have truly lost nor for bourgeois conceptions of freedom which would uproot them and make them into free, but disconnected atoms. They fight for a radical notion of freedom *within* community, which neither the feudal past nor the capitalist future are capable of providing. Thus the lower middle classes in both the cities and in the countryside are inherently radical, yet fit neither of the traditional camps on revolution neatly.

Inherently radical and also, sadly, almost inevitably unsuccessful. This history of the lower-middle-class urban revolution has almost always been a history of failure; the consolidation of the new regime has often been based on the failure of the lower-middle-class revolt. This is less true of peasant revolutions, of which there have been several notable successes, including those of China, Vietnam, Cuba, and Nicaragua. But even here, several radical peasant revolutions were suppressed by the consolidation of the new regime, as in Mexico or Algeria. These radical groups, urban and/or rural, often form the shock troops of the revolution, pushing the remnants of the old regime out of the way, and articulating an entirely new and fresh vision of social reconstruction, which often gets buried along with their incipient radicalism by the elites of the new regime.

In part, defeat stems from the contradictory perspectives that reactionary radicals bring to their movements of resistance. Locally based, they can draw upon local support, but often have difficulty making alliances with other potential discontents in the cities who might join a revolutionary coalition. The moral boundaries of locally based resistance "are what give it is local staying power." This type of movement is however, strategically outmatched by the elite culture, which can draw on national resources (Scott, 1977c: 219).

In defeat, these reactionary radicals are eloquent: "Even if we got nothing, that's not important. What's important is that we *had* to fight back. And we fought so well that the big people and the government will never forget us again . . . No strike, no demonstration, no rebellion fails. Protest against injustice always succeeds." So spoke a Filipino rebel after the failure of the Huk rebellion (cited in Walton, 1984:69). In defeat, these groups often bequeath a legacy to future generations of revolutionaries, who find themselves in similar structural positions, facing the same structural transformation of their lives by industrial capital and the centralizing state, and who articulate a similar moral vision to guide their rebellion. For this reason, as Moore writes (1966:505): "the chief social basis of radicalism has been the peasants and the smaller artisans in the towns. From these facts one may conclude that the wellsprings of human freedom lie not where Marx saw them, in the aspirations of classes about to take power, but perhaps even more in the dying wail of a class over whom the wave of progress is about to roll."

The Value of the Moral Economy Model

The moral economy of revolutionary movements offers several important insights that are extremely useful in our theoretical understanding of revolution. First, the model provides a notion of peasant resistance as one end of a continuum of peasant behavior in the face of threatened erosion of the coherence of everyday life. Thus revolution is not such an aberrant event, but rather the "high-end" expression of discontent that is already present as peasants lose autonomy and community. The expression of this discontent as participation in revolutionary social movements is more a result of favorable structural circumstances – collapse of the state, intra-elite struggle, increased geopolitical and military pressure from abroad – than the intensity of the discontent of the peasantry themselves.

When such structural conditions are not present, the peasants have an ingenious set of methods of ''everyday resistance'' to their worsening situation. These methods are ''what people do short of organized confrontation that reveals disgust, anger, indignation, or opposition to what they regard as unjust or unfair actions by others more wealthy or powerful than they'' (Kerkvliet, 1986: 108). These forms of resistance include foot-dragging, false compliance, pilfering, feigned ignorance, slander, arson, sabotage, dissimulation pamphlets, vernacular newspapers, satirical cartoons, double entendres in speech, gestures of contempt or mockery, and, above, all, flight (see Adas, 1981; Scott and Kerkvliet, 1986). These forms of everyday resistance, however, were gradually rendered less effective by the increasing structural transformation taking place outside the village. ''As precolonial contests states were gradually transformed into highly centralized bureaucracies which increasingly impinged on local and village affairs, the usual peasant defense mechanisms were greatly reduced in effectiveness or rendered completely impotent'' (Adas, 1981: 240). As a result, ''peasant reliance on evasion, patron protection, and avoidance shifted to forms of protest expression that involved more direct challenges to and clashes with the wielders of power'' (Adas, 1981: 246). Thus peasant participation in revolutionary movements occurs when traditional forms of resistance break down for structural reasons, and the moral economy of participation and mobilization remains anchored in structural analysis.

The moral economy model thus helps us distinguish between the types of peasant movement that we observe and also between the possible varieties of political response to these large-scale structural shifts. This is shown in figure 7.1, where we can see that the particularity of a revolutionary mobilization of lower-middle-class city-dwellers or peasants depends on the confluence of the sources of their vision and their outlook. Where rebels are rooted in tradition and yet reactionary, their rebellion is likely to be sporadic, an occasional uprising which is incapable of being sustained. Their solidarity is conservative, their ability to unite with others sharply diminished. Where the outlook of the rebels is modern, reactionary social movements are likely to be fascistic efforts to subdue the rising militance of the urban working class. The working class is radical, yet its outlook is also modern, seeking a proletarian state. Only when rebellion is both radically visionary and rooted in tradition is the particular form of solidarity and organizational capacity present which sustains the rebellion and allows for revolutionary participation. This is the radical solidarity that underlies the moral economy of revolutionary participation.

Source of solidarity among rebels

		Traditional	Modern	
Reactionary		Sporadic uprisings from below Conservative solidarity	Fascist social movements Revolution from above	**Political ideology of rebels**
Radical		Moral-economy-based movement Social revolutionary movement	Working-class radicalism Trade-union reforms	

Figure 7.1 Sources of solidarity and political orientations of social movements: effects on type of movement.

Another significant advantage of the moral economy approach is methodological, and concerns the notable resistance of scholars to reify structural relationships into analytic categories that serve as the "empty theoretical boxes" that Smelser employed. Classes, states, and even international economies are not things, but *relations* between social actors. They are created, maintained, and sustained through the interaction of people. English historian E. P. Thompson makes a similar case for the understanding of the term class, when he writes that class is not a structure, or even a category, but "something which in fact happens in human relationships." In fact, he argues,

> this notion of class entails the notion of historical relationship. Like any other relationship, it is a fluency which evades analysis if we stop it dead at any given moment and anatomize its structure. The finest-meshed sociological net cannot give us a pure speciment of class, any more than it can give us one of deference or of love. The relationship must always be embodied in real people and in a real context. Moreover, we cannot have two distinct classes, each with an independent being, and then bring them *into* relationship with each other. We cannot have love without lovers, nor deference without squires and labourers. And class happens when some men, as a result of common experiences (inherited or shared), feel and articulate the identity of their interests as between themselves, and as against other men whose interests are different from (and usually opposed to) theirs. The class experience is largely determined by the productive relations into which men ar born – or enter involuntarily. (1963: 9)

Perhaps the central value of this approach is that it brings people back into the revolutionary equation again – not as the sole vehicle by which revolutions are explained, but within the context of the larger-scale structural shifts we have been identifying throughout this book. The revolutionary equation now must include structural causes, social processes of mobilization and resistance within the revolutionary events themselves, and the structural reconsolidation of political power following the revolution. None of these can be reduced to any of the others, and each deserves separate yet unified analytic inquiry.

The Tilly Synthesis

The work of Charles Tilly and his many colleagues and students comes, perhaps, as close to a synthesis of structure and process, of human agency within an institutional framing, as that of any contemporary theorist of revolution. Tilly's work, elaborated over the past quarter-century, has ranged over counter-revolutionary peasants during the French Revolution, civil violence and contention in seventeenth-and eighteenth-century British and French cities and countryside, and comparative theoretical accounts of the dynamics of state-building. Such work has challenged many accepted principles of sociological analysis. It replaces neutral states with states acting as individual contenders for legitimate political power. Tilly takes discontent within the population as a constant, and seeks to specify the conditions under which motivation can become *mobilization*. Thus a level of organization is the necessary intervening variable between people's anger and their political action. These three terms – contention, mobilization, organization – form the analytic core of Tilly's work on revolution. His is a theory of contention as conventional politics, in which revolution is but an extreme expression of everyday competition for resources; of the mobilization of discontents into a political struggle with power-holders; and of their level of organization as a chief predictor of their capacity to succeed.

Theoretically, Tilly's work fuses several strands of classical theory. He is, as he puts it, "doggedly anti-Durkheimian" in his insistence on the collective rationality of social action and the purposiveness of revolutionary behavior; "resolutely pro-Marxian" in his understanding of the centrality of social classes and capitalism in the development of revolutionary situations, and his insistence that the state is an interested party that may represent the interests of a ruling class; "sometimes indulgent to Weber" in his belief that the state is a pivotal actor in the revolutionary equation, a contender in its own right: and, finally, "sometimes reliant on Mill" in the claims that revolutionary action, like all other social action, is rational (Tilly, 1978: 48).

Tilly's dogged anti-Durkheimianism leads him to carefully demarcate his theory from those earlier models that stress collective behavior or frustration and aggression in aggregate psychological theories of revolutionary behavior. Several followers of Durkheim, notably the aggregate social psychology of Davies, Gurr, and others, or the breakdown of the functional social system theories of Smelser, Johnson, and others, stress either the irrationality of movements or the inherent legitimacy of the state. Tilly assumes neither. The movements are as rational as any social scientist who attempts to study them, and the state appears legitimate only because power-holders are, for the time being, in power. Legitimacy is *always* problematic for Tilly, as power-holders are constantly seeking to expand their purviews. Movements that rise in opposition to the state are collectively rational attempts to wrest power from others. Contrary to Durkheimian notions, Tilly sees states not in some vaguely Hegelian way as the transcendent repositories of the good and the right, but as greedy institutions always seeking to augment their power.

Like many of the theorists we have discussed in this chapter, he takes classes and international events seriously. But, above all, Tilly's theory of revolution is a political theory, a theory that revolves around the state. Tilly defines revolution as ''a transfer of power over a state through armed struggle in the course of which at least two distinct power blocs make incompatible claims to control the state, and some significant portion of the population subject to the state's jurisdiction acquiesces in the claims of each bloc'' (Tilly, 1989: 3). The crucial elements of this definition are structural – armed struggle, two or more power blocs, transfer of state power. This definition is also composed of temporal processes: a revolutionary situation, in which power blocs emerge making incompatible claims for political power, and a revolutionary outcome, in which the transfer of power is carried out from those who hold state power to some group that formerly did not hold state power. Tilly notes that ''few revolutionary situations have revolutionary outcomes,'' thus allowing for revolutions to fail.

Despite Tilly's structural definition, a crucial element remains the allegiance of some portion of the population to each of the contending power blocs. Unlike Skocpol and other structural theorists of the state and revolution, Tilly also takes people's motivations and aspirations seriously, not so much as independent forces – as earlier non-structuralist theories did – but within the context of political struggle which constitutes the daily life of all societies:

> Despite the many recent attempts to psychologize the study of revolution, by introducing ideas of anxiety, alienation, rising expectations, and the like, and to sociologize it by employing notions of disequilibrium, role conflict, structural strain, and so on, the factors which hold up under close scrutiny are, on the whole, political ones. The structure of power, alternative conceptions of

justice, the organization of coercion, the conduct of war, the formation of coalitions, the legitimacy of the state – these traditional concerns of political
thought provide the main guides to the explanations of revolution. (Tilly,
1973: 447)

Tilly thus takes sharpest aim at non-structural accounts of revolution. He
draws a sharp distinction between collective behavior – the blind irrationality
of the crowd – and collective action – "joint action in pursuit of common
ends" (Tilly, 1978: 84). Collective action is purposive, pro-active, and political, and the main determinants of a group's mobilization are "its organization, its interest in possible interactions with other contenders, the current
opportunity / threat of those interactions and the group's subjection to repression" (Tilly, 1978: 56). Revolutionary movements are to be located at one
end of the spectrum of political activity; they are not qualitatively different
events. Instead, "political violence is essentially a by-product of omnipresent
processes of political conflict among mobilized – that is, organized and
resource-controlling – groups and governments" (Skocpol, 1976a: 165).

To Tilly, a revolution is the expression-as-crisis of political struggle that
occurs all the time. Chiding theorists who stress social disintegration, Tilly
argues

> that revolutions and collective violence tend to flow directly out of a popula-
> tion's central political process, instead of expressing diffuse strains and
> discontents within the population; . . . that the specific claims and counter-
> claims being made on the existing government by various mobilized groups are
> more important than the general satisfaction or discontent of these groups, and
> that claims for established places within the structure of power are crucial.
> (1973: 436)

As Aya (1979: 68) puts it, "for all the violent passion and passionate violence
they entail, revolutions, rebellion, and lesser forms of coercive civilian
conflict are best understood as (to adopt Clausewitz's venerable definition of
war) 'a mere continuation of politics by other means'."

If revolution is but the crisis expression of "politics as usual," we must
inquire what "politics as usual" looks like to Tilly. Here the two key themes
of the centrality of the state and the rationality of collective action are
evident. Each of these analytic linchpins is a determined response to the two
major schools of non-structural theories of revolution. Against the aggregate
social psychologists, Tilly asserts the rationality of collective action, and
against theories of systemic breakdown he insists on the historical and analytic
specificity of capitalism and the state. His model "seeks the genesis of revolutions . . . in the competing interests and aspirations of embattled power
groups. Like war, revolutions and collective violence arise from ongoing

contests for resources, influence, and hegemony previously managed within existing diplomatic channels'' (Aya, 1979: 68).

In contrast to theories of systemic breakdown, which stress the unevenly distributed dislocating experiences of modernization, Tilly emphasizes more concrete processes of capitalism and state-building. This emphasis can be summarized in several propositions (see Hunt, 1984: 262–3). (1) Changes labelled modernization, he argues, had no uniform effects on the level, focus, form, or timing of political conflict. One need not search for revolutionaries among the newly disenfranchised groups, those whose lives are disrupted by modernization. In contrast, he writes, ''the motors of militancy are set in motion not by the marginal, the unintegrated, and the recently arrived, but by workers who belong to firmly established networks of long standing at the core of industrial society'' (Shorter and Tilly, 1974: 272–3). (2) In the short run, rapid urbanization and industrialization – the two chief mechanisms of social dislocation to the systemic breakdown theorists – generally depressed the level of collective violence. (3) Urbanization and industrialization were able to stimulate conflict when they diverted resources from established groups that retained their internal organization. (4) The emergence of industrial capitalism transformed the identities and interests of the major contenders for power as well as the form of their collective action. (5) The frequency and outcome of collective conflict depends on the operation of the state.

The analytic centrality of the state in Tilly's schema leads us naturally to ask how he views the state. States are not the passive administrative units of Durkheimian theory, nor are they the instruments of class rule that Marxist theory implies. States are omnivorous and autonomous institutions, whose agents constantly seek to expand their purview both domestically and internationally. This expansion is both horizontal, extending state control over increasingly large geographic areas, and vertical, bringing greater numbers of social groups throughout the social hierarchy under state control. Statemakers are ''coercive and self-seeking entrepreneurs,'' whose personal mobility becomes enmeshed in state expansion (Tilly, 1985a: 169). Typically, Tilly argues (1985a: 181), state activity involves four mutually reinforcing activities:

1 War-making: eliminating or neutralizing their own rivals outside the territories in which they have clear and continuous priority as wielders of force.
2 State-making: eliminating or neutralizing their rivals inside those territories.
3 Protection: eliminating or neutralizing the enemies of their clients.

4 Extraction: acquiring the means of carrying out the first three
   activities – war-making, state-making, and protection.

All four of these activities, Tilly tells us, depend on a state's capacity to
monopolize the means of coercion. Thus the building of armies and police
forces is a vehicle by which to maintain the level of extraction of resources for
the states to pursue their own ends. Extraction, which includes everything
from outright plunder to standard tributes, to bureaucratized forms of taxation, creates the capability of the state to pursue those ends.

These four activities are never uncontested, however. In fact, in Tilly's
model, state expansion is both what strengthens the regime, and what leaves
the society vulnerable to revolution. "Revolutions have occurred especially in
times of state expansion, when the drive to build the state's military power
has expanded its agents' claims on its subject populations yet the state has
remained vulnerable to counterclaims from subjects and creditors, and to
costs imposed by war" (Tilly, 1989: 10). This is another expression of revolution as a continuation of politics-as-usual. The business of the state is to
expand, but that expansion is eventually what leaves it vulnerable to
contenders from below.

Surely, here is a model that is far less sanguine about politics than those
earlier models which stressed legitimacy, value consensus, and solidarity. The
state is essentially an insatiably greedy protection racket. No wonder Tilly
makes an analogy between state-building and organized crime (see Tilly,
1985a).

Perhaps most centrally, both organized crime and state-building are
dramatically transformed by the advent of capitalism. The expansion of
capitalism, Tilly argues, creates new resources and frees up old resources
which state-builders can then capture for their own state-building projects.
Tilly relies on his historical explorations to suggest a model of an omnivorous
and bellicose state which moves simultaneously to advance its position in the
global geopolitical arena and to subdue domestic opposition. One of the
best mechanisms that states have developed to accomplish both these
ends – perhaps the best mechanism ever invented – is capitalism, which subordinates a domestic population to what appear to be non-political regimens,
such as factory discipline and wage labor, and can also generate entrepreneurial activity and promote the power of a state against international rivals.
Capitalism and state-building are mutually reinforcing historical processes in
Tilly's mind, and their combined effect is the cause of revolution in the
modern world.

Historically, the growth of industry "produced profitable markets for big
agricultural producers" and thereby the "conditions for political alliance
between great landlords and aspirant state-makers" (Tilly, 1975: 72). This

historical alliance between capitalism and state-building also suggests why eras of capitalist expansion and of dramatic state-building often go together.

It also explains why those eras are usually eras of ideological transformation, since ideology and culture are responsive to these larger-scale structural shifts. "The elaboration of new ideologies, new theories of how the world works, new creeds, is part and parcel of both paths to a revolutionary position: the emergence of brand new challengers and the turning [to revolutionary goals] of existing contenders" (Tilly, 1975: 526; see also Skocpol, 1976a: 167). So , for example, when Tilly discusses mid-seventeenth-century Europe, he suggests that the "drift towards government adoption of liberal doctrines . . . grew not only from the accession of capitalists to political power and the penetration of market relations into everyday life, but also from the experience of statesmen seeking to put larger and larger resources at the disposition of the state" (Tilly, 1975: 73). In discussing the impact of capitalism on the peasantry, Tilly is clear that capitalism and the state often mutually reinforce one another, and that the state becomes central to the process of capital accumulation:

> Capitalism was not some inexorable force that simply swept away existing institutions through the very force of the market mechanism. In many societies, social organization had been a means to insulate peasants from direct or sustained contact with the international market. For peasants to produce what the market demanded they produce, there had to be an additional force insuring compliance, with the market's demands. That force was the state. (Tilly, 1985b: 73)

For it was the state, Tilly tells us, whose armies and police forces could enforce the discipline of the new market, and could undo or prevent the traditional methods of peasant organization.

Of course, capitalism and state-building do not always act in concert. "Capitalism and national states grew up together and presumably depended on each other in some way, yet capitalists and centers of capital accumulation often offered concerted resistance to the extension of state power" (Tilly, 1985b: 140). But in the main, only the state can provide capitalists with the muscle to enforce their transformation of traditional agricultural arrangements, and only capitalism can appear to legitimately extract sufficient resources to finance the state's projects without raising significant opposition.

Tilly's analysis also explains why eras of capitalist expansion and state-building are often eras of war. War looms large in Tilly's account of revolution, since war-making is one of the state's chief activities and the extraction of domestic resources and pacification of the domestic population are necessary for a successful war effort. Here, too, capitalism and the state often find themselves working in a mutually reinforcing tandem, since capitalist expansion requires safe overseas markets for production and distribution which states can provide by conquest or diplomatic treaty, and the increased revenues generated by capitalist expansion can further finance state-sponsored expansion projects.

Expanding capitalism, expanding states, and wars form the structural foundations of Tilly's analysis of revolutions. These are the structural forces that provide the context of revolution. But Tilly argues that we must go further. We must also account for human agency. We must bring people back into the revolutionary equation.

Revolutions are enormously complex events, "whose occurrence probably depends upon a convergence of several relatively independent processes;" thus, explanations of revolution must be, above all, historically grounded in order to make sense of this complex totality (Skocpol, 1976a: 166). As Tilly wrote in his first book, "a revolution is a state of a whole society, not of each segment of society" (Tilly, 1964: 159). Since revolutionary situations emerge in specific historical contexts, the theoretical explication of revolutions must likewise be historically grounded. Explanations of revolution, Tilly argues, must be historically specific, and recognize the analytic centrality of both the state and its discontents. Thus the political struggle among contenders for power is the centerpiece of his work. Revolutions occur not because of a breakdown in a functional system, but because forces of opposition find common cause with one another and join coalitions in response to increased pressure from the state. "Revolutionary action becomes likely when, in the presence of vulnerable power-holders, potential opponents those power-holders communicate with each other sufficiently to recognize that they have the collective capacity to overturn the existing structure" (Tilly, 1985b: 32). Here, Tilly adopts Trotsky's notion that the revolutionary moment happens when a society experiences *multiple sovereignties*, a power struggle among contending groups, one of which is the state.

In a revolutionary situation, several contenders advance mutually exclusive claims for political power, and a significant segment of the population commits itself to the claims of the alternative groups. "A revolutionary situations begins when a government previously under the control of a single, sovereign polity becomes the object of effective, competing, mutually exclusive claims on the part of two or more distinct polities" (Tilly, 1978: 191). The existing repressive apparatus of the government proves itself incapable of or unwilling to suppress this alternative. As Gottschalk wrote earlier, "[d]espite the universal demand for revolutionary change, despite the intense hopefulness of success, unless those who wish to maintain the status quo are so weak that they cannot maintain themselves, there is little likelihood of a successful revolution" (Gottschalk, 1944: 7). Thus several contenders all carve out a claim for political power (Tilly, 1978: 200; see also

Hunt, 1984: 264).

Revolutions, therefore, happen when the structural forces create the possibility for mobilization of a relatively constant level of discontent or where these forces make possible the mobilization of new pockets of opposition and discontent. When a revolutionary situation develops, and there emerge two or more centers of political legitimacy, then the events of a revolution may unfold. Tilly proposes that revolutions follow a relatively easily discernible pattern or sequence (1978: 216–71): (1) the mobilization of contenders; (2) an increase in the number of people accepting the new claims; (3) unsuccessful efforts by the government to suppress the alternative coalition; (4) the establishment by the alternative coalition of effective control over some portion of the government; (5) struggles of the alternative coalition to maintain or expand that control; (6) the reconstruction of a single polity through the victory of the alternative coalition; (7) the reimposition of routine governmental control throughout the subject population.

As we can see, Tilly's argument focuses on the motivations of the participants at the same time as it underscores the importance of the state in political conflict. Tilly reverses Gurr's earlier inversion of the relationship between the state and the individual or social group. To Tilly, "the revolutionary moment arrives when previously acquiescent members of that population find themselves confronted with strictly incompatible demands from the government and from an alternative body claiming control over the government, or claiming to be the government" (Tilly, 1978: 192). And the final condition for revolution, he writes, "is the formation of . . . coalitions between polity members and revolutionary challengers" (Tilly, 1973: 443). This difference's view of between Tilly's and Gurr the sequence and timing of the revolutionary event can be expressed graphically. Gurr uses a tension-release model of frustration and aggression to explain the timing of revolution; his model would look something like figure 7.2. Tilly's model of the timing of a revolution would look quite different (see figure 7.3). From

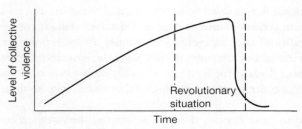

Figure 7.2 The tension-release model of collective violence. *Source*: Tilly (1978: 218).

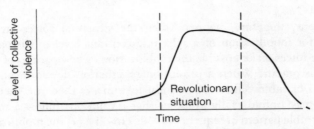

Figure 7.3   The contention model of collective violence.   *Source*: Tilly (1978: 218).

Tilly's account, then, it would appear that it is not the failure of the government to live up to people's expectations but the sudden increase in governmental demands that is likely to spark a revolutionary moment.

For example, in seventeenth-century France, "the dominant influences driving the French peasants into revolt were the efforts of authorities to seize peasant labor, commodities, and capital. Those efforts violated peasant rights, jeopardized the interests of other parties in peasant production and threatened the ability of the peasants to survive as peasants" (Tilly, 1984:   ). This is crucial: revolutionary coalitions are forged in response to increased exactions from governments in crisis.

In this way, Tilly preserves both the analytic centrality of the state as well as human agency and motivation. Far from psychologizing revolution, Tilly places his political psychology within structural transformations of capitalist expansion, state-building and war. Curiously, though he claims to be resolutely pro-Marxian, his analysis bypasses the placing of class struggle at the level of production on the same causal plane as state-building or capitalist expansion in the global arena. Perhaps he downplays class struggle between lords and peasants or between capitalists and workers because he believes it to be such historical constant that it is simply assumed, or perhaps it is because he believes that class struggle needs some additional force to kick it into gear (see also Skocpol, 1976a: 166).

Tilly's work has been subject to several levels of criticism, which has tended to focus on four central questions. As I noted above, Tilly is curiously silent on the centrality of class struggle in his model of revolution. He is never analytically clear about the role of class struggle, nor does he elaborate a central theoretical place for it. Thus it is only in his historical accounts of various forms of contention and revolution that classes take on some analytic power.

Second, critics have examined Tilly's account of the causes of revolution. Some, like Goldfrank, deconstruct Tilly's account of mobilization, and argue that Tilly "falls back on member discontent and the development of new ideologies in accounting for the commitment of large numbers to revolutionary contenders" (Goldfrank, 1979: 140). After all, Tilly argues that potential contenders are always available for potential revolt, "in the form of millenial cults, radical cells, or rejects from the positions of power. The real question is when such contenders proliferate and/or mobilize" (Tilly, 1975: 525). Skocpol goes even further, criticizing Tilly's reliance on such non-structural themes as ideology and religion as potential mobilizing forces. Thus, social psychological variables, particularly discontent, "re-emerge[s] as a central explanatory factor – only with the dependent variable no longer violent behavior, but, instead, acquiescence in the support of revolutionary elite, coalition, or organization" (Skocpol, 1976a: 167).

A third arena of critique is Tilly's account of the process of revolution, the revolutionary moment itself. Here, again, Tilly appears to rely on non-structural factors; the resolution of the crisis of multiple sovereignty in Tilly's model is the voluntary commitment of a large segment of the population to the new regime. The consolidation of the new regime depends, it appears, on member satisfaction and the development of new ideologies. Gone, it would appear, is the model of the state as omnivorous and repressive.

Finally, Skocpol suggests that Tilly's emphasis on multiple sovereignty as the moment of revolution has the odd effect of "trivializing" the role of the state in revolution.

> The state is not seen as determining by its own strength or weakness whether or not a revolutionary situation can emerge at all. Instead it is portrayed as an organization competing for popular support on more or less equal terms with one or more fully formed revolutionary organizations or blocs. Societal members are envisaged as able to choose freely and deliberately whether to support the government or a revolutionary organization, with their choices determining whether or not a revolutionary situation occurs. (Skocpol, 1976a: 167–8)

These criticisms are searching, but not compelling enough to dismiss Tilly's efforts at synthesizing the structural and the normative, and his efforts at replacing human agency in a theory revolution *within* parameters that are simultaneously institutionally drawn and historically specific. Skocpol and others' disagreements with Tilly can be most easily expressed metaphorically. As I argued earlier, Skocpol's metaphor of revolution is the structurally unsound bridge, which strains and eventually collapses from the increased pressure of foreign competition and more advanced social forces. Once collapsed, new elites rebuild a structure far stronger and capable of withstanding far more pressure.

Tilly, by contrast, sees political life, both everyday and during revolutions, along the lines of the child's game "King of the Hill." At the top, power-holders use whatever resources they can to maintain their power, constantly fighting off potential challenges and securing their fortress. But these power-holders may overdo it, extend themselves too far, try to build up their power too much, and, as a result, they become vulnerable to attack by a concerted coalition of revolutionary opposition. By carefully building up their resources, this coalition challenges existing power-holders for the top position.

Tilly's model of revolution can take us a long way towards understanding that complex phenomenon. He restores human agency to the equation without sacrificing the primacy of structure, thus achieving an important synthesis. In addition, his deliberate historical excavations of the ways in which people have resisted political domination in Europe situates the search for theoretical models within the historical record. It is an admirable achievement.

8

Conclusion

Now, as for the revolution . . . Well, above all, it's virtue. In the revolution, you've got to have virtue. Why did we win? Because we had virtue. *Duc Luc Nao Cung Thang!* Virtue always wins!

> Fifty-seven-year-old peasant farmer, Quang Ngai Province,
> Vietnam, March 1975[1]

This book has examined a large number of twentieth-century social scientific approaches to the phenomenon of revolution. I have identified a set of critical areas that must be analyzed and shown how each theoretical perspective, by stressing one set of structures or institutions over others, often fails to achieve a theoretical synthesis that would completely explain revolution. Non-structural theories present significant problems; aggregate social psychological models emphasize individual motivations, but lose sight of social structural preconditions of revolution; and structural-functionalist reliance on value consensus in a stable social system incorporates cultural analysis into a discussion of mobilization, but underplays the critical causal role of social classes, the world market, or the state as a repressive institution.

The three structural perspectives each focus our attention on a critical arena for analysis that we must incorporate into our discussion. We saw how the international arena – the world economy, global geopolitical and military competition – forms the contextual frame for revolutionary events within a single country. Yet world systems models downplay the causal role of class relations at the level of production, and the autonomous roles of culture and politics. A more traditionally Marxist focus on these class relations devalues the autonomous role of the state, and may, although it need not, decontextualize the revolutionary society from a larger international frame. (Paige, for example, remains sensitive to the commercialization of agriculture as a world process.) The state-centered theories of revolution are as structurally sound as the states they analyze are unsound, locating the revolutionary moment as a moment of state collapse and reconstruction in the aftermath of class-based struggles from below. But even here, Skocpol and others tend to overlook the significance of conscious human activity in the process of revolution.

Tilly's synthesis comes closest to addressing all the major issues and allowing for a multidimensional model of revolution. But even he under-values class struggle as well as world-economic variables. In fact, in generating a model of political contention that places the state at the analytic center and observes the ways in which groups mobilize themselves and their resources to struggle with the state, Tilly undervalues economic variables altogether, giving less causal weight to the world economy as well as to class struggle at the level of production. When he does, quite successfully, discuss the inter-national context, it is as an arena for geopolitical and military competition.

Space and Time: Structure and History

Before concluding this essay it might be wise to summarize the theoretical and methodological themes that have emerged as central in the analysis of revolution. I will offer this summary in connection with issues of both historical time and societal space. Spatial and temporal issues frame the occurrence of revolution, and they must construct our analyses of revolution. By "spatial" I mean the levels of analysis of social structures that exist within, between, and among societies located within a global context. By "temporal" I mean locating the revolutionary society, as well as the phenomenon of revolution itself, within historical time.

As we have seen, the first spatial arena to be understood is that locating the revolutionary society within a larger, international, frame of reference. Not only is the capitalist world economy the arena towards which states and economic elites orient themselves; the global arena of political, military, and diplomatic competition is also the arena in which the constraints on indi-vidual states are articulated. The international arena places political, military, and economic constraints and pressures on the old regime, as well as offering enticing new opportunities for political initiatives, military conquest, and economic expansion.

In discussing contemporary revolutions, we must further ask what position the society plays in the global context, what "zone" it occupies in the spatial division of the international division of political power, production and distribution. Here Wallerstein's terms "core" and "periphery" are valuable heuristic devices to locate the society. Revolutions in the core will have dramatically different trajectories from revolutions in the periphery.

To take but one example of this difference, consider the ideological differences between revolutionary movements in the core and in the periphery. In the core, revolutionary movements are often motivated by "socialist" ideologies, which involve enlarging political participation, redistribution of wealth, and a more international outlook on global coopera- tion. Often revolutionaries in the core are opposed by reactionaries and conservatives, who employ nationalistic arguments against global coopera- tion. But in the periphery, nationalism is an ideology of the revolutionaries, not of the counter-revolutionaries. Nationalists seek to rid the nation of foreign domination, and begin a path of autonomous national development. (That nationalist revolutionaries in the periphery often appear to power- holders in the core as socialist may be more a result of the fact that revolu- tionaries in the core espouse socialist ideas than any genuine socialism among periphery revolutionaries. Of course, many revolutionaries in the periphery do find that the ideology of socialism galvanizes their anti-imperialist senti- ments and coincides with nationalist ideals.)

What is crucial here is that, as an ideology, nationalism is remarkably fluid, capable of serving as a justification for imperialism in the core and of inspiring anti-imperialist struggle in the periphery. The example suggests that the experiences of revolutionaries in the core cannot be easily exported to the periphery, and what is more, that the experiences of revolutionaries in the periphery are not models for revolution in the core. (Thus the ironic pathos of American students emulating Fidel Castro or Che Guevara during the 1960s, or the often tragic efforts of students in the periphery attempting to "reason" like liberal individualists with foreign dominators.)

The international arena also has a temporal dimension, since more than just goods and armies move across international boundaries. The migration of ideas across national lines may put pressure on the old regime state, as well as providing inspiration for those who seek revolutionary solutions. Past revolutions in some societies may inspire revolutionaries in others:

> Revolutions belong to a tradition of historical action in the strong sense that virtually all revolutions in the present century have imitated – or at least set out to imitate as best they could – other revolutions of an earlier date. The condi- tions of revolutionary possibility are extensively determined by the under- standing held by existing ruling groups of what dangers they have to face and how easy these are to surmount, and by the understanding held by potential revolutionaries of the circumstances in which they might be able to seize power and the uses to which it might be put. Plainly as revolutionary forces wax and wane from decade to decade in one part of the world or another, the morale and repertoire of both revolutionary and counter-revolutionary forces will alter constantly. Revolutions may become possible in conditions in which they would have previously been inconceivable. (Dunn, 1972: 232)

Dunn's argument suggests that historical revolutions may not adequately serve as models for contemporary revolutionary events, and that efforts to simply apply those models will be woefully inadequate. I have argued that we must distinguish "early" revolutions from "late" revolutions, and that both of these might well be distinguished from revolutions in contemporary Third World societies, which are adequately labelled "dependent" revolutions. Again these three revolutions will have different configurations of state, class, and international arena, and thus different forms of political contention and different forces of political mobilization.

For one thing, the relationship between state and society differed dramatically between the early revolutions – England and France – and contemporary revolutions. In earlier societies, the revolutionary problematic was "one of liberating a dynamic society and growing economy from within an inhibiting political framework" (Hermassi, 1976: 11). By contrast, contemporary revolutions have occurred in developing societies, which were "marked by relative stagnation and backwardness, and their aim has been to employ the massive apparatus of state power in order to catch up with developments abroad" (Hermassi, 1976: 11). Thus models drawn from the experience of earlier revolutions will be fundamentally flawed and incapable of accounting for the dramatic variation in the line-up of forces – classes, political contenders, the state – that will characterize societies in a different world context and with a different internal configuration. And, of course, given the academic biases and countries of origin of most social scientists, not to mention theorists of revolution, most of the theories of revolution that we have examined have erred on this dimension.

What we conclude, therefore, is that an adequate sociological explanation of revolution must be historically sensitive, not only to the historical development of the particular society under scrutiny, but to the historical development of the world system as a whole and the shifting positions of individual units within that whole.

The Centrality of the State

It is clear that an adequate theory of revolution will have to be comparative. We have identified the structural forces that will need to be compared: international arena, class relations, and the state. Comparisons of the relationships between state and civil society are central, since the state is really the revolutionary vortex, the place where the external pressures and opportunities of the international arena and the domestic pressures of traditional class arrangements are joined. A revolution often begins when the state is no longer able to relieve the pressure of international competition or domestic struggle by passing its problems off to foreign competitors or to domestically subordinate classes. In short, revolutions begin because of the structural inability of the state to resolve its crisis.

If this is so, then we can reasonably approach the problem of revolution by beginning with the collapse of the state. This focus is useful for a number of reasons. First, we can read backward to understand the ways in which the increased international pressure coincided with and reinforced the increased domestic constraints on the ability of the state to handle this pressure, thus setting up the revolutionary situation. At the same time, taking a middle-range focus on the shorter-run precipitants of the revolutionary collapse of legitimate authority does not prevent the analysis of culture and ideology and the motivations of individual participants in a revolutionary event, but stresses that they be understood in the context of longer-run structural preconditions. Finally, a discussion of the crisis of the state and the solutions that the old regime adopts to resolve this crisis allow us to analyse the state in relative autonomy from either international economic considerations or domestic class relations. Thus although we may therefore be seeing the state as more autonomous than it really is, when properly contextualized within an international and domestic frame, we are able to observe the policy options open to the state at any one time, the limits on those policies, and the rationales developed for them.

A Comparative Historical Method

Methodologically, we can approach the comparative analysis of states and revolution from two directions, each outlined by John Stuart Mill in his *A System of Logic*. Using the "Method of Agreement," (see figure 8.1) students can attempt to show that several cases of revolution have in common a similar causal pattern. Seeking the similarities between otherwise diverse

Case 1	Case 2	Case n	
a	d	g	⎫
b	e	h	⎬ Overall differences
c	f	i	⎭
x	x	x	⎫ Crucial
y	y	y	⎭ similarity

Figure 8.1 Mill's Method of Agreement. Key: x = causal variable; y = phenomenon to be explained. *Source*: Skocpol and Somers (1980: 184). The uses of comparative history in macrosocial inquiry. *Comparative Studies in Society and History* 22(2). © Cambridge University Press.

Positive case(s)	Negative case(s)	
a	a	
b	b	} Overall
c	c	} similarities
x	not x	
		} Crucial
y	not y	} difference

Figure 8.2   Mill's Method of Difference. Key: x = causal variable; y = phenomenon to be explained.   *Source*: Skocpol and Somers (1980: 184). The uses of comparative history in macrosocial inquiry. *Comparative Studies in Society and History* 22(2). © Cambridge University Press.

cases may bring one closer to understanding the crucial causal variables that are present in each case. By contrast, the "Method of Difference" invites students to examine those cases in which the phenomenon to be explained and what we take to be the causes of the phenomenon are compared with other cases in which neither the phenomenon nor the hypothesized causes are present. Thus, by comparing a positive with several negative cases, one can isolate the causal factors. We can see this in figure 8.2. Although the Method of Difference is, by itself, a more powerful analytic strategy, both of these methods are useful in constructing a comparative model of revolution.

What is essential, however, is that models of revolution be neither solely comparative or historical, but *both* comparative *and* historical. Given the differences in the world context between, say the French and the Cuban Revolutions, what good would an ahistorical comparison be? And given the differences in the line-ups of structural forces in mid-seventeenth-century England and late-twentieth-century Nicaragua – the pervasiveness of the capitalist world economy, the domination of the international political arena, and the distortion of particular national economies and polities by imperialism – a strictly historical analysis of revolution would be equally thin. A comparative and historical analysis of revolution can set the revolutionary society within its framing contexts, both temporal and spatial, and observe the mechanisms that form the revolutionary situation.

Within a comparative historical framework, the motivations and beliefs and experiences of individuals become more comprehensible. These non-structural factors of revolution are necessary to an adequate understanding, but they can only be understood in context. Ideologies of political opposition, whether they are grounded in competing visions of political justice or religious cosmologies, become analytically important at the moment that a state collapses, at the moment of the vacuum of power, when competing world views may articulate their visions of social reconstruction and for social acceptance at the same time that they contend for political power.

Only within such a context can non-structural variables such as psychological factors and voluntaristic notions of human behavior become comprehensible. Trotsky understood this dilemma well, when he wrote in the Preface to his massive *History of the Russian Revolution* that although the masses go into a revolution without a prepared plan for social reconstruction, they do have a sharp feeling that they can no longer endure the old regime. But, he cautions, they need organization. "Without a guiding organization, the energy of the masses would dissipate like steam not enclosed in a piston box. But nevertheless what moves things is not the piston or the box but the steam" (Trotsky, 1959: x–xi). Ideology and discontent without organization cannot be revolutionary; organization without revolutionary fervor becomes another bureaucratic iron age.

The Analytic Posture

Finally, a word about ourselves as students of revolution. Our analysis of revolution must be both distanced and sympathetic: distanced enough to understand the interplay of complex spatial and temporal forces and sensitive enough to hear the voices of the participants, and their often transcendent, timeless cries for freedom. How can we help but hear them – those who uttered those cries intended them to reach across time and space and touch us whenever we live, because the issues they raise are so essential and fundamental. "Revolution may destroy many things of value with its cruelty and violence, but it may also give expression to the unquenchable spirit of freedom" in people all over the world at different periods of time (Zagorin, 1982, vol. 1: 208).

These are surely the sentiments of the revolutionaries themselves, and analyses of revolution that are simply dispassionate accounts of the rise and fall of classes or states are as bloodless as their subjects are passionate. Neither is complete. The revolutionaries hope that their message may become a clarion call to others in similar circumstances. On the eve of his death, for example, Thomas Jefferson offered these thoughts on the potential meaning of the Declaration of Independence as a revolutionary document (cited in Calvert, 1970: 71):

> May it be to the world, what I believe it will be (to some parts sooner, to others later, but finally to all) the signal of arousing men to burst the chains under which monkish ignorance and superstition have persuaded them to bind themselves, and to assume the blessings and security of self-government. The form which we have substituted restores the free right to the unbounded exercise of freedom and opinion. All eyes are opened or opening to the rights of man. The

general spread of the light of science has already laid open to every view the power of truth, that the mass of mankind has not been born with saddles on their backs, nor a favored few, booted and spurred, ready to ride them legitimately, by the grace of God.

(Modern readers may not easily identify these last few lines as readily as Jefferson's contemporaries might have. Jefferson is here illustrating the remarkable capacity of revolutionary slogans to traverse historical and geographical boundaries by quoting from the writings of John Lilburne and other Levellers during the English Revolution.)

Such hopes are both historically emergent and timeless; societally specific and transcendent. And always, there are people waiting for their turn, their chance to taste the possibility of freedom. Pedro Martinez, Oscar Lewis's celebrated peasant informant, is as eloquent as any:

> I believe that all the revolutions that we see on this earth come to us already destined from up above. The *next revolution* is already written . . . Since Zapata, many have tried but nothing happens. Everything is crushed because God has not given the word yet. Then suddenly we'll see the revolution of the poor against the rich in Mexico. Not now, I don't think, but it will come. I can't say who will be the leader, but it must be someone. (Lewis, 1964: 457)

Future generations will invariably be inspired by the words of today's revolutionaries and will find within them some transcendent truths that speak to their particular oppression together with the inspiration to organize themselves to overthrow that oppressive system. For the circumstances may change dramatically from generation to generation, and from country to country, but the well-springs of human emotion from which revolutions must inevitably draw are constant in their effort to articulate a language of freedom and dignity.

Notes

Chapter 1 Revolutions in the Sociological Imagination

1 This poem can be found in *Selected Poems and Two Plays of William Butler Yeats*, M. L. Rosenthal, ed. New York: Collier, 1962, p. 91.
2 Eckstein (1965) includes only preconditions and precipitants; a precipitant is defined by him as "an event which actually starts the war, much as turning the flintwheel of a cigarette lighter ignites the flame." I believe that it makes more sense to distinguish among the three levels of temporal analysis I have indicated here (see also Stone, 1972).

Chapter 2 On the Shoulders of Giants: Classical Sociological Perspectives on Revolution

1 Despite this, many perceptive sociologists have missed or ignored this fact. Thus does Robertson ask (1985: 236) '[w]hy is it that the modern founders of sociology, while being deeply concerned with religion, did not deem revolution to be a topic of great importance?" I shall endeavor to demonstrate that the founders of modern sociology found revolution to be *at least* as important.
2 Later in *The Manifesto* Marx underscores this point, noting that "every form of society has been based . . . on the antagonism of oppressing and oppressed classes" (1978: 483).
3 This is so important that Skocpol includes the part of the peasantry as the feature that distinguishes a political revolution from a social revolution (see Skocpol, 1979a).
4 In this last phrase, Tocqueville introduces a theme that dominates his magisterial work on the United States, *Democracy in America* (1966) – that material progress leads not to contentment and satisfaction but to restlessness.
5 I would be remiss did I not mention that Tocqueville also incorporates some non-structural variables into his analysis. After a long and elaborate structural and historical analysis, Tocqueville closes both *The Old Regime and the French Revolution* and *The European Revolution* with descriptions of French national

character, and its contribution to the revolution. In the latter, he writes that the French "love liberty, but only as the least of their possessions" and that in France "there is more genius than common sense, and more heroism than virtue" (1959: 159, 160). In the concluding passage to *The Old Regime* he notes:

Ordinarily, the French are the most routine-bound of men, but once they are forced out of the rut and leave their homes, they travel to the ends of the earth and engage in the most reckless ventures. Undisciplined by temperament, the Frenchman is always readier to put up with arbitrary rule, however harsh, of an autocrat than with a free, well-ordered government by his fellow citizens, however worthy of respect they be. At one moment he is up in arms against authority and the next we find him serving the powers-that-be with a zeal such as the most servile races never display. So long as no one thinks of resisting, you can lead him on a thread, but once a revolutionary movement is afoot, nothing can restrain him from taking part in it . . . The Frenchman can turn his hand to anything, but he excels in war alone and he prefers fighting against odds, preferring dazzling feats of arms and spectacular successes to achievements of the more solid kind. He is more prone to heroism than to humdrum virtue, apter for genius than for good sense, more inclined to think up grandiose schemes than to carry through great enterprises. Thus the French are at once the most brilliant and the most dangerous of all European nations, and the best qualified to become, in the eyes of other peoples, an object of admiration, of hatred, of compassion, or alarm – never of indifference.

6   Tocqueville's direct participation makes a statement like Hereth's (1986: 80), that "no matter how eagerly he greeted and accepted the republican results of revolutions from time to time, he likewise kept his distance from revolution itself", seem not only a mystification ("from time to time?" "revolution *itself*?") but inaccurate.

7   The enduring legacy of Tocqueville's analysis, then, is not to be sought in the "relative deprivation" theorists who claim him (and to whom I shall turn in the next chapter), but rather in the structural analysis of revolution provided by Skocpol and Tilly.

8   This position is in direct contrast to the perspectives of functionalists, who argue that Weber was concerned with legitimacy more than power. Parsons even translated Weber's German term for domination as "imperative coordination" stressing the coordinated element as opposed to the coerced mechanism of coordination. This depoliticization of Weber also occurs in his theory of stratification, which strikes me as an analysis of the various hierarchies along which people are arrayed and thereby dominated by those in superior (class, status, party) positions, as well as the types of resources (economic, social, political) that groups may mobilize in their efforts to gain some form of mobility within a structure of domination.

9   Although throughout this volume I have not used the masculine pronoun as generic and universal, I believe that with Freud such use is essential, since his theory depends so heavily on the psychological development of the male child

into manhood. I thus use the masculine pronoun here specifically, not generically.

10   Freud thus develops a multidimensional perspective on the relationship of demands and the institutional capacity to meet them. As we shall see in the next chapter, the relative deprivation theorists embrace Freud's notion of aggression following the frustration of libidinal demands (and the incapacity of political institutions to meet those demands), but do not follow his understanding that sometimes states can ask for too much from their subjects.

Chapter 3   Stages, Systems, and Deprivation: Non-Structural Theories of Revolution

1   See also Schwartz (1972), Hopper (1950), and Krejci (1983) for further elaboration of this position.

2   This formulation also borrows from Goldstone (1982: 191–2) and Schwartz (1971: 112).

3   This, despite Smelser's earlier assertion (1962: 282) that *some* degree of organization is necessary, that "the discontented must have *some* degree of access to some method of affecting the normative order."

4   This entire paragraph also appears verbatim on p. 177 of this poorly edited volume (Eisenstadt, 1978).

5   This definition is restated in Davies (1971: 133).

Chapter 4   Revolution in an International Context: Geopolitical Competition and the Capitalist World Economy

1   Trotsky himself does not use the term "multiple sovereignty" to describe a revolutionary situation. Tilly transformed Trotsky's notion of "dual power" or "dual sovereignty" into multiple sovereignty after reading an article by Peter Amann (Tilly, personal communication, 1989).

2   I shall develop this question of geopolitical and military competition between states in greater detail in chapter 6.

Chapter 5   Class Struggle and Revolution

1   In the following chapter I will also discuss Lenin's theory of the relationship between revolution and the state, which also diverges significantly from that of Marx. Here, however, I want to concentrate on those elements of Lenin's class theory that are consistent with and diverge from those of Marx.

2   Moore's theory of the revolutionary character of the peasantry is also a theory of the peasantry as tragic actors, as both the makers of revolution and its first and chief victims. This is a theme to which I shall return below.

3   This discussion of Moore's theory draws on a schematic analysis of the theory presented by Collins (1973: 202–3).

4   This typology is presented by Taylor (1984: 26–31).

5   See also Moore (1966: 438–41) for a more detailed theoretical elaboration of this schema.

6. I am indebted to Martin Spencer for this formulation, as well as much of the political and cultural critique of Moore.

Chapter 6   The State and Revolution

1   Lenin is here quoting the definition of the state provided by Engels in *The Family, Private Property and the State*, which Lenin cited (1970: 7):

> The state is, therefore, by no means a power forced on society from without . . .
> [I]t is a product of society at a certain stage of development; it is the admission that this society has become entangled in an insoluble contradiction with itself, that it is cleft into irreconcilable antagonisms which it is powerless to dispel. But in order that these antagonisms, classes with conflicting economic interests, might not consume themselves and society in sterile struggle, a power seemingly standing above society became necessary for the purpose of moderating the conflict, of keeping it within the bounds of "order"; and this power, arisen out of society, but placing itself above it, and increasingly alienating itself from it, is the state.

2   Weber's separation of means and ends in his definition leaves him with a less historically specific theory than he thinks. Certainly, the monopoly over the means of legitimate violence is as essential ingredient in the formula. But the state must be located within an historical process. When viewed historically, we can observe that certain social formations did not develop a "state" proper, while others did. This would lead us to inquire what was common among those societies that did witness the development of a state (in whatever form it did develop). The Greek and Roman city-states, the feudal monarchies, and later absolutist states as well as the capitalist state do not only share the common element of monopoly of the legitimate use of violence. They also share, in general, a common end: the maintenance of the class nature of the society in which they arose. The common end of states, as political organizations, is, in this more Marxian sense, the maintenance of class domination and the suppression of class struggle. Control over the means of repression is a necessary but not sufficient part of the definition; the existence of a state implies the application of that means of violence towards a particular end.

3   We will return to the question of absolutism and the absolutist state later in this chapter.

4   In explicating Gidden's theory of revolution, I have been greatly helped by both the formal work of and informal communication with Ira J. Cohen; see, for example, Cohen (1987 and 1989).

5   Much of this section is drawn from Kimmel (1988: 9–17).

6   This last position, that absolutism has "no class character, is most often associated with non-structuralist theorists, who argue for the state as an institution without class character in general. One French historian, Roland Mousnier, argues that the absolute monarchy was independent of social class:

> By dividing functions between two classes, but reserving the most important of them to the lesser class, the bourgeoisie, and systematically raising up this class

and counterposing it to the other stronger class, the King brought the class struggle to a point of equilibrium between classes, which ensured his personal power, and, in the government and the state, unity order, and hierarchy. (Mousnier, 1980: 236).

Because in large part this position is concerned with the state as the embodiment of political legitimacy, I will concentrate on the two positions that claim a class character for the state.

7   In a conciliatory response to this definition, Wallerstein writes that he could "accept Anderson's entire statement if the adjective 'feudal' were dropped" (Wallerstein, 1980: 32). This strikes me as analogous to accepting Marx's epigrammatic notion that "[t]he history of all hitherto existing societies is the history of class struggle" if the adjective "class" dropped. Unfortunately, as I read it, the operative term in the statement is the adjective "feudal," and the differences between Wallerstein and Anderson remain salient and fundamental to their specific arguments.

8   This is the subject of *Absolutism and its Discontents* (Kimmel, 1988).

9   Much of this section is based on Himmelstein and Kimmel (1981).

10 I will deal with Tilly's work in the next chapter.

11 For example, ideology is important in the French Revolution, not only in its capacity to mobilize revolutionary activities, but also for setting long-term trends in motion. The process of 'revolutionary de-Christianization'', discussed by Michel Vovelle, that dominated French theological thought between 1760 and 1790 transformed a world view that was concerned with "Baroque piety" into a more secularized view, which had an independent effect in loosening traditional bonds among various classes and between those classes and the state (see Vovelle, 1973).

Chapter 8   Conclusion

1   The farmer is quoted in Martin (1973: 8).

References

Adas, Michael (1979) *Prophets of Rebellion: Millenarian protest movements against the European colonial order*. Chapel Hill, NC: University of North Carolina Press.
——(1981) From avoidance to confrontation: peasant protest in precolonial and colonial Southeast Asia. *Comparative Studies in Society and History*, 23(2).
——(1982) Bandits, monks, and pretender kings: patterns of peasant resistance and protest in colonial Burma, 1826–1941. In *Power and Protest in the Countryside: studies of rural unrest in Asia, Europe and Latin America*, (Robert Weller and Scott Guggenheim, eds.) Durham, NC: Duke University Press.
Adorno, Theodor, Frenkel-Brunswik, Else, Levinson, Daniel J., and Sanford, R. Nevitt (1950) *The Authoritarian Personality*. New York: Schocken Press.
Anderson, Perry (1974) *Lineages of the Absolutist State*. London: New Left Books.
Arendt, Hannah (1965) *On Revolution*. New York: Viking Press.
Aya, Roderick (1979) Theories of revolution reconsidered: contrasting models of collective violence. *Theory and Society*, 8(1).
Baecheler, Jean (1975) *Revolution*. New York: Harper and Row.
Bell, David V. J. (1973) *Resistance and Revolution*. Boston: Houghton Mifflin.
Berger, John (1972) *Ways of Seeing*. New York: Penguin.
Bloch, Marc (1967) A contribution towards a comparative history of European Societies. In *Land and Work in Medieval Europe*. New York: Harper and Row.
Block, Fred and Somers, Margaret (1984) Beyond the economistic fallacy: the holistic social science of Karl Polanyi. In *Vision and Method in Historical Sociology*, T. Skocpol, ed. New York: Cambridge University Press.
Bonnell, Victoria (1985a) *Roots of Rebellion: workers' politics and organizations in St Petersburg and Moscow, 1900–14*. Berkeley: University of California Press.
——, ed. (1985b) *The Russian Worker: life and labor under the tsarist regime*. Berkeley: University of California Press.
Braudel, Fernand (1986 [1979]) *Civilization and Capitalism, 15th–18th Century*, vol. 3: *The Perspective of the World*. New York: Harper and Row.
Brinton, Crane (1965) *The Anatomy of Revolution*. New York: Harper and Row.
Calhoun, Craig (1980) Community: towards a variable conception for comparative research. *Social History*, 5(1).

—(1982) *The Question of Class Struggle: social foundations of popular radicalism during the industrial revolution*. Chicago: University of Chicago Press.

—(1983) The radicalism of tradition: community strength or venerable disguise and borrowed language? *American Journal of Sociology*, 88(5).

—(1988) The "retardation" of French economic development and social radicalism during the Second Republic: new lessons from the old comparison with Britain. In *Global Crises and Social Movements: artisans, peasants, populists and the world-economy*, Edmund Burke III, ed. Boulder, CO: Westview Press.

Calvert, Peter (1970) *Revolution*. London: Macmillan.

Chorley, Katharine (1973) *Armies and the Art of Revolution*. Boston: Beacon Press.

Cohen, Ira J. (1987) Structuration theory and social *praxis*. In *Social Theory Today*, Anthony Giddens and Jonathan Turner, eds. Cambridge: Polity Press.

—(1989) *Structuration Theory: Anthony Giddens and the constitution of social life*. London: Macmillan.

Collins, Randall (1973) Letter to the editor. *Contemporary Sociology*, 2(1).

—(1981) *Sociology Since Midcentury*. New York: Academic Press.

—(1986) *Weberian Sociological Theory*. New York: Cambridge University Press.

Colton, Ethan (1935) *Four Patterns of Revolution*. New York: Association Press.

Davies, James C. (1962) Toward a theory of revolution. *American Sociological Review*, 6(1).

—(1969) The "J" curve of rising and declining satisfaction as a cause of some great revolutions and a contained rebellion. In *Violence in America*, H. Graham and T. Gurr, eds. New York: Signet Books.

—(1971) *When Men Revolt and Why*. New York: Free Press.

Dollard, John, Doob, Leonard, Miller, Neal, Mowrer, O. H. and Sears, Robert (1967) *Frustration and Aggression*. New Haven, CT: Yale University Press.

Downs, Anthony (1957) *An Economic Theory of Democracy*. New York: Harper and Row.

Draper, Hal (1978) *Karl Marx's Theory of Revolution*. New York: Monthly Review Press.

Dunn, John (1972) *Modern Revolutions: an introduction to the analysis of a political phenomenon*. New York: Cambridge University Press.

Durkheim, Emile (1957) *Professional Ethics and Civic Morals*. London: Routledge and Kegan Paul.

—(1958) *The Division of Labor in Society*. New York: Free Press.

—(1951) *Suicide*. New York: Free Press.

—(1961) *Moral Education*. New York: Free Press.

Eastman, Max (1936) Differing with Sigmund Freud. In *Enjoyment of Living*. New York: Harper and Row.

Eckstein, Harry (1964) *Internal War*. New York: Free Press.

—(1965) On the etiology of internal wars. *History and Theory*, 4(2).

Edwards, Lyford (1972) *The Natural History of Revolution*. Chicago: University of Chicago Press.

Edwards, Thomas (1982) *Combined and Uneven Development*. London: New Left Books.

Eisentadt, S. N. (1978) *Revolution and the Transformation of Societies*. New York: Free Press.

Ellwood, Charles (1905) A psychological theory of revolutions. *American Journal of Sociology*, 11(1).

Engels, Frederick (1970 [1884]) *The Origins of the Family, Private Property and the State*. New York: International Publishers.

Engels, Frederick (1971 [1878]) *Anti-Duhring*. New York: International Publishers.

Evans, Peter (1975) Industrialization and imperialism: growth and stagnation on the periphery. *Berkeley Journal of Sociology*, 20.

Evans, Peter, Rueschemeyer, Dietrich and Skocpol, Theda, eds (1985) *Bringing the State Back In*. New York: Cambridge University Press.

Feierabend, Ivo and Feierabend, Rosalind (1972) Systemic conditions of political aggression: an application of frustration – aggression theory. In *Anger, Violence and Politics*, Ivo Feierabend, Rosalind Feierabend, and Ted Robert Gurr, eds Englewood Cliffs, NJ: Prentice-Hall.

Fenton, Steve (1984) *Durkheim and Modern Sociology*. New York: Cambridge University Press.

Freire, Paulo (1972) *Pedagogy of the Oppressed*. New York: Seabury Press.

Freud, Sigmund (1959) *Group Psychology and the Analysis of the Ego*. New York: Norton.

——(1961) *Civilization and its Discontents*. New York: Norton.

——(1965) *The Interpretation of Dreams*. New York: Avon.

Friedland, William (with Barton, Amy, Dancis, Bruce, Rotkin, Michael, and Spiro, Michael) (1982) *Revolutionary Theory*. Totowa, NJ: Allenheld and Osmun.

Friedrich, Carl J., ed. (1966) *Revolution*. New York: Atherton.

Fulbrook, Mary and Skocpol, Theda (1984) Destined pathways: the historical sociology of Perry Anderson. In *Vision and Method in Historical Sociology*, Theda Skocpol, ed. New York: Cambridge University Press.

Gabriel, Yiannis (1983) *Freud and Society*. London: Routledge and Kegan Paul.

Gamson, William, Fierman, Bruce, and Rytina, Steven (1982) *Encounters with Unjust Authority*. Homewood, IL: Dorsey Press.

Geschwender, James A. (1968) Explorations in the theory of revolutions and social movements. *Social Forces*, 42(2).

Giddens, Anthony (1973) *The Class Structure of the Advanced Societies*. New York: Harper and Row.

——(1985) *The Nation State and Violence*. Berkeley: University of California Press.

Gillis, John (1970) Political theory and the European revolutions, 1789–1848. *World Politics*, 22(3).

Goldfrank, Walter (1975) World system, state structure and the onset of the Mexican Revolution. *Politics and Society*, 5(4).

——(1979) Theories of revolution and revolution without theory: the case of Mexico. *Theory and Society*, 7(1).

Goldstone, Jack A. (1980) Theories of Revolution: The Third Generation. *World Politics*, 23(3).

——(1982) The comparative and historical study of revolutions. *Annual Review of Sociology*, 8.

Goodspeed, D. J. (1962) *The Conspirators*. London: Macmillan.

Goodwin, Jeff and Skocpol, Theda (1988) Explaining revolutions in the contemporary Third World. Paper presented at a conference on Comparative Politics: Research Perspectives for the Next Twenty Years. New York: The Graduate Center, CUNY, 7–9 September.

Gottschalk, Louis (1944) Causes of revolution. *American Journal of Sociology*, 50(1).

Granovetter, Mark (1978) Threshold models of collective behavior. *American Journal of Sociology*, 83(6).

Greene, Thomas H. (1984) *Comparative Revolutionary Movements: the search for theory and justice*. Englewood Cliffs, NJ: Prentice-Hall.

Grotanelli, Christiano (1985) Archaic forms of rebellion and their religious background. In *Religion, Rebellion and revolution*, Bruce Lincoln, ed. New York: St Martin's Press.

Gurr, Ted Robert (1968a) A causal model of civil strife: a comparative analysis using new indices. *American Political Science Review*, 62.

——(1968b) Psychological factors in civil violence. *World Politics*, 20.

——(1970) Sources of rebellion in western societies: some quantitative evidence. *Annals of the American Academy of Political and Social Science*, 391 (September).

——(1971) *Why Men Rebel*. Princeton, NJ: Princeton University Press.

——(1976) *Rogues, Rebels and Reformers*. Beverly Hills, CA: Sage Publications.

Hagopian, Mark N. (1974) *The Phenomenon of Revolution*. New York: Dodd, Mead.

Halpern, Manfred (1966) The revolution of modernization in national and international society. In *Revolution*, Carl Friedrich, ed. New York: Atherton.

——(1971) A redefinition of the revolutionary situation. In *National Liberation: revolution in the Third World*, Norman Miller and Roderick Aya, eds. New York: Free Press.

Hechter, Michael (1977) The lineages of the capitalist state: a review essay of Anderson's *Lineages of the Absolutist State*. *American Journal of Sociology* 82(4).

Hereth, Michael (1986) *Alexis De Tocqueville: threats to freedom in democracy*. Durham, NC: Duke University Press.

Hermassi, Elbaki (1976) Toward a comparative study of revolutions. In *Comparative Studies in Society and History*, 18(2).

——(1980) *Third World Revolution Reassessed*. Berkeley: University of California Press.

Higham, Robin, ed. (1972) *Civil Wars in the Twentieth Century*, Lexington, KY: University of Kentucky Press.

Himmelstein, Jerome and Kimmel, Michael S. (1981) Skocpol's structural model of revolution. *American Journal of Sociology*, 86(5).

Hintze, Otto (1975) *The Historical Essays of Otto Hintze*, Felix Gilbert, ed. New York: Oxford University Press.

Hobsbawm, Eric (1962) *The Age of Revolution, 1789–1848*. New York: New American Library.

——(1975) Revolution. Paper presented to the XIV Congress of Historical Sciences, San Francisco, CA.

——(1986) Revolution. In *Revolution in History*, R. Porter and M. Teich, eds.

Cambridge: Cambridge University Press.

Hopper, R. D. (1950) The revolutionary process. *Social Forces*, 28(3).

Hunt, Lynn (1984) Charles Tilly's collective action. In *Vision and Method in Historical Sociology*, Theda Skocpol, ed. New York: Cambridge University Press.

Huntington, Samuel (1968) *Political Order in Changing Societies*. New Haven, CT: Yale University Press.

Ireland, T. (1967) The rationale of revolt. *Papers in Non-market decision making*. 1.

Jenkins, J. Craig (1982) Why do peasants rebel? Structural and historical theories of modern peasant rebellions. *American Journal of Sociology*, 88(3).

Johnson, Chalmers (1964) *Revolution and the Social System*. Stanford, CA: Hoover Institution Studies.

——(1966) *Revolutionary Change*. Boston: Little, Brown.

——(1973) *Autopsy on People's War*. Berkeley, CA: University of California Press.

Kerkvliet, Benedict J. Tria (1986) Everyday resistance to injustice in a Phillipine village. In *Everyday Forms of Peasant Resistance in South-East Asia*, James Scott and Benedict J. Tria Kerkvliet, eds. London: Frank Cass.

Kiernan, Victor (1986) Imperialism and revolution. In *Revolution in History*, R. Porter and M. Teich, eds. Cambridge: Cambridge University Press.

Kimmel, Michael S. (1977) Wallerstein's *Modern World System*: a critique. *Contemporary crises*, 2(3).

——(1982) Review of Wallerstein's *Modern World System*, vol. II. *Theory and Society*, 11(2).

——(1984) Toward the republic of virtue: the ideology and organization of the Levellers and the *sans-culottes*. *Research in Social Movements, Conflict and Change*, 7.

——(1988) *Absolutism and its Discontents: state and society in seventeenth century France and England*. New Brunswick, NJ: Transaction Books.

Krejci, Jaroslav (1983) *Great Revolutions Compared: the search for a theory*. New York: St Martin's Press.

Le Bon, Gustav (1913) *The Psychology of Revolution*. New York: Putnam's.

——(1960) [1895]) *The Crowd*. New York: Viking.

Leiden, Carl and Schmitt, Karl M. (1968) *The Politics of Violence: Revolution in the Modern World*. Englewood Cliffs, NJ: Prentice-Hall.

Lenin, V. I. (1929) Letters on tactics. In *Collected Works*, vol. 20. New York: International Publishers.

——(1970) *The State and Revolution*. Peking: Foreign Language Press.

Lewis, Oscar (1964) *Pedro Martinez: a Mexican peasant and his family*. New York: Random House.

Lowy, Michael (1982) *The Politics of Combined and Uneven Development: the theory of permanent revolution*. New York: New Left Books.

Lukacs, Georg (1971) *History and Class Consciousness*. Cambridge, MA: MIT Press.

Lupsha, Peter (1971) Explanations of political violence: some psychological theories versus indignation. *Politics and Society*, 2(1).

Luxembourg, Rosa (1970) *Reform or Revolution*. New York: Pathfinder Press.

Mao Zedong (1967) *Quotations from Chairman Mao*. Peking: Foreign Language Press.

Mann, Michael (1986) *The Sources of Social Power*, vol. 1. New York: Cambridge University Press.

Martin, Earl (1978) A journey to My Lai and beyond. *Bulletin of Concerned Asian Scholars*, 10(4).

Marx, Karl (1963) *The Eighteenth Brumaire of Louis Bonaparte*. New York: International Publishers.

Marx, Karl (1964) *Pre-Capitalist Economic Formations*. New York: International Publishers.

——(1971) *Revolution and Counter-Revolution*. New York: Capricorn.

——(1978) *The Marx – Engels Reader* (2nd ed.), Robert Tucker, ed. New York: Norton.

Mathias, Peter (1985) Concepts of revolution in England and France in the eighteenth century. *Studies in Eighteenth Century Culture*, 14.

Meusel, Alfred (1934) Revolution and counter-revolution. In *Encyclopedia of the Social Sciences*. New York.

Migdal, Joel S. (1974) *Peasants, Politics and Revolution*. Princeton, NJ: Princeton University Press.

——(1982) Capitalist penetration in the 19th century: creating conditions for new patterns of social control. In *Power and Protest in the Countryside: studies of rural unrest in Asia, Europe and Latin America*, Robert P. Weller and Scott Guggenheim, eds. Durham, NC: Duke University Press.

Miliband, Ralph (1977) *Marxism and Politics*. New York: Oxford University Press.

Miller, Norman and Aya, Roderick, eds. (1971) *National Liberation: revolution in the Third World*. New York: Free Press.

Mintz, Sidney (1982) Afterword: peasantries and the rural sector – notes on a discovery. In *Power and Protest in the Countryside: studies of rural unrest in Asia, Europe and Latin America*, Robert P. Weller and Scott Guggenheim, eds. Durham, NC: Duke University Press.

Mitchell, Edward (1967) *Land Tenure and Rebellion: a statistical analysis of factors affecting government control in South Vietnam*. Memorandum RM-5181-ARPA (abridged), prepared for the Advanced Research Projects Agency, ARPA Order No. 189–1. Santa Monica, CA: The Rand Corporation.

Moore, Barrington (1962) *Political Power and Social Theory*. New York: Harper and Row.

——(1966) *The Social Origins of Dictatorship and Democracy: lord and peasant in the making of the modern world*. Boston: Beacon Press.

——(1978) *Injustice: the social bases of obedience and revolt*. White Plains, NY: M. E. Sharpe.

Mousnier, Roland, (1970) The Fronde. In *Preconditions of Revolution in Early Modern Europe*, R. Forster and J. P. Greene, eds. Baltimore, MD: Johns Hopkins University Press.

——(1980) *The Institutions of France under the Absolute Monarchy, 1598–1789*, vol. 1: *Society and State*. Chicago: University of Chicago Press.

Neumann, Sigmund (1949a) The international civil war. *World Politics*, 1(3).

——(1949b) The structure and strategy of revolution: 1848 and 1948. *Journal of Politics*, 11.

Olson, Mancur (1965) *The Logic of Collective Action*. New York: Schocken Books.

Paige, J. (1975) *Agrarian Revolution*. New York: Free Press.

Park, Robert Ezra (1955) *Society*. Glencoe, IL: Free Press.

Parsons, Talcott (1955) *The Social System*. New York: Free Press.

Pettee, George Sawyer (1938) *The Process of Revolution*. New York: Harper and Brothers.

Platt, Gerald M. (1980) Thoughts on a theory of collective action: language, affect and ideology in revolution. In *New Directions in Psychohistory: the Adelphio Papers in Honor of Erik Erikson*, Mel Albin, ed. Lexington, MA: D. C. Heath.

Platt, Gerald M. and Weinstein, Fred (1969) *The Wish to be Free*. Berkeley: University of California Press.

——and——(1973) *Psychoanalytic Sociology*. Baltimore, MD: The Johns Hopkins University Press.

Polanyi, Karl (1957) *The Great Transformation*. Boston: Beacon Press.

Pope, Whitney (1986) *Alexis de Tocqueville: his social and political theory*. Beverly Hills, CA: Sage Publications.

Popkin, Samuel (1979) *The Rational Peasant*. Berkeley: University of California Press.

Porter, Roy and Teich, Mikulus, eds (1986) *Revolution in History*. Cambridge: Cambridge University Press.

Rejai, Mostafa (1977) *The Comparative Study of Revolutionary Strategy*. New York: David McKay.

Roazen, Paul (1968) *Freud: political and social thought*. New York: Vintage.

Robertson, Priscilla (1965) *Revolutions of 1848: a social History*. New York: Harper and Row.

Robertson, Roland (1985) The development and modern implications of the classical perspective on religion and revolution. In *Religion, Rebellion, Revolution*, Bruce Lincoln, ed. New York: St Martin's Press.

Robinson, Paul (1969) *The Freudian Left: Wilhelm Reich, Geza Roheim, Herbert Marcuse*. New York: Harper and Row.

Ruiz, Ramon Eduardo (1980) *The Great Rebellion: Mexico, 1905–24*. New York: W. W. Norton.

Rule, James B. (1989) *Theories of Civil Violence*, vol. 1. Berkeley: University of California Press.

Salert, Barbara (1976) *Revolutions and Revolutionaries*. New York: Elsevier.

Schwartz, David C. (1971) A theory of revolutionary behavior. In *When Men Revolt and Why*, James Davies, ed. New York: Free Press.

——(1972) Political alienation: the psychology of revolution's first stage. In *Anger, Violence and Politics*, Ivo Feierabend, Rosalind Feierabend, and Ted Robert Gurr, eds. Englewood Cliffs, NJ: Prentice-Hall.

Scott, James C. (1976) *The Moral Economy of the Peasant*. New Haven, CT: Yale University Press.

——(1977a) Hegemony and the peasantry. *Politics and Society*, 7(3).

——(1977b) Peasant revolution: a dismal science. *Comparative Politics*, 9(2).

——(1977c) Protest and profanation: agrarian revolt and the little tradition (two parts). *Theory and Society* 4(1, 2).

Scott, James and Kerkvliet, Benedict J. Tria, eds. (1986) *Everyday Forms of Peasant Resistance in South-East Asia*. London: Frank Cass.

Shorter, Edward and Tilly, Charles (1974) *Strikes in France*. New York: Cambridge University Press.

Skocpol, Theda (1976a) France, Russia, China: a structural analysis of social revolutions. *Comparative Studies in Society and History*, 18(2).

——(1976b) Old regime legacies and communist revolutions in Russia and China. *Social Forces*, 55(2).

——(1977) Review of Wallerstein's *Modern's World System*. *American Journal of Sociology*, 82(2).

—— (1979a) *States and Social Revolutions*. New York: Cambridge University Press.

——(1979b) Review of Eisenstadt's *Revolution and the Transformation of Societies*. *Contemporary Sociology*, 8(3).

——(1982) What makes peasants revolutionary? In *Power and Protest in the Countryside: studies of rural unrest in Asia, Europe and Latin America*, Robert P. Weller and Scott Guggenheim, eds. Durham, NC: Duke University Press.

—— ed. (1984) *Vision and Method in Historical Sociology*. New York: Cambridge University Press.

Skocpol, Theda and Somers, Margaret (1980) The uses of comparative history in macrosocial inquiry. *Comparative Studies in Society and History* 22(2).

——and Trimberger, Ellen Kay (1977) Revolution in the world historical context of capitalism. *Berkeley Journal of Sociology*, 22.

Smelser, Neil (1959) *Social Change and the Industrial Revolution*. London: Routledge and Kegan Paul.

——(1962) *A Theory of Collective Behavior*. New York: Free Press.

Somers, Margaret and Goldfrank, Walter (1979) The limits of agronomic determinism: a critique of Paige's *Agrarian Revolution*. *Comparative Studies in Society and History*, 21(3).

Sorokin, Pitirim (1967) *The Sociology of Revolution*. New York: Howard Fertig.

Stinchecombe, Arthur (1978) *Theoretical Methods in Social History*. New York: Academic Press.

Stone, Lawrence (1972) *The Causes of the English Revolution, 1529–1642*. New York: Harper and Row.

Taylor, Stan (1984) *Social Science and Revolutions*. New York: St Martin's Press.

Thomas, Keith (1975) Review of Wallerstein's *Modern World System*. *New York Review of Books*, October.

Thompson, E. P. (1963) *The Making of the English Working Class*. New York: Vintage.

Thompson, F. M. L. (1963) *English Landed Society in the Nineteenth Century*. London: Routledge and Kegan Paul.

Thucydides (1956) *The Peloponnesian War*. Harmondsworth: Penguin.

Tilly, Charles (1964) *The Vendée*. Cambridge, MA: Harvard University Press.

——(1973) Does modernization breed revolution? *Comparative Politics*, 5(3).

——(1974) Town and country in revolution. In *Peasant Rebellion and Communist Revolution in Asia*, John Lewis, ed. Stanford, CA: Stanford University Press.

——ed. (1975) *The Formation of National States in Western Europe*. Princeton, NJ: Princeton University Press.

——(1978) *From Mobilization to Revolution*. Reading, MA: Addison-Wesley.

——(1982) Routine conflicts and peasant rebellions in 17th century France. In *Power and Protest in the Countryside: studies of rural unrest in Asia, Europe and Latin America*, Robert P. Weller and Scott Guggenheim, eds. Durham, NC: Duke University Press.

——(1985a) War making and state making as organized crime. In *Bringing the State Back In*, Peter Evans, Dietrich Reuschemeyer and Theda Skocpol, eds. New York: Cambridge University Press.

——(1985b) *Big Structures, Large Processes, Huge Comparisons*. New York: Russell Sage Foundation.

——(1989) Changing forms of revolution. Working paper 80, Center for Studies of Social Change, New School for Social Research.

Tocquerille, Alexis de (1959) *The European Revolution and Correspondence with Gobineau*, John Lukacs, ed. New York: Anchor.

——(1966) *Democracy in America*, 2 vols. New York: Anchor.

——(1955) *The Old Regime and the French Revolution*. New York: Anchor.

——(1970) *Recollections*, George Lawrence, trans. London: Macdonald.

——(1980) *On Democracy, Revolution, and Society*, J. Stone and S. Mennel, eds. Chicago: University of Chicago Press.

Trimberger, Ellen Kay (1978) *Revolution from Above: military bureaucrats and development in Japan, Turkey, Egypt and Peru*. New Brunswick, NJ: Transaction Books.

Trotsky, Leon (1930) *My Life*. New York: Pathfinder Press.

——(1959 [1932]) *The History of the Russian Revolution*. New York: Doubleday.

Tucker, Robert (1966) The Marxian revolutionary idea. In *Revolution*, Carl J. Friedrich, ed. New York: Atherton.

Urry, John (1973) *Reference Groups and the Theory of Revolution*. London: Routledge and Kegan Paul.

Vovelle, Michel (1973) *Piété baroque et déchristianization en Provence au XVIIIe siècle: les attitudes devant la mort après les clauses des testaments*. Paris: SEVPEN.

Wallerstein, Immanuel (1974) *The Modern World System*, vol. 1. New York: Academic Press.

——(1979) *The Capitalist World Economy*. New York: Cambridge University Press.

——(1980) *The Modern World System*, vol. II. New York: Academic Press.

——(1984) *The Politics of the World Economy*. New York: Cambridge University Press.

——(1989) *The Modern World System*, vol. III. San Diego, CA: Academic Press.

Walton, John (1984) *Reluctant Rebels: comparative studies of revolutions and undevelopment*. New York: Columbia University Press.

Weber, Max (1951) *The Religions of China*. New York: Free Press.

——(1958) *From Max Weber*, (H. Gerth and C. W. Mills, eds. New York: Oxford University Press.

——(1961) *General Economic History*. New York: Collier.

Weber, Max (1962 [1904]) *The Protestant Ethic and the Spirit of Capitalism*. New York: Scribner.

Weber, Max (1978) *Economy and Society*, 2 vols. Berkeley, CA: University of California Press.

Weller, Robert P. and Guggenheim, Scott, eds (1982) *Power and Protest in the Countryside: studies of rural unrest in Asia, Europe and Latin America*. Durham, NC: Duke University Press.

Willer, David and Zollschan, George K. (1964) Prolegomenon to a theory of revolutions. In *Explorations in social change*, G. Zollschan and D. Willer, eds. Boston: Houghton Mifflin.

Wolf, Eric (1969) *Peasant Wars of the Twentieth Century*. New York: Harper and Row.

——(1982) *Europe and the People Without History*. Berkeley: University of California Press.

Wolfenstein, E. Victor (1971) *The Revolutionary Personality: Lenin, Trotsky, Gandhi*. Princeton, NJ: Princeton University Press.

Wood, Gordon (1973) The American revolution. In *Revolutions: a comparative study*, L. Kaplan, ed. New York: Vintage Books.

Zagorin, Perez (1976) Prolegomena to a comparative history of revolution in early modern Europe. *Comparative Studies in Society and History*, 18(2).

——(1982) *Rebels and Rulers*, 2 vols. Cambridge: Cambridge University Press.

Index

abdication of nobility   26–31
above, revolution from   153–6
absolutism   113–14, 228–9
  and state   151, 162, 163–70
accelerated deprivation   78
accelerators of revolution   56
action *see* collective behavior
Adas, M.   199–201, 204
administration *see* bureaucracy
Adorno, T.   72
Africa   25
  and class struggle theories   139,
    142–3
  and international context   84, 102
  and non-structural theories   52, 76
  and state   153
  and structural social psychology   203
aggregate social psychological models of
    mass discontent   47, 73–82
aggression
  classical sociological perspectives of
    40–1, 43
  non-structural theories of   70–3,
    80–1
  agreement, method of   221
agriculture   135
  agronomic determinism   136–44
  commercialization of   121, 122, 136–
    41, 198, 217
  politics of production   120–3

and state   152, 172, 173–5, 183
typology of revolution   123–9
see also peasantry
'agronomic determinism'   136–41
  limits of   141–4
Algeria   25, 203
alienation   36, 148
  of intellectuals   48–9, 52, 63
Amann, P.   227
ambivalence, revolutionary   25–33
America *see* United States
analytic posture   223–4
anarchist revolution   58
anatomical references *see* physiological
Anderson, P.   93, 150, 153, 163–70,
    192, 229
Angola   25, 52, 84, 139, 142–3
anomie   37, 75
anthropomorphism   111
Arendt, H.   8, 16, 190, 201–2
aristocracy *see* ruling classes
Aristotle   4, 9
artisans *see* proletariat
Asia   203; *see also* China; India; Japan;
    Vietnam
aspirational deprivation   77
atomization   28
authoritarianism   178
authority
  classical sociological perspectives of

242 *Index*

Moore's theory, politics of agricultural production 120–3; state autonomy and cultural variation 129–36; typology of revolution 123–9
and state 147–8, 171, 177–8, 179, 182, 183
world system and 136–41
see also bourgeoisie; proletariat; ruling classes
classical sociological perspectives *see* sociological perspectives
Clausewitz, K. von 208
coalitions 11, 129
non-structural theories of 50, 52
cognitive dissonance 73
Cohen, I.J. 162–3, 228
Colbert, J.B. 169
collapse of social system *see* disequilibriated social system
collective behavior/action
irrational *see* irrationality
non-structural theories 50, 53, 60, 66–9; as pathology 39, 41–2, 67–8
and structural social psychology 194, 206–8, 213–14
see also revolution
Collins, R. 150, 153, 180, 190, 227
on class conflict 109, 123
on elation 192
on loss of legitimacy 190
on revolution as geopolitical failure 156–61
colonialism *see* imperialism
Colton, E. 118
combined and uneven development 89–91, 109
commercialization of agriculture 121, 122, 136–41, 198, 217
communism 195
and class struggle theories 122, 126, 127–8
classical sociological perspectives of 16, 43
non-structural theories of 48
and state 175, 177, 186–7

comparative study, need for 13, 83–4, 221–3; *see also* international context
competition
military 7
political 92–4
conduciveness, structural 57, 59
confusion 75
consensus 55
consequences of revolution 12
conspiracy 79
contemporary revolution *see* Africa; Asia; Central America; South America *and under* peasantry
contention model of collective violence 213
core and periphery concept 100–8, 110, 113, 155, 218
ideologies different 218–19
Netherlands as true core country 102–3; 110, 113, 114
see also semi-periphery
cotton 111
counter-determinants 59
counter-revolution 5, 132
coup d'État 6, 23, 58
craze 59
crime, organized 210
crisis 17
acute 48, 49
era of (1300–1450) 101–3
fiscal 92–3, 151, 170, 173
and state 151, 170, 173–5, 180
crowds *see* collective behavior
Cuba 25, 84, 203, 222
culture 132, 134, 190–1, 211
role undervalued 114

Davies, J.C. 75–6, 78–80, 207, 227
Declaration of Independence (USA) 223–4
decremental deprivation 77
defense *see* military; war
definitions of revolution 4–7
democracy

and class struggle theories 122, 123, 130

classical sociological perspectives of 20, 22

illusory 148

institutionalization of 32, 33, 34–6

and liberty, conflict between 95

Denmark 93, 160

'dependent' revolutions *see* developing countries

deprivation, theories of 75–82

despair 12, 192

determinism, agronomic 136–44

developing (relatively backward) countries 63

and class struggle theories 128–9, 131, 134

nationalism in 60, 66

revolution in 85, 89–91, 103–10 *passim*

and state-builders 153–6

see also semi-periphery

deviant behavior 56

dictatorship 123

difference, method of 222

Diggers 105, 202

discontent *see* mass discontent

disease metaphors 5, 47–8, 51, 56

disequilibrated social system theories of revolution 47, 53–67, 74–5

division of labor and solidarity 36, 38

Dollard, J. 73

Dorr's Rebellion 76

Downs, A. 69

Draper, H. 17, 116

Dreyfus affair 15

Dunn, J. 5, 85, 93, 146, 191–2, 219

Durkheim, E. 3, 14, 15, 33, 46, 55, 65, 196, 209

on anomie 75

anti-Durkheimianism 206–7

sociological perspective 36–9

Eastman, M. 39

Eckstein, H. 13, 225

'economism' 97, 119

economy *see* capitalism; production; world system

Edwards, L. 47–51, 53, 117

Edwards, T. 89, 90

ego 42

Egypt 76, 84, 153

1848 revolutions 15, 23–4, 29–31, 93

Eisenstadt, S.N. 54–5, 60–2, 227

elites *see* intellectuals; leaders; ruling classes

Ellwood, C. 54

emotions 12, 159, 192

endogenous changes 55

Engels, F. 16, 20, 22, 116, 164, 228

England 111, 114

Revolutions of 1640–60 and 1688 222, 224; class struggle 117, 122–4, 128–30, 132, 135, 140; classical sociological perspectives 19, 49, 52; international context 84, 85, 93–4, 102–5, 109; state 152, 160, 167, 171, 174–5, 177, 181; structural social psychology 190, 202, 206

textile industry 66

equality 28, 32

equilibrium lost *see* disequilibrated social system

Europe

absolutism 114

capitalism 102–3, 122–3

political competition 93

see also England; France; Germany; Italy; Netherlands; Russia; Spain

Evans, P. 107

'everyday resistance' 204

eviction of peasantry 122–3, 124

exogeneous changes 55

expansion *see* imperialism

expectations 36; *see also* mobility, upward

exploration, age of 102; *see also* imperialism

external relations *see* international context

hope 12, 192
Hopper, R.D. 50–1, 70, 227
hostile outburst 59
Huk rebellion 203
Hunt, L. 209, 213
Huntington, S. 5, 55, 62–5, 146, 178
Hutchinson, L. 49

ideas, importance of 7, 28, 132–3, 159
ideologies 222
  and class struggle 118
  different in core and periphery 218–19
  like religion 42
  non-structural theories of 49, 57, 59
  reflecting economic and political reality 105
  and structural social psychology 190, 211, 215
immiseration 21, 27, 75, 85, 90–1, 173, 198
  and class struggle theories 118–19, 139, 142
imperatives, revolutionary 16–25
imperialism 61, 88, 172
  and class struggle theories 127, 140
  and international context 88–9, 96, 99–100, 102, 105–8
  and structural social psychology 194, 201, 206–8, 208, 213–14
improvement in conditions prior to revolution
  classical sociological perspectives of 27–8, 30
  non-structural theories of 48, 75–6
inclusion 178–9
India 106, 127–8, 133, 135, 198
indignation 80
individuals 68–9, 88; *see also* psychology
industrial 'revolution' as misleading term 104–5
industrialization *see* capitalism
inequality 9; *see also* class struggle
inferiority, upper class, non-structural theories of 49, 54, 56–7
inquiry method 13–14

institutionalization of democracy 32, 33, 34–6
institutions
  transnational 7
  see also bureaucracy; state
integration, insufficient 36–7
intellectuals, alienation of 48–9, 52, 63
international revolutionary movements 60, 66
internal war 79
international context, revolution in 3, 83–115, 217, 218, 227
  capitalism as history 101–6
  geopolitical failure, revolution as 156–61
  Marxist background 87–91
  Polanyi and world market 94–8
  political competition among states 92–4
  and state 150–60, 165, 173, 180–1
  structural analysis, need for 83–7
  and structural social psychology 199, 209, 211–12
  see also war; world system
intransigence of elite 56–7
Iran 84
Ireland 68, 93
Ireland, T. 69
irrationality of collective action 207
  classical sociological perspectives 39, 41–2
  non-structural theories of 60, 68, 74–5
isolation 28
Italy 93, 103, 122, 167

Jacobin revolution 57, 58
jacquerie 58
James I, king 49
Japan
  class struggle 122–5, 127, 128, 130, 131, 135
  state 155–6, 171, 173–5, 177
  war: with China 181; with Russia 159
J-curve model 76, 78